Anthropology & Philosophy

Anthropology & ...

Anthropology has a history of sometimes troubled relations with neighboring disciplines, yet at the same time there have been major efforts both within anthropology and within various related disciplines for cross-fertilization and for advancing interdisciplinary work. Anthropology has been cited as a source of inspiration for new perspectives and new scholarly developments by scholars in history, literary criticism, sociology, political science, economics, demography, gerontology, legal studies, education, women's studies, art history, music, and other fields. This series addresses the need for works that examine the intersection of anthropology and these other academic fields.

Anthropology & Law
James M. Donovan and H. Edwin Anderson, III

Anthropology & Mass Communication: Media and Myth in the
  New Millennium
Mark Allen Peterson

Anthropology & Political Science: A Convergent Approach
Myron J. Aronoff and Jan Kubik

Anthropology & Philosophy: Dialogues on Trust and Hope
Edited by Sune Liisberg, Esther Oluffa Pedersen, and Anne Line Dalsgård

Anthropology & Philosophy
Dialogues on Trust and Hope

Edited by
Sune Liisberg, Esther Oluffa Pedersen
and Anne Line Dalsgård

berghahn
NEW YORK · OXFORD
www.berghahnbooks.com

First published in 2015 by
Berghahn Books
www.berghahnbooks.com

Library of Congress Cataloging-in-Publication Data

Anthropology & philosophy : dialogues on trust and hope / edited by Sune Liisberg,
Esther Oluffa Pedersen, and Anne Line Dalsgård.
    pages cm. — (Anthropology & —)
Includes bibliographical references and index.
    ISBN 978-1-78238-556-1 (hardback : alk. paper) — ISBN 978-1-78533-752-9
(paperback) — ISBN 978-1-78238-557-8 (ebook)
    1. Philosophical anthropology. 2. Anthropology—Philosophy. 3. Trust.
4. Hope. I. Liisberg, Sune, editor of compilation. II. Pedersen, Esther Oluffa,
editor of compilation. III. Dalsgård, Anne Line, 1960– editor of compilation.
IV. Title: Anthropology and philosophy.
    BD450.A497 2015
    301.01—dc23

                                                                    2014019641

British Library Cataloguing in Publication Data

A catalogue record for this book is available from the British Library

ISBN: 978-1-78238-556-1 hardback
ISBN: 978-1-78533-752-9 paperback
ISBN: 978-1-78238-557-8 ebook

CONTENTS

ACKNOWLEDGMENTS

Anne Marie Pahuus was a significant person in the initial preparations for the book but withdrew from further engagement in the project due to other work. We wish to thank her for her inspiration along the way. Cheryl Mattingly and Michael D. Jackson have each in their own way been very supportive of the project. Heidi Flegal and Alexander Heape improved the readability of our texts and three anonymous reviewers contributed advice, corrections, and moral support. We, the three editors, wish to thank them all.

INTRODUCTION
Trust and Hope

Esther Oluffa Pedersen and Sune Liisberg

Trusting and hoping alike are conjectural modes of understanding. They relate to the practical identity of human beings as persons. Who can I trust? What may I hope? Although both trust and hope are related to factual understandings of past experiences, they equally imply a move toward the future that depends on the imaginary anticipation of the imminent. They concern future states that exceed the immediate control of the person trusting or hoping. But whereas trust typically concerns near and probable futures that mostly meet our expectations, hope may very well paint a scenario of a possible and radically different future. Hope in the radically new is a mode of existence that can persist without trust in its realization. But if I hope for events and phenomena that lie closer to my immediate life-world, my hope seems to be backed up by some kind of trust in these things being possible to realize. Trusting someone or something implies that I also hope for the realization of the trusted. My hope, however, can be completely convoluted and implicit in trust in a way that makes a re-description of trust in terms of hope misleading. In this sense, trusting is a mode of existence that shapes our outlook on the near future; a future that will probably develop according to implicitly or explicitly expressed expectations. Hope, conversely, is a perspective toward a future that I wish were possible, but about which I may also have a troublesome feeling that it may not be realized. This difference in the subjunctive space taken up by trust and hope, respectively, is important and constitutes the basis for a difference in the approaches taken when researching trust and hope.

There is a significant and increasing interest in studying trust, whereas hope as a research topic is not favored with the same attention. A prevalent approach to studying trust in the social sciences is to perform quantitative survey studies of generalized trust in different entities, ranging from trust in political institutions, over trust in the economy, to trust in other individuals. On the background of large-scale, quantitative survey studies into trust, social scientists talk about low-trust and high-trust nations and communities. Such measurements of trust are common, and the results are often mentioned in the public debate. But when it comes to hope, we do not find a similar level of attention. There are examples of quantitative measurements of hope, but they are rare. The difference surely has something to do with the fact that while high/low degrees of trust indicate traits about the general behavior of the members of a given group, this would not be as apparent with measurements of hope. There seems to be a fairly robust correlation between measuring high degrees of trust in a population and high levels of social collaboration. Similar correlations between hope and behavior are much looser—if, indeed, they can be tracked at all. Basically, hope does not lend itself as easily to quantitative measurement as trust does.

In the context of this book there will be little focus on quantitative approaches to the study of trust and hope. In its place the reader will find conceptual and qualitative analyses of trust and hope, viewed from within a specific context and as a phenomenon pertaining to the first-person perspective, which takes a central position in the chapters that make up this volume. The common foundation for all of the chapters is the double approach of, firstly, developing a mode of collaboration between anthropology and philosophy and, secondly, analyzing either trust or hope from the viewpoint of the association between the specific anthropologist and philosopher. Accordingly, all chapters are the result of collaboration between an anthropologist and a philosopher, who have discussed a common angle and a shared interest in trust and hope. Some of the contributing anthropologists and philosophers take their point of departure in developing or sustaining a distinctive theoretical understanding of trust and hope. Others seek to understand a specific cultural context through the perspective of either trust or hope, while yet others engage in developing empirical and conceptual bridges between trust and hope.

The participating anthropologists and philosophers, working in pairs, have discussed and developed their specialized academic research angles, focusing their encounters on a shared topic. In so doing, this anthology goes against the current, that is, it counteracts the scarcity of direct dialogue between the two disciplines. Presupposing and aiming to show that a huge potential exists and can be uncovered by jointly exploring these topics, the anthology seeks to pave the way for further collaborative efforts by bringing anthropologists and philosophers together in the shared exploration of trust and hope. The underlying premise of the book is that the phenomena of trust and hope can best be examined and analyzed when standing upon a strong empirical foundation and reaching outward to perform an equally strong conceptual exploration. The dialogues collected in this anthology seek to substantially develop the current understanding of trust and hope in anthropological and philosophical research. We hope that the different models of cooperation between anthropologists and philosophers represented here may inspire other anthropologists and philosophers to engage in interdisciplinary projects, discussions, and work. In this sense, we consider the very format of the book to be paradigmatic and encouraging for new possibilities of interdisciplinary research into the human condition.

The Context for Bringing Anthropologists and Philosophers into Dialogue

The conception of this anthology dates back to 2009, a period of time at Aarhus University where anthropologists and philosophers from Denmark and the United States had the opportunity to do interdisciplinary work and exchange their views. Anthropologists and philosophers alike experienced their exchange of ideas as being so productive that it was suggested that we should build on this creative moment to shape something more enduring. Thus, the idea behind the anthology was born. Contributors were soon invited, and work began. As with most anthologies, the process of actualizing the content has, at times, been challenging. Some of these challenges were purely practical, while others had to do with the form that we had chosen for the book: The contributions should, in one form or another, be a dialogue between an anthropologist and a philosopher. We had no recipe for this kind of partnership, so every pair of contributors had to find their own way of doing it. We have found these challenges worthwhile and valuable because the results of the encounters between representatives of anthropology and philosophy demonstrate how both disciplines can benefit from such interdisciplinary work.

Within a Danish context, trust and hope have a prominent history as privileged topics of research. It is almost impossible to discuss trust without mentioning the Danish philosopher and theologian Knud Ejler

Løgstrup (1905–1981), a former professor at Aarhus University. His book *The Ethical Demand* (Løgstrup [1956] 1997), has had a lasting significance for the understanding and discussion of the phenomenon of trust. According to Løgstrup, trust is naturally given. Our immediate and unbiased reaction to another human being is characterized by trust. Trust is thus the original moral sentiment that forms human encounters. Only subsequently do we pass judgment on one another, and only subsequently are we in need of moral principles to guide our actions. Løgstrup argues that the human life-world is permeated with the silent, radical, and unarticulated ethical demand that we take care of the exposed, vulnerable life placed into our hands by another person, "the other." Building on this premise, Løgstrup launches a critique not only of traditional moral theories such as Immanuel Kant's (1724–1804) conception of the categorical imperative based on reason to guide and motivate moral actions, or utilitarianism's conception of morality as the principle of the greatest happiness, but also what Løgstrup (1968) refers to as the "subjectivism" of the Danish philosopher and theologian Søren Kierkegaard (1813–1855).

Løgstrup finds that Kierkegaard has misrepresented not only the relations between human beings, but also the human relation to the world and God. We are, according to Løgstrup, placed in a shared life-world, which is imbued with the responsibility to safeguard the fragility of life. Løgstrup focuses on the permeating goodness of Creation, arguing that we are all placed in this world with a mutual responsibility to sustain it. For his part, Kierkegaard understood human life as radically individual, in that a true relation to God is characterized by passion and can be established only from the point of view of subjectivity. Where Løgstrup concentrates on trust as a phenomenon closely related to everyday life, Kierkegaard examines the everyday despair of the human being. In Kierkegaard's view, despair is only dissolvable by the Christian possibility of faith. A key assumption in Kierkegaard is therefore the assertion that life would be nothing but despair, were there no eternal consciousness (Kierkegaard [1843] 1983), and this assertion is important to Kierkegaard's notion of futurity and the possibility of hope.

In his famous analysis of anxiety from 1843, Kierkegaard (1992) defines anxiety as a dizzy experience of freedom that confronts us with possibility as such, and possibility is linked with futurity, since having existential possibility is defining for having a future. In this radical experience of freedom, the human being is confronted with the idea of God as representing a person's possibility of being forgiven and, at the same time, as the limit of reason to which the human subject can relate only in faith. According to Kierkegaard ([1843] 1990), faith is concerned with eternity in the form of being an expectation of victory. However, the victory of faith simply consists in *having* the expectation now, in *this* concrete life—existentially it does not concern a victory in another, distant life. Faith, being the expectation of victory, in this way entails hope as a modus of human life as well. So, in Kierkegaard, one could say that from the depths of anxiety and despair we are thrown back into the life that we have before us, our own life, but in a qualitatively different way, namely as something that is subjected to a choice, and which can exclusively be realized authentically as chosen. Only against this background—and this would be the existentialist argument against Løgstrup—can trust and hope as everyday features of the human social world qualify as features of what we have chosen more fundamentally, namely our life.

In the present volume, several contributors, American and Danish, critically discuss Løgstrup's theory of trust. Kierkegaard, among other existentialist and existential-political thinkers, is also addressed here by some as a central thinker, especially with regard to the theme of hope. From another angle, namely the French sociological tradition, comes a figure that is central for a number of contributors: the anthropologist Marcel Mauss. His widely acknowledged book *The Gift* from 1925 (Mauss 2010) seems to capture a very essential feature of trust relations: the structure of gift exchange. The exchange of gifts is what Mauss has called "a total social phenomenon," meaning that it lies at the root of, and is implied in, every social enterprise and comes across as a more basic structure of sociality than the *homo oeconomicus* of our days; and so it is that Mauss suggests that we should take as a principal aspect of our life what has been, and always will be, the principle: Go beyond yourself, donate, freely and obligatorily; one has nothing there to risk (see Mauss [1925] 2010). In its capacity of being a total social phenomenon, the structure of gift exchange might as well be identified as lying at the root of inter-human trust relations. One could say that when people trust one another, we actually exchange a piece of our freedom with the other person.

The above-mentioned authors do not exhaust the theoretical sources of inspiration for investigations of trust and hope in the area where anthropology and philosophy intersect. The dialogues presented in this anthology are a vivid illustration of this. Nevertheless, by pointing to a discrepancy between Løgstrup's propensity to hold an affirmative and optimistic worldview, on the one hand, and Kierkegaard's more gloomy and individualistic stance to the world, on the other hand, we can indicate a larger question concerning how to approach the phenomena of trust and hope that needs to be dealt with in one way or another.

That question is: Will we take as our starting point an affirmation of the actuality and relevance of trust and hope, or will we commence to question what trust and hope may be within the modern world? The dialogues in this volume present different answers. The theoretical framework of gift-giving elaborated on by Mauss offers a possible way to obviate the choice itself (between a tendency to hold generally optimistic or pessimistic views concerning the instantiation of investigations into trust and hope) by focusing on the structure of giving and receiving gifts. The French tradition of Mauss thereby gives primacy to an analysis of the structure, preferring it over an investigation into the individual perspective. As regards a discussion of agent versus structure, the dialogues in this volume once again present a variety of different takes on how to tackle such methodological issues.

The Results of the Meetings Between Anthropologists and Philosophers in Their Writing

Commencing on a joint endeavor between anthropologists and philosophers is only possible when the partners from the two disciplines are open toward the way questions are asked and answers are sought by the anthropologist and the philosopher respectively. Thus the discussion of possibilities of collaboration should not be conducted on a too abstract level. It needs to be grounded in either an approach to practicing anthropological and philosophical analysis or in a specific topic. The seven pairs presented here can be said to develop seven distinct approaches to the joint venture of anthropologists and philosophers. The different modes of collaboration will hopefully be interesting for others to read both because of their different ways of handling the interdisciplinary work and because of the analyses that arise out of the experiment.

The opening dialogue, *Practical Philosophy and Hope as a Moral Project among African-Americans,* between anthropologist Cheryl Mattingly and philosopher Uffe Juul Jensen, reflects upon the relations between anthropology and philosophy. It argues for the rewards of this encounter, and shows how a fruitful encounter can take place by elaborating on the fieldwork done by Mattingly. They have approvingly taken on the recommendation of interdisciplinary work between anthropologists and philosophers and have composed a jointly authored chapter, "What Can We Hope For? An Exploration in Cosmopolitan Philosophical Anthropology." The text is structured around two parts in which Mattingly and Jensen first discuss how collaboration between anthropologists and philosophers may develop and enhance both if it rests on a mutual recognition of the insights of each discipline. The authors note that both disciplines seem to keep a distance to each other. But instead of lamenting the lack of collaboration in spite of the many shared interest in subject matter, they propose a way of initiating the conversation between anthropology and philosophy that begins in philosophy, but should be equally important for anthropology. Firstly, going back to Aristotle, they point out how philosophy, in order to philosophize about the world, needs to go beyond itself and look to other disciplines that produce valuable knowledge. Secondly, they invoke Sartre, who emphasized that philosophizing in the armchair and doing exegesis of texts is not enough if one really wants to philosophize about important matters. One needs to pay attention to the social practices themselves, and one must also be changed personally by the practice of philosophizing. In other words, the development of social theory—whether it be philosophical or anthropological—demands engagement with social world practices. Learning and understanding the "real" social world entails a change of personality in the sense of a change of perspective and a deepening of one's understanding that does not leave everything as it was. Jensen and Mattingly thirdly argue that recapturing the distinction between "exegetical" and "cosmopolitan" forms of philosophy, the distinction which Kant drew, makes it possible to retain a space for the important practice of exegesis within philosophy without discrediting one's involvement in theorizing about worldly affairs. The philosophical anthropology of Kant is devoted to investigating popular concepts used by ordinary language users, and, in this sense, it covers Kant's idea of a cosmopolitan philosophy as well as the discipline of contemporary anthropology. Although neither Jensen nor Mattingly are prone to accept Kantian philosophy as methodologically contemporary, they argue that his idea of a cosmopolitan philosophical anthropology makes a convincing starting point for fruitful encounters between the modern disciplines of anthropology and philosophy.

The second part of the joint chapter is an exposition of how a cosmopolitan philosophical anthropology might look. Focusing on the ethnographic material from the fieldwork done by Mattingly and her group in Los Angeles among African-American families caring for children with severe medical conditions, the authors develop a study of hope. The concept of hope concerns future time in the subjunctive mode, and it can only be understood by taking the first-person perspective of the person(s) hoping for the future. To study the concept of hope goes against one of the major trends in current anthropology and current philosophy, namely the structuralist and poststructuralist frameworks that downplay personhood. Jensen and Mattingly show—making a direct reference to Sartre's claim that we ought not to employ theoretical positions without acknowledging how these theories develop as reactions to other paradigms and positions—how this interest in hope intersects with contemporary social theory. They develop a variant of virtue ethics rooted in Aristotle, but in employing it they stress that the perspective of hope only emerges if we look at the processes of acting and becoming as ends in themselves. Subsequently, the authors examine a concrete ethnographic instance of the process of becoming hopeful in spite of profound despair.

The dialogue *Existential Anthropology and the Category of the New*—between anthropologist Michael D. Jackson, author of the chapter "The Reopening of the Gate of Effort: Existential Imperatives at the Margins of a Globalized World," and philosopher Thomas S. Wentzer, author of the chapter "The Eternal Recurrence of the New"—explores the question of an existential imperative concerning the desire to live a rich and fulfilled life. Jackson, drawing upon the material from his fieldwork in Kuranko villages in Northern Sierra Leone, focuses on the equivocality that pertains to our wishes for a better future. We address the powers that be *both* in the hope that some good will come of it *and* in the knowledge that our petitions will probably come to nothing. This realistic knowledge is attenuated under the conditions of life as it is lived by people on the margins of the globalized world, such as the Kuranko people. But it is, according to Jackson, an existential experience pertaining to human life as such, since it concerns the distribution and redistribution of the scarcest of all goods: life itself. We aim for a life of well-being, but this is never a settled state. It is an ongoing struggle. Humans hardly ever feel completely satisfied with their lot, which is why they almost always strive to improve their situation socially, spiritually, or materially. This feeling of want, in proportion to what we think life ought to yield to us, is what Jackson calls "existential dissatisfaction" and it is an irreducible part of the human condition.

Jackson invokes two significant episodes from his recent fieldwork in Kuranko. First there is the letter from Ferenkay, a young Kuranko man from the village of Firawa, urging the recipient of the letter to take him along and give him a job and enable him to work. On the one hand this letter raises the ethical issue of why some people have so much more than others, and on the other hand it appeals to a conception of natural justice whereby all human beings are entitled to partake of the good things in life. Ferenkay appeals to "Mr. White Man" as a power mighty enough to be able to create a radical change and a new and better beginning for his life. This letter, along with the second episode, a direct appeal that Jackson gets from another young man, Fasili, to take

Fasili with him to America, depict very clearly the dilemma that Jackson, as a comparatively rich person, experiences when confronted with the existential demand from another person to assure him a fair deal, or some kind of natural justice. For how can one help the other in need without leaving oneself destitute? Fasili embodies the equivocality of the existential demand in his simultaneous patient stoicism toward the desperate conditions of his life, and his impatient and urgent desire for transformation of his situation. It is precisely this duality of hope toward the future that Wentzer's contribution subjects to a conceptual analysis. Wentzer relates his philosophical analysis of the new to the concrete fieldwork of Jackson.

Arguing for an existential understanding of the new, Wentzer underscores that the predicate "new" or the ontology of change concerns our emotive and conceptual stances toward our lives, which are brought into play while we cope with a changing world. According to Wentzer, we only articulate novelty if it comes across as the opening of an opportunity for us, while we resign and suffer the occurrences of the world whenever they work against us. To underline this existential attitude toward the new the ideal type attitudes of the stoicism of Seneca, and the historicism of Hegel are invoked. Thus Wentzer argues that the language of the new is solely employed when we want to understand the future and our life as our own doing. Wentzer interprets the right to experience the event of a new beginning in one's life as an existential demand in human life. This demand represents an imaginative doorway to a new lifetime—we hope for a new beginning and thus hope for the possibility of doing things differently. It is therefore an optimistic hope to get a grip on one's own life, felt from the first-person perspective. This hope, however, may—if realized—turn out disappointing. It is not given that a new beginning—even such a radical one as Fasili dreams of by asking Jackson to bring him to America—will bring about a better life-situation. It may turn out to be another experience of suppression and structural violence. According to Wentzer, the new should be understood as an attitude toward one's future lifetime rather than an actual event. The new is real only as a mode of experiencing significant possible change in life. It is, as such, an integral part of the human condition as an intentional stance toward the occurrences in one's life.

Wentzer and Jackson join forces to develop and explore the possibilities of an existential anthropology that focuses on the common human condition and the shared wish to live in the world as if it were one's own. The existential attitudes toward life and the narrating effort to understand life both as stoic fate and as possible new and better beginnings where we are subjects of our lives, instead of subjected to the happenings of life, the authors argue, ought not to be reified as different social formations or different forms of humanity.

Philosopher Esther Oluffa Pedersen and anthropologist Lotte Meinert anchor their dialogue *Intentional Trust in Uganda* in a common interest in understanding the attitudes of trust and distrust as these are formed in, and of, the social sphere of human life. Through discussions during the writing process the two authors have taken mutual inspiration from each other. Their chapters are the result of a coordination and cooperation between two independent lines of research. Pedersen's chapter, entitled "An Outline of Interpersonal Trust and Distrust," develops a conceptual framework for understanding trust and distrust as attitudes that are highly sensitive to the social environment of the individual. Meinert's chapter, "Tricky Trust: Distrust as a Point of Departure and Trust as a Social Achievement in Uganda," is based on ethnographic fieldwork carried out in Uganda primarily since 2008—which was the year when "peace broke out," as the Ugandans in the northern part of the country jokingly call the general peace treaty in Uganda. Pedersen and Meinert have worked at corroborating the theoretical model of trust suggested by Pedersen with the insights from the fieldwork conducted by Meinert. As a result of the discussions they have developed a common understanding of both Pedersen's theoretical framework and Meinert's interpretation of her own fieldwork. In her theoretical conception of interpersonal trust, Pedersen strives to develop a framework within which both the individual experience of developments and changes in trust relationships between persons, and the general and more broad sociological atmosphere of trust or distrust between peers is taken into account. In order to achieve this goal she develops three main concepts. The first concept is "prima facie trust/distrust" by which Pedersen denotes the immediate way in which a person tends to meet social situations, trustfully or distrustfully, on the background of "things taken for granted" by that person. Important to Pedersen's notion of prima facie trust/distrust is—in opposition to Knud E. Løgstrup—that it does not imply the assumption of an ontological or moral hierarchy between the attitudes of either trust or distrust. Rather, whether a person as a default attitude meets others with trust or distrust depends on her past experience and social environment—brought up in an atmosphere of distrust between peers, distrust will also become the prima facie attitude in encounters with others. Pedersen's second main concept, "reflective trust/distrust," covers situations in which a person's social world of "things-taken-for-granted" erodes and a decision about whether to act trustfully or distrustfully is required. Here, the situation and the comprehension hereof by the person experiencing it will force a reflective consideration of whether displaying trust or distrust toward others is appropriate. Thus in experiencing a breach in the expectancies the person is forced to reflect over her placement of either trust or distrust in others and under certain circumstances. While the first two concepts are meant to apply from a first-person perspective, the third concept of Pedersen's conceptual framework, the "locus of trust," only applies from a third-person perspective and involves a description of the trust situation and the place of the trust relationship. This concept in particular has been developed through the discussions between Meinert and Pedersen. The idea is to try to capture the whole scene of trustful and distrustful interactions by schematizing features of each interacting individual with respect to questions about conventions of social action, institutions and social structure, collective worldviews, and ways of behaving toward nature and social entities. Thus, the locus of trust is "the interface of all participating agents' individual trust diagrams in concrete time and place."

Meinert opens her chapter by critically discussing the Danish theologian K. E. Løgstrup's assumption that trust is an ontologically (or naturally) founded and therefore basic attitude of human interaction, whereas distrust simply denotes a lack of trust. Meinert's ethnographic fieldwork in Uganda suggests, in contradiction to Løgstrup, that developing trust is a vulnerable and tricky human enterprise that may be preconditioned by distrust. In fieldwork observations in Uganda, Meinert argues that the atmosphere of trust is permeated by distrust so that the human social world is, at the outset, taken to *be* untrustworthy. The trust in one another has no ontological status but is something we continually have to establish, to will into existence, and to fight for. During the period of 2008 to 2011, Meinert has conducted interviews with two young Ugandan men, Peter and Oloya, who were both, in different ways, victims of the long-lasting armed conflict between the rebel Lord's Resistance Army (LRA) and the Ugandan government. In 2008, after several years of unsuccessful peace negotiations, an agreement to cease hostilities was finally signed between the conflicting parties. At that time the conflict had lasted for twenty-two years, and it left behind a Ugandan people who were deeply divided and beset with new uncertainties. This is the situation in which Meinert, in a local video shop, and over a period of three years, meets with Peter and Oloya, who both make music to express their state of uncertainty and despair, but also their hopes for a better future characterized by trust and truthfulness. In her interpretations and conclusions Meinert draws on the texts that accompany Peter's and Oloya's music, and also on their life stories as told to her by them, gradually revealing a deep rooted and all-embracing distrust. This finally leads Meinert to suggest that we cannot take trust to be the ontologically basic feature of inter-human relations as suggested in Løgstrup's theory of trust.

As for the dialogue between the two chapters, Pedersen incorporates Meinert's cases as striking examples that illustrate the difference between the levels of prima facie and reflective trust/distrust. Likewise, Meinert applies the conceptual framework of Pedersen's chapter in order to grasp the differences between, on the one hand, the prima facie distrust that characterize the two young men and, on the other hand, their quest for a better future, which comes to the fore in their music. In their music, the young men reflectively strive after developing trust. This Meinert views as an example of Pedersen's differentiation between a prima facie attitude of distrust and a reflective strive to build up trusting attitudes toward others.

Whereas Meinert's fieldwork in Uganda draws attention to a social environment where distrust is predominant, anthropologist Nils Bubandt's fieldwork in Indonesia points to another complicated feature of trust relationships, namely the interconnections between trust, inauthenticity, and power. In the dialogue *Trust, Ambiguity, and Indonesian Modernity,* Bubandt and philosopher Sune Liisberg explore the question whether inauthenticity and self-deception may be contained within trusting relationships. The cooperation in this dialogue consists of complementary investigations based on Bubandt's analyses of fieldwork material from Indonesia and Liisberg's philosophical analyses of the relation between trusting behavior and tolerance of ambiguity. Even though their chapters do not draw common conclusions, the shared effort to take the endeavor of the other into account opens the perspectives of anthropologists and philosophers to complementary readings. Throughout their chapters, Bubandt and Liisberg make meta-commentaries to each other that are meant to invite the reader also to engage in such meta-discussions of fruitful pathways between anthropology and philosophy. It is made clear that Liisberg's interpretation of trust as linked to tolerance of ambiguity through a benign form of self-deception and Bubandt's discussion of the complex intertwinement between trust, authenticity, inauthenticity, power, and forgery in Indonesia may be read together in a manner that enhances both.

In his chapter, "Trust in an Age of Inauthenticity: Power and Indonesian Modernity," Bubandt presents his fieldwork from Indonesia as what he calls a "counter-ethnography," which serves to point out that the accustomed Western story of universal structures of trust and authenticity in modernity are far more complex. Bubandt endorses an idea of multiple modernities to elucidate the circumstances pertaining to Indonesian understandings of power and authenticity. The aporia of Indonesian conceptions of power, trust, and novelty is that the new is politically claimed to be authentic by virtue of power, but that power is inherently inauthentic. Bubandt illustrates his assumption by discussions of, firstly, the theme park *Taman Mini Indonesia Indah,* where the political power of the "New Order" of president Suharto installed itself as the authentic source of interpretation—and construction—of Indonesian culture. Secondly, Bubandt invokes the example of forgery to discuss the role played by *aspal,* or "authentic-fake," products in Indonesian ordinary, fiscal, and political life. Bubandt accounts for the lethal role played by a fake letter in the riots and unrest between Muslims and Christians in North Maluku in 2001. The letter, although suspected of being a forgery, still had a social effect. It reverses the logic of the "authentic-fake" state; a state that bestows authenticity upon objects simply by fiat and through its actual power. As a result, in Indonesia one can trust the givenness of power even while, at the same time, claims as to the authenticity of power and its authoritative signs are entirely untrustworthy.

Liisberg, in his chapter, "Trust as the Life Magic of Self-Deception: A Philosophical-Psychological Investigation into Tolerance of Ambiguity," embarks on a methodologically very different route by conferring his energy into an interpretation of Jean-Paul Sartre as a philosopher of trust. Liisberg shows how Sartre's concepts of good and bad faith equally are instances of self-deception. Within the core of trustfulness there lies a certain type of self-deception in the form of good faith. It concerns a positive illusion about the other, which is needed to be able to trust in spite of an uncertainty, at least principal, about the intentions of the other—as they are merely probable—and about the future. This positive illusion can, according to Liisberg, be understood as a way of tolerating ambiguity. Since the happenings of the world are never known beforehand, the future is exposed to uncertainty. Trusting others in good faith is consequently something we can do when the ambiguities of the world stay on the fringes of our consciousness, while distrusting behavior potentially arises from an acute awareness of these ambiguities. The recourse to self-deception as bad faith is an attempt to overcome the meta-stable structure of human existence, namely the way our existence is stretched out between a facticity and a transcendence of the given. In bad faith we either reify our transcendence by identifying with our facticity in a role—Sartre's famous example being the waiter, who believes himself to be essentially a waiter in an attempt to escape his inevitable freedom—or we endeavor to understand ourselves as pure consciousness or pure transcendence—where Sartre offers the example of a woman who denies the fact that she is on an obviously romantic date with a man by insisting that the man is entirely interested in having an intellectual conversation with her. The essential point that Liisberg makes is that we ought to employ the differentiation between good and bad faith not as a differentiation between authentic and inauthentic beliefs, but rather between self-deceptive ways in which we try to cope with the inherent ambiguities of life, whereby trust can be interpreted as a certain benign form of self-deception based on positive ideas about the other.

Bubandt and Liisberg find throughout their meta-discussions of the work of the other fruitful ways of including the concepts and phenomena of each other. Different from such a model of cooperation, the dialogue between philosopher Sverre Raffnsøe and anthropologist Hirokazu Miyazaki is molded as Miyazaki's response to Raffnsøe's concepts and ideas. As the title, *Gift-Giving and Power Between Trust and Hope,* suggests, Raffnsøe and Miyazaki investigate the relations between trust and hope through the lens of gift-giving and the social power it entails. Miyazaki's contribution, "Hope in the Gift—Hope in Sleep" is partly based on ethnographical fieldwork done in Fiji. It takes the form of a comment to Raffnsøe's chapter, "Empowering Trust in the New: Trust and Power as Capacities." Raffnsøe's aim is to develop a new conception of power—which he calls "Power II"—a conception that enables us to consider trust as something which involves power, and vice versa, especially in the context of management. Without power there can be no management. The question is, however, whether the classical understanding of power, which consist in an "either–or" model—either you are in power and do not trust, or you trust at the price of having power—can serve as a model in a time like ours, where management tends to become management of self-management. Raffnsøe's suggestion is that management needs to adopt an idea of "both–and," since in practical terms management needs both power and trust in order to function. If we want to place our "trust in trust" within management, we need to know how trust and power are internally compatible with each other. In opposition to the classical notion of power, which can also be defined by "the four Cs" (command, coercion, control, and calculation), the more refined concept of power that Raffnsøe presents is defined as a capacity to affect "the dispositions and the conduct" of others, which leads us to focus on the virtual. This means that we can conceive of trust as an anticipatory affect: Instead of calculating and controlling future scenarios by means of command and coercion, we rely on trust as the means to "conduct the conduct of others" by affecting their dispositions *through* the trust we place in them. Against this backdrop, trust becomes associated with hope and is turned toward the new as a form of negotiating the future, that is, as a form of the exchange of gifts, following Marcel Mauss's model of primitive societies.

In his comment on Raffnsøe's chapter, Miyazaki, on the basis of his fieldwork among indigenous Fijians, focuses on the gift as a model of trust. Gift-givers place trust in gift-receivers, and this is anchored in hope, namely the hope for the efficacy of the gift. Furthermore, to the Fijians the exchange of gifts is a means to obviate uncertainty, unknowability, and indeterminacy, which in addition generates hope for God's mercy—the gift of eternal life—and obviates the unknowability of the efficacy of the gift-giving itself. Thus, hope is allowed anew as a motivator of trust. As an alternative to understanding trust in terms of interaction, Miyazaki suggests the model of sleep as a non-interactional and non-relational model for comprehending the way trust and hope are constantly being made anew as capacities. If it is true that the gift is continual work, then sleep is an appropriate supplement to the gift. These considerations finally serve as a backdrop for Miyazaki's reflections upon the crisis of trust in Fukushima, which followed the earthquake, tsunami, and nuclear disasters that hit Japan in March 2011. As the Japanese government launched a campaign of *kizuna* (bonds) to unite forces throughout the nation to relieve the victims of the disasters, it was expecting a form of reciprocal trust, i.e. gift-giving between the government and the citizens. Miyazaki's analysis is concerned with the managerial motives of the "kizuna campaign" and the question why the campaign failed and instead engendered a sense of distrust in the government.

The dialogue *With Kierkegaard in Africa* is dedicated to a double investigation into hope as an existential structure in human life. Philosopher Anders Moe Rasmussen and anthropologist Hans Lucht take as their common starting point the perspective of the Danish philosopher Søren Kierkegaard, and more specifically his book *Fear and Trembling* from 1843. Though Kierkegaard functions as a shared theoretical framework, Rasmussen and Lucht differ in the employment and analysis of Kierkegaard. Rasmussen is concerned with an interpretative elucidation of the existential structure of hope in Kierkegaard's text, whereas Lucht can be said to unfold the meaning of this structure in lived experience by invoking it in his analysis of fieldwork material. In this sense their chapters complement each other as two different types of readings of Kierkegaard and of the existential experience of hope. Thereby they also enhance the scope of Kierkegaard's philosophy.

Rasmussen opens his chapter, "Self, Hope, and the Unconditional: Kierkegaard on Faith and Hope," by noticing how a discourse of hope

seems to have regained standing in our political and social life—a notable example of this tendency being the 2008 Obama campaign in
the United States. The concept of hope has traditional roots in religious discourse, where it denotes the hope of an afterlife. The modern condition, however, is one of secularization and breaking away
from tradition. Therefore it becomes acutely relevant to ask whether
the notion of hope is possible to keep up without any connotations of
something that transcends, and hence is "not of this world." According
to Rasmussen, Kierkegaard is a most interesting witness to this question because he vividly invokes the two pitfalls in modernity, namely
nihilism and orthodox religiosity/traditionalism. Confronted with the
nihilistic nightmare that life is completely devoid of meaning, religious
orthodoxy offers no remedy. Until Kierkegaard arrived on the scene, religious thought had managed to keep the nihilistic danger at a distance.
But that path is no option for Kierkegaard. Instead, he attaches new
meaning to the concepts of faith and hope, making them responsive to
nihilism and turned against religious orthodoxy. Understood as a "paradox of existence," faith is inscribed with a notion of distance or transcendence. This feature of faith Kierkegaard elucidates through what
he calls the double movement of faith. The double movement consists
in, firstly, a transcendence of the finite and thus a grasp of the infinite
in the ethical stance. However, this infinite ethical security has to be
transcended by the second movement leading to a return to the finite
on the strength of the absurd. This double movement underscores that
faith and hope are to be understood in terms of self-relation, or anthro-
pologically. They denote the possibility of a radical change of attitude
toward life as a whole; a change that accepts finitude only against the
backdrop of the possible. Kierkegaard's concept of hope is therefore an
embracement of transitory reality as the place where something radically new can happen.

    In the chapter "Kierkegaard in West Africa: Hope and Sacrifice in
a Ghanaian Fishing Village," Lucht employs the structure of hope as
defined by Kierkegaard in the double movement of resigning everything and winning it back "on the strength of the absurd," using it
to elucidate the rationale behind anthropomorphisms. Responding by
anthropomorphizing the world that one has been thrown into involves
a re-figuration of that world to encompass moral concerns, so that the
world can be trusted to respond to one's yearnings and demands. Accordingly, human existence is based on the anguish involved in giving
up everything to powers beyond one's control in order to institute a
moral structure on the indifferent outside world. Lucht interprets the
struggles of Ghanaian fishermen in accordance with this structure of

hoping that the outside world will react responsively to their sacrifices. The canoe fishermen offer the sea not only the sacrifice of a bull, but also their unmitigated practical involvement in fishing, and they expect to get something in return from the sea's understanding that it is obliged to give them something back. In this sense, the traditional fishermen regard their toil with the sea and the fish as imbued with moral claims. However, the decline in canoe fishing in the coastal villages of Ghana compromises this worldview. Without any reason to believe that the sea, by yielding a catch, will restore the engagement of the fishermen, they fall into despair. The hopeless situation leaves many in a state of nihilism. One fisherman expresses this to the anthropologist as follows: "Come back in ten years, and you'll find nothing here." As an alternative, the hope of a better life in Europe spurs many to attempt high-risk immigration to Europe. The wave of African immigrants may be understood as gift-giving and sacrifice in a shape that poses a potential threat to the political systems of Europe, in the sense that willingness to give up everything may disturb that power structure because it cannot be reciprocated. If power is based on some kind of reciprocity, the underlying power structure cannot be upheld when gifts given to it consist in utter self-sacrifice. But Lucht remarks that for this to be the case, the risks taken by African immigrants would have to be interpreted as sacrifices, and this is far from the case. Rather, in Europe migrant stories are conveyed through a filter of distance that takes the deaths and the suffering of migrants crossing the Mediterranean sea out of their moral contexts and inscribes them in the happenings of the unresponsive world; a world to which Europeans seem to have no obligation.

Finally, in their epilogue "Anthropology and Philosophy in Dialogue?" anthropologist Anne Line Dalsgård and philosopher Søren Harnow Klausen discuss some of the complexities involved in the dialogue between philosophers and anthropologists, which both disciplines have only recently embarked upon, for instance in the present volume and a few other initiatives. Their chapter is therefore a meta-reflection upon, on the one hand, the biased presumptions of the two disciplines toward one another, and, on the other hand and in spite of these presumptions, the motivating factors in commencing such interdisciplinary engagement between philosophy and anthropology. Over the last two decades, philosophers have increasingly been finding that they ought to relate to, and maybe even integrate, empirical findings into their conceptually orientated work; in this respect, the philosopher's most obvious choice for an empirical research field has normally been the cognitive sciences. However, Klausen and Dalsgård argue, there are shortcomings linked with this combination, since most of the empirical findings in the cognitive sciences have been the result of experimental, and so more or less de-contextualized, research settings. Here anthropology, based on ethnographical fieldwork, offers a quite different sort of research material for philosophers to dialogue with—if they dare—namely real-life research findings concerned with a salient topic, specifically the question: "What are human beings?" This question is also very central in philosophy, only in philosophy it is mostly posed in a generalizing form aiming at the essence of what *the* human being is. This difference therefore, and by the same token, invokes a classical example of how and where the two disciplines typically get into trouble when they confront each other, at least in the form of biases: On one side, anthropology, there is an emphasis on particular, contextualized points of view; on the other side, philosophy, there is an ambition of generalizing points of views into, ideally, an argument for one point of view. Nevertheless, anthropologists have always found inspiration in philosophy, and there are also examples of philosophers owing their inspiration to anthropology, one notable instance being the theoretical debt that French poststructuralism owes to structural anthropology. The ideal that Klausen and Dalsgård ultimately envision for the dialogue between anthropology and philosophy is that "philosophy could be prompted by the findings of anthropology to ask new questions, which would then be subjected to fieldwork by anthropologists."

The present book is no ordinary anthology. It is a workroom in which anthropologists and philosophers have commenced on a dialogue on the two research topics, trust and hope, that are important for the field of anthropology as well as for the field of philosophy. The interdisciplinary efforts of the contributors demonstrate how the coming together of anthropologists and philosophers can result in new and challenging ways of thinking about trust and hope. We hope this endeavor of starting a closer dialogue between anthropology and philosophy will be a source of inspiration for others to work in the productive intersection between anthropology and philosophy and to investigate further into the social phenomena of trust and hope.

References

Kierkegaard, Søren. (1843) 1983. *Fear and Trembling*. Translated by Howard V. Hong and Edna H. Hong. Princeton, NJ: Princeton University Press.

———. (1843) 1990. *Eighteen Upbuilding Discourses.* Translated by Howard V. Hong and Edna H. Hong. Princeton, NJ: Princeton University Press.

———. (1843) 1992. *The Concept of Anxiety.* Translated by Reidar Thomte. Princeton, NJ: Princeton University Press.

Løgstrup, Knud E. 1968. *Opgør med Kierkegaard.* Copenhagen: Gyldendal.

———. (1956) 1997. *The Ethical Demand.* Translated by Theodor I. Jensen and Gary Puckering, revised by Hans Fink and Alasdair MacIntyre. Notre Dame, IN: University of Notre Dame Press.

Mauss, Marcel. (1925) 2010. The Gift : *The Form and Reason for Exchange in Archaic Societies.* London: Routledge Classics.

PRACTICAL PHILOSOPHY AND HOPE AS A MORAL PROJECT AMONG AFRICAN-AMERICANS

JOINT STATEMENT

Cheryl Mattingly and Uffe Juul Jensen

The two authors of this chapter, one a philosopher (Uffe Juul Jensen) and the other an anthropologist (Cheryl Mattingly), have been in conversations over the past two decades. We have decided to write this together as part of our long project of discussion. Some of our observations about the challenges and possibilities of cross-disciplinary dialogue are informed by our own history of conversation (Jensen and Mattingly 2009). Some parts of this chapter are also being further developed in forthcoming books. The structure of our chapter is as follows. After a brief review of some crucial challenges to an interdisciplinary dialogue, the subsequent sections move us into the heart of the chapter. We begin by sketching a possible solution that involves a reframing of the philosophical enterprise. We then try to put this reframing to use, concretely, in an analysis of ethnographic cases that explore hope as a moral practice. This case material is drawn from a research project that Cheryl Mattingly and her colleagues have been conducting for many years in Los Angeles (Mattingly 2010, 2014).

WHAT CAN WE HOPE FOR?
An Exploration in Cosmopolitan Philosophical Anthropology

Cheryl Mattingly and Uffe Juul Jensen

This chapter proposes a cosmopolitan philosophical anthropology to consider a particular human problem—the problem of hope. In light of the ethnographic material presented, we consider hope as a cosmopolitan (or "indigenous") concept, examining how it reveals itself in practice and, especially, the kinds of ethical demands it poses. Before carrying out this theoretical and interpretive exercise, however, we begin the chapter by stepping back to reflect—in broad strokes—upon the challenges posed by carrying out an interdisciplinary conversation between the two disciplines. We first take up this matter from the perspective of anthropology, and subsequently from a common philosophical point of view.

Philosophy: A View from Anthropology

Anthropologists are often uneasy or even outright dismissive of philosophy as an enterprise. They may cite a philosopher or two where it seems advantageous to their arguments, but by and large they have expressed the view that philosophers are too prone to universal abstractions to be of much help in exploring the historically and culturally situated circumstances of the people they study. The examples that philosophers use are too thin, denuded of real world weight and heft, they complain. Even when philosophers tell them that they are drawing upon "ordinary language" or "ordinary experience," anthropologists find their exemplars strangely rarified and parsed, as though plucked out of the conversations and events of the world and set into some pristine space. Anthropologists also make a second key objection. Western philosophy—being Western, after all—is especially ill equipped to illuminate the life-worlds of non-Western peoples. How can a Kant, Hegel, or Locke do justice to the indigenous epistemologies, ontologies, ethics, and metaphysics of peoples who have cultivated decidedly non-Western modes of life? In fact, one of anthropology's contributions to the sociology of knowledge has precisely been an ongoing critique of Western philosophy—especially its worrisome propensity to turn the particularities of European history and culture into material for grand theories.

Despite these anthropological misgivings about misleading universalities or "Eurocentric" biases, it would be quite wrong to say that anthropologists have shunned philosophy altogether. For one thing, some philosophers, at least some of the time, have been exempt from this general line of anthropological attack. Anthropologists have mined a select few with immense enthusiasm, finding ways to apply their frameworks within a vast array of social and historical circumstances. Most popular are those philosophers who have formulated commentaries and critiques of the European project of modernity itself (including its universalisms) and looked skeptically at both the primary ideals of Western thought and its social practices and institutions. A few decades ago, Marx served as such a philosopher. In contemporary times, Michel Foucault immediately comes to mind. And, as Dalsgård and Klausen point out later in this volume, anthropologists have drawn freely upon continental phenomenology and hermeneutics in examining cultural practice and the cultural body as lived experience. Even anthropologists who are resolute in their suspiciousness of philosophical abstractions or grand theorizing have a difficult time escaping philosophy altogether. For it is simply the case that anthropology as an enterprise has had ambitions not unlike philosophy even if its methods have been so very different: to expose and explore deep structures of human thought, language, and cognition, for example, or meaning-making as a universal cultural practice, or lived experience, processes of human socialization, strategies of power, and forms of economic exchange. The list could go on and on.

Even the most relativist of anthropologists, those most committed to describing local realities without reference to a universal human condition or human capacities, tend to have ambitions to speak in a more generalizing way—to at least create theories or interpretive schemes that could be applied elsewhere, to other peoples in other places. Thus the vast majority of anthropologists are not content merely to describe or catalogue a local scene (however remote and exotic) and view this as an end in itself. To quote a remark made by Clifford Geertz (in his ironic way), "We (anthropologists) don't go around the world to count the cats in Zanzibar" (Geertz 1973: 19). The recent trend in anthropology to explore situations as both local and also nested within larger global systems that belong to a world history might seem an escape from philosophy. Perhaps anthropology can understand itself along more empirical lines, as contributing to a documentation of the historical dispersion of forms of modernity around the world or to the complexities of import/export dynamics: the locally inflected indigenizing of technologies, religions, therapies, media cultures, sciences, and institutional forms in a post-colonial world. And yet, even this historical trend is not without its philosophical inspirations—the voices of Foucault, Derrida, Deleuze, Hacking, even some faint echoes of Marx, are very much part of the conversation.

If anthropologists are not only doing a kind of interpretive work that bears some kinship to philosophy, not only asking questions that philosophers might ask, but also drawing upon philosophers in the asking of those questions, then why is conversation between the two disciplines so troubled? Where is the rub? Here, again, a view from anthropology. Anthropologists feel challenged by a philosophical complaint that when they draw upon philosophy, they tend to cherry-pick. Anthropologists are sensitive to being portrayed as conceptual amateurs, or dabblers. A harsh philosopher might put it this way. There is an anthropological rule of thumb in how to use philosophy: Take a little of this and a little of that and mix it into your interpretive stew as you wish. Do not worry if the philosophers you draw upon describe themselves as incommensurably at odds with one another. Do not trouble yourself to learn the history of ideas that a philosopher is speaking to, or against, or with. And do not worry about being too "true" to a philosopher's system of thought. Just draw upon those arguments of a philosopher that illuminate your ethnographic material and ignore those arguments that do not.

One anthropological response to this charge is that this approach to theory (philosophical or otherwise) is central to the entire disciplinary enterprise, even central to how anthropology can contribute theoretically to questions that philosophers are also concerned with. Most essentially, there is the matter of the sheer thickness, the nuance, of ethnographic examples. The methods of anthropology produce slices of the world that overflow, elide, slip away from the systematic purity of theory. This penchant for messiness is no accident; in fact its production in fieldnotes and monographs is a matter of some disciplinary pride. Part of the job of the anthropologist in the field is to undergo a form of immersion in some local reality (or realities), compelling her to rethink, modify, or even discard the theoretical frameworks she has learned. This is not because theory is without merit. It is simply because theory, being general, cannot be expected to capture the nuance of the particular events that the fieldworker is documenting. In an effort to do justice to this kind of phenomenal complexity, the anthropologist may draw upon a variety of theorists, but the field itself—the people, the events, the experiences that the anthropologist has—all this messy "reality" (for want of a better term)—is *expected to talk back*. It is expected to resist, to surprise, to call for new questions, to undo assumptions. This is the hope and the challenge of the anthropological method.

The theoretical innovation that an anthropologist can contribute to philosophy comes from this dialogue between the theoretically informed expectations and questions that the ethnographer brings to the field and what emerges as salient once she has spent time there. Salience is guided by several criteria. Most centrally, it means that in some way, the ethnographer's questions are meant to intersect with matters that are "at stake" for the people she studies. Or, if her questions and interests veer sharply away from their concerns, this is a matter to be explained and justified. But salience is also more broadly understood in terms of the local material, the social and historical conditions that are of significance to the people living in that field.

What does this difference in approach mean in terms of how anthropologists make use of philosophy? As already noted, the questions are often as radical or basic as those of philosophers. For example: What does it mean to be a person? To have an experience? To know something? To distinguish truth from falsehood? To be social? To live temporally? To trust? To hope? But answers emerge through methods that defy philosophical lines in the sand. What if it turns out that the ethnographic scene seems to be in some ways Foucauldian, in some ways Marxian, in other ways, Heideggerian? What if it appears that both Sartre and Bourdieu have something to say that illuminates a particular situation, even if Bourdieu, with great explicitness, rejects Sartre's formulations? This is the anthropological dilemma: Being loyal to the ethnographic density of the situation either leaves one theory-less (stranded in "mere description") or calls for some manner of cherry-picking through various theoretical positions. Purism simply will not do; it is too reductive. The conceptually innovative anthropologist is very likely to have "borrowed" and indigenized theoretical voices drawn not only from various schools of philosophical thought but from other disciplines as well.

Anthropology: A View from Philosophy

Philosophers have not been as concerned with anthropology as anthropologists have with philosophy. Few influential contemporary philosophers take anthropological studies into account in their work. Those who specialize in philosophy of social science may consider or analyze examples from anthropological research, but do this mostly to illustrate conceptual points or epistemological distinctions (for instance between explanatory and interpretive approaches) or to criticize epistemological or ethical implications (a few examples of which will be mentioned below). Philosophy students seldom study or show serious interest in anthropology. They may learn about experimental methods in science, but rarely about anthropological fieldwork.

In a way this is no surprise. Philosophy is an old discipline, probably the oldest scholarly discipline in Western culture. Reading texts is an important part of studying and doing philosophy. Studying philosophy is not (as will be made clear below) *only* about reading and understanding texts, but the canonized texts are crucial to philosophy. Most of the texts are difficult. Reading and understanding thinkers like Plato, Aristotle, Aquinas, Descartes, Spinoza, Leibniz, Hume, Locke, Kant, and Hegel takes a great deal of time, skill, and discipline. You can become a medical doctor without studying Hippocrates, Paracelsus, or Sydenham. You cannot, however, become a philosopher without knowing the works of the great philosophers of the past. Perhaps Whitehead was not completely right when he claimed that all philosophy is a footnote to Plato. Nevertheless, to understand modern philosophers such as Nietzsche, Marx, and Bergson or to understand great philosophers of the twentieth century (like Wittgenstein, Heidegger, Dewey, Arendt, Deleuze, and Foucault) you have to have knowledge of, and insight into, the philosophical tradition.

However, philosophers' widespread neglect of anthropology is not just a consequence of their preoccupation with interpretive work and conceptual scrutinizing of the canonized works of philosophy. After all, contemporary philosophers have recognized that doing serious epistemology or metaphysics implies acquiring knowledge of relevant parts of mathematical logic, semantics, or even modern physics. So how is it that so many philosophers write about social life, culture, and practice without being concerned with contemporary research in anthropology and sociology? According to the German philosopher Michael Theunissen, a former professor at Freie Universität in Berlin and an expert on Hegel and Kierkegaard, standards of philosophy change over time. He addresses the question: How is it possible to do philosophy today in an age so heavily dominated by science and technology? (Theunissen 1989). When Marx lived in London and frequented the British Museum for ten years to study economics, he set a new standard for philosophy, Theunissen argues. The philosopher still has to know the philosophical tradition and know how categories and conceptual frameworks have developed. But this is no longer sufficient. To contribute to a philosophical understanding of society and social practice, the philosopher also has to study the research being conducted in the field.

Today, according to Theunissen, a philosopher would be seen as a charlatan if he tried to present a philosophy of social life without also having adequate knowledge of scientific or scholarly research of relevance to his study. However, this does not seem to hold true in all areas. Even prominent philosophers still write about society and social practice without considering anthropological or sociological research. John Searle, just to mention one example, does not consider any works by sociologists or anthropologists at all in his book *The Construction of Social Reality* (Searle 1995). Some philosophers have decried institutionalized philosophy for ignoring anthropology and sociology. One of the most notable examples is Pierre Bourdieu, who left philosophy to become an anthropologist and sociologist. He ridiculed philosophers for believing that they could say anything illuminating about society without studying it (Bourdieu 1997).

But are abandoning the philosophical discipline or acquiring competence in multiple disciplines (philosophy *and* sociology, for example) the only viable alternatives? This is not a very practical suggestion; it takes years of training to carry out sophisticated and theoretically nuanced fieldwork. And, of course, it also takes many years of study to become philosophically proficient, so this is not an obvious route for the anthropologist. We consider some other possibilities for working between philosophy and disciplines dedicated to the study of social practice.

Aristotle's Division of Philosophical Labor

Aristotle offers one promising start. He promoted the idea of philosophy as the queen of the sciences. He attributed a special role to philosophy but, at the same time, acknowledged the sciences as relatively independent fields or practices that developed knowledge by methods fit for the problems within their specific domains. He abandoned Plato's idea of the Philosopher King, contending that philosophers should have neither sovereign power in the state nor power over the arts and sciences.

Aristotle offers a model for fruitful collaboration between philosophers and researchers in contemporary interdisciplinary research, namely a strategy for a division of labor. Philosophers are to carry out conceptual analysis, making crucial distinctions between categories, articulating epistemological standards, and so on. Researchers for their part (for example in anthropology and sociology), are to conduct their concrete studies informed by the results of the (sometimes abstract) conceptual and epistemological analyses, and at the same time contribute to conceptual development and epistemological reflection.

A few examples can help to illustrate this idea of a division of labor between philosophy and anthropology. Ludwig Wittgenstein criticized James Frazer's account of magical and religious views in *The Golden Bough.* Frazer made these views appear as *errors,* but according to Wittgenstein (1967), "truth" and "falsehood" are only applicable to propositions or stated theories. Religious and magical practices are not stated as theories, and they are not to be changed through argument. Wittgenstein's critique was based upon a conceptual analysis of truth and falsehood. He did not, however, give an a priori criticism of Frazer for not living up to specific *scientific* standards. His analysis of Frazer does not imply a criticism of anthropology as, say, not meeting standards of scientific practice. Rather, Wittgenstein was attempting to contribute to developing an anthropological approach to human practices.

Bernard Williams's (1985) and Gilbert Ryle's (2009a, 2009b) distinction between "thick" and "thin" descriptions is another example of philosophers trying to highlight an important conceptual distinction that holds relevance outside philosophy. Ryle illuminated this distinction through a typical ordinary language analysis, but its broader relevance is illustrated in the way it was subsequently taken up by Geertz, where it served a crucial role in furthering his interpretive approach to anthropology and his well-known theory of "thick description" (Geertz 1973). Here, philosophy was used to promote epistemological reflection within anthropology.

A third example may further illustrate the fruitful division of philosophical labor between philosophers and anthropologists. Marcel Mauss's famous essay "A Category of the Human Mind: The Notion of Person; The Notion of Self" has been analyzed, discussed, and criticized by anthropologists and philosophers (such as Carrithers et al. 1985). Mauss's text is quite complex and difficult. In a book dedicated to Mauss's article, Steven Lukes launches his concluding remarks as follows: "A magnificent answer—but what was the question? That is how a reflective reader might reasonably respond to Mauss's provocative and perplexing essay" (Lukes 1985: 282). Lukes does not, however, assume the role of Philosopher King in condemning Mauss for having written an obscure, perhaps even incoherent, text. Rather, he approaches it as textual material and, along with other contributors to the same volume, he brings Mauss into dialogue with philosophers (including Kant and Strawson) as well as other sociologists, illuminating Mauss by situating his analysis historically and socially. Lukes's contribution (and the edited book more generally) can be seen as a realization of an Aristotelian model for interdisciplinary collaboration between philosophers and anthropologists.

So there are a few examples. But once again the question is: Why so few? If Aristotle provided a promising starting point for collaboration, why are there not more examples of this kind of interdisciplinary collaboration? Is there something about the culture of philosophy and the way it is taught that impedes this?

Why Philosophers Ignored Aristotle's Division of Labor

Jean-Paul Sartre offers a suggestive answer to our questions, drawing upon his own experience of learning (Sartre 1963). Like any other philosophy student, Sartre had studied all the major Western philosophers: Plato, Aristotle, Descartes, and Kant. But at a crucial point in his education he discovered something important about learning and understanding philosophy: something he did, in fact, get from his teachers at the university. What he realized was that at any time, depending upon social and political conditions, there was a selection even among the "great" or "canonized" philosophers about who ought to be read, and how they ought to be received. In 1925, when Sartre was twenty years old, there was such a "horror of dialectics ... that Hegel himself was unknown to us" (Sartre 1963: 17). Of course, Sartre continues, the students were allowed to read Marx. They were even advised to read him; one had to know Marx "in order to refute him."

Sartre read Marx, and he found "everything perfectly clear" (Sartre 1963:18), but, as he adds, "I understood absolutely nothing." Sartre explains this apparent contradiction. "To understand is to change, to go beyond oneself." Reading Marx did not change him. Rather, change came with experiencing the social world he was living in, specifically the reality of Marxism, the workers who lived and practiced Marxism. It was their practice that began changing Sartre. What he also discovered, then, was that philosophical enquiries are not only to be carried out in the armchair or at the desk. Coming to understand *how* philosophy plays a role in changing social practice paves the way for a personal change, and so for an understanding of the philosophy that is at play "out there" in a practice.

Sartre was not just writing about understanding Marx. "Every philosophy is practical, even the one which at first appears to be the most contemplative. Its method is a social and political weapon" (Sartre 1963: 5). As an example, Sartre mentions Cartesian rationalism. In line with Sartre's claims, but speaking about ethics, Moody-Adams argues that "Some of the most important moral inquiry ... takes place in the difficult context of everyday life." Understanding the context of moral inquiry, according to Moody-Adams, requires "a kind of moral ethnography" (Moody-Adams 1997: 189).

In light of this recognition that philosophers need to engage with and understand ordinary social practice, they should not only be less arrogant toward anthropologists who may lack their exegetic skills, but even welcome anthropologists as companions in interdisciplinary efforts to promote the understanding of philosophy: an understanding achieved through the interplay of engaging with the complexity of everyday practice and personal change. In fact, Sartre's perspective on understanding philosophy may point to a shortcut for anthropologists trying to integrate philosophical inquiries with their fieldwork. Anthropologists generally do not possess the exegetic skills that philosophers acquire through years of reading and analyzing philosophical texts, but they do have access to, and skills for interrogating, social practices. The texts they produce as a result, and the practices they work with to describe and interpret, may well embody philosophical ideas and perspectives, just as Sartre learned when he observed Marx's workers.

However, there still is a danger here for the anthropologist eager to connect philosophical ideas to examinations of local, social practices. Let us say the anthropologist identifies philosophical challenges in concrete practices. She accounts for a reasoning in practice that apparently embodies a philosophical strategy. She articulates what she assumes is the implicit philosophy of everyday actors by using relevant philosophers' concepts and, in so doing, redescribes the practice she is studying. Sartre has a warning: Intellectuals who apply a philosophical system "to conquer new territory not yet fully explored, those who provide practical applications for the theory and employ it as a tool to destroy or to construct—they should not be called philosophers" (Sartre 1963: 8).

What can we learn from Sartre here? Doing *philosophy in practice* is different from *applying* philosophical theories' frameworks or standards. Philosophies emerge from social practices undergoing transformation. A philosophy is alive and effective as long as the practices and the tensions that it articulates and illuminates are alive. Periods ripe with philosophical revolutions are rare. Descartes's and Locke's epochs are such periods. So is Kant's and Hegel's and, according to Sartre, the Marxian period. Philosophizing in practice is not in general as creative and critical as pathbreaking philosophical revolutions. But the structure of such paradigm changes can serve as a model for philosophizing in practice in a more general way.

This brings us back to a basic feature of philosophy mentioned earlier: philosophy as mediated in texts embodying positions, perspectives, and sometimes theoretical systems developed in negotiation, opposition, or struggle with other (earlier or simultaneous) positions or systems. The important point to underscore is this: No particular perspective (say an existentialist or phenomenological perspective) should *ever* be used for interpreting or conceptualizing empirical material *in abstraction from* or by *neglecting* this dialectics between philosophical positions. Sartre illustrates this by pointing out how Kierkegaard's existentialism should not be seen as a self-contained answer to the question of what a human being is. He warns against hypostasizing Kierkegaard's account of the responsible, individual human being. Kierkegaard's existentialism has to be understood in its dialectical relation to Hegel and the struggle between these two perspectives as reflecting or articulating a culturally and historically situated conflict.

Sartre's point and his illustration are so crucial to the general claim of this chapter that they merit further elaboration. Kierkegaard insists unrelentingly on the irreducibility and specificity of what is lived. The lived subjective life can never be an object of knowledge. Our inwardness in its infinite depth, a subjectivity discovered beyond language, is the kernel of Kierkegaard's existentialism (Sartre 1963: 10–11). How is Kierkegaard's account of the human condition to be understood, and how could it inform anthropologists studying contemporary human practices? Sartre stresses that Kierkegaard is inseparable from Hegel. For Hegel, our inward paradoxes, ambiguities, and dilemmas are manifestations of an unhappy consciousness that can be surpassed or transcended in knowledge. The pure, lived aspect of tragic experience that Kierkegaard focuses upon is—in Hegel—"absorbed by the system as a relatively abstract determination which must be mediated, as a passage towards the absolute, the only genuine concrete" (Sartre 1963: 9). In Hegel's philosophy, knowledge is ascribed eminent dignity.

Contextualizing Kierkegaard's "anthropology" as a position in philosophical controversies is a demanding task, however. It points to an urgent need to foster collaboration between philosophy and the social sciences. In interdisciplinary research, this is probably primarily a task for the trained philosopher. Yet anthropologists, sociologists, and historians do have important tasks to carry out in *understanding* Kierkegaard, that is, understanding potentials in his thinking for *changing us* and our approach to human practices today. Kierkegaard is inseparable from Hegel and, according to Sartre, "his vehement negation of every system can arise only within a cultural field entirely dominated by Hegelianism—The Dane feels himself hemmed in by concepts, by History, he fights for his life, it is the reaction of Christian romanticism against the rationalist humanization of faith" (Sartre 1963: 12).

Our cultural, social, and political situation is very different from the situation in which the Hegel–Kierkegaard controversy was situated and developed. But might there be similarities between that situation and our present situation, and conflicts between hegemonic institutions structuring and constraining our individual lives *and* individuals' and communities struggling to get their suffering and subjectivity recognized? Anthropologists addressing and trying to answer such questions are not *applying* philosophy from yesterday to contemporary life and practices, but contributing to developing philosophy by studying social life today.

Anthropology as Part of a Cosmopolitan Practical Philosophy: The Kantian Bridge

The philosophical role just ascribed to anthropology was partly inspired by Sartre's reflections both on Marx and, more broadly, on the relations between philosophy and social practice. There are, however, reasons for accepting and promoting that role without relying on or accepting the materialist perspective adopted by Sartre in his late work. We turn to Immanuel Kant to further develop this claim. Kant lectured on anthropology beginning in 1772 and during all the years while writing his three critiques—*Critique of Pure Reason, Critique of Practical Reason,* and *Critique of Judgment*—which have influenced philosophical thought ever since. In 1798 he published *Anthropology from a Pragmatic Point of View* based upon his lectures.

The lectures were very popular and the book was also widely read at the time. Strangely enough, Kant's work has rarely been mentioned in histories of anthropology, although among philosophers there has been, and still is, a discussion about the relation between Kant's critical philosophical work and his reflections on anthropology. However, this is not our concern here. What is of interest for our purposes is Kant's *distinction* between two different approaches to philosophy. This delineation is introduced in a chapter on method already present in his *Critique of Pure Reason*. Kant distinguishes between two kinds of philosophy, corresponding to two different kinds of concepts. On the one hand, there are scholastic concepts, which today we call "expert concepts," that are specified, defined, and justified within a scientific or systematic framework. On the other hand, we have cosmopolitan or popular concepts (*Weltbegriffe*), meaning concepts shared by all language users and related to our human life and our ends.

Scholastic philosophy is concerned with scholastic concepts. Doing scholastic philosophy is analyzing concepts and arguments in philosophical texts (including what we earlier characterized as the exegetic work of philosophy). Here, the consistency and coherence of concepts, arguments, and systems are assessed without considering the meaning or relevance of those concepts to life or social practice. Cosmopolitan philosophy, alternatively, examines the relevance and meaning of concepts in relation to our life. For Kant, anthropology plays a crucial role in developing this latter cosmopolitan (practical) philosophy. Kant's cosmopolitanism suggests a unification of anthropology and philosophy in analyzing popular concepts embedded in everyday practice. Most of Kant's philosophy, his metaphysics as well as his ethics, is, however, abstract, and a priori, and detached from everyday experience, so how could he possibly be an inspiration for a practical philosophy-cum-anthropology today?

There is an ongoing discussion of Kant's cosmopolitanism and how to understand it in relation to his whole critical project as developed in his *Critique of Pure Reason* and *Critique of Practical Reason*. That discussion is beyond the scope of this chapter. We would, however, remind readers of Kant's own understanding of the relation between his more abstract (transcendental) philosophical analyses and a cosmopolitan philosophy. Kant's three famous questions—What can I know? What should I do? What may I hope? (Kant 1998: 677)—are respectively answered in metaphysics, ethics, and religion. But all three questions belong to anthropology, according to Kant, because they refer to a fourth question: "What is man?" As stressed by Martin Heidegger, Kant never came to a clear understanding of the peculiarity of that question and its relation to metaphysics, "for anthropology is an empirical-ontic science and as such cannot afford to found ontology and philosophy in general" (Heidegger 1997: 48).

Other interpreters of Kant's anthropology have been less concerned with the problem of understanding the relation between metaphysics and Kant's cosmopolitan approach. Foucault, for example, reads Kant's anthropology as a kind of a paradigm for reflecting on and accounting for human practice. Foucault highlighted important aspects of Kant's position in his complementary doctoral thesis: *Introduction to Kant's Anthropology.* Foucault stressed that, according to Kant, "*Anthropology* is ... neither a history of culture nor an analysis of successive forms, but the practice, at once immediate and imperative, of a culture already given in advance. It teaches man to recognize, within his own culture, what the world teaches him" (Foucault 2008: 54).

Foucault does not discuss an important presupposition Kant makes in his understanding of anthropology and its role—that a philosophy of human nature is to be combined with a philosophy of history. Kant advocated an optimistic Enlightenment philosophy of continuous historical progress. We are, as human beings, destined to live in a society with other human beings, to cultivate and civilize ourselves. We are constantly under the influence of our desires and our inclinations, but we are still destined to make ourselves worthy of humanity (Wilson 2006: 38). Today, few would adopt Kant's teleological philosophy of history and his vision of continuous and inevitable historical process toward a just cosmopolitan world order. One might reasonably ask: Why then draw upon Kant at all? If we reject Kant's idea of transcendental freedom, his a priori principles, *and* his teleological philosophy of history, do we not need another philosophical framework to secure the role of cosmopolitan anthropology ascribed by Kant?

Although in this chapter we cannot address this objection, we would still claim that Kant's demarcation of a special kind of philosophical inquiry that is, in its essence, practical and anthropological is an exceedingly important one. Furthermore, his three questions ring every bit as true, and every bit as profound, today as they were when he asked them. In the second part of the chapter we consider one of them—"What can I hope for"—in a particular historical and ethnographic context where the question is not posed by a philosopher, but by people struggling to live their lives. In so doing, we will try to contribute a cosmopolitan philosophy, inspired by Kant's, but in some respects quite different from it.

Anthropology as Cosmopolitan Philosophy

To summarize thus far: We have puzzled over, and suggested some reasons for, the difficulties that have kept anthropologists and philosophers from engaging in fruitful conversations, despite their many shared interests and concerns. More optimistically, we have outlined three claims proposed *within philosophy* that provide some support and guidance for how anthropology and philosophy might develop their conversation in more promising directions.

First, we noted that Aristotle, even while promoting philosophy as queen of the sciences, rejected Plato's Philosopher King, and offered an intellectual division of labor that, although obviously in need of amendment to fit our current historical situation, provides a useful starting point. Aristotle acknowledged that the sciences were relatively independent fields that developed their own methods to fit the problems specific to them. Thus, he announced the necessity of contributions from disciplines and methods outside philosophy for the production of knowledge. Obviously, this recognition suggests the need for philosophy to look beyond itself to other disciplines and other methods in order to do its work.

Second, drawing upon Sartre, we took up his challenge that to really do philosophy, and even to understand philosophy, one could not simply read texts or do armchair-based exegetical exercises. He makes two important amendments. Even as a philosopher, he argued, one also needed to observe (or perhaps even participate in) social practices themselves. Sartre was, of course, particularly concerned with social practices that were directed toward changing society. But Sartre also offers another challenge that would take philosophy outside the library or its task of exegesis: that to actually understand or learn philosophy—not only a practical activist like Marx, but even more "contemplative" philosophers like Descartes—one must be changed personally. While anthropologists would not necessarily agree with Sartre's focus on practices that are specifically directed to social change, they would certainly strongly support his view that the development of social theory demands engagement with "real world" social practices, both through closely observing them and through participating in them. What is more, many anthropologists would also strongly support Sartre's view that learning, and even the understanding of texts themselves, not to mention social practices, involves not only the cultivation of skills, methods, and theoretical sophistication but indeed personal transformation. Certainly it has been part of the folk wisdom of anthropology that the experience of doing work "in the field" will, and should, change you.

Thirdly and finally we discussed Kant's useful distinction between "exegetical" or "scholastic" and "cosmopolitan" forms of philosophy. Unlike Sartre, Kant offers a legitimate place for the sort of armchair philosophy that anthropologists have so often critiqued. However, he also proposes a version of philosophy that is, precisely, anthropological. His cosmopolitan philosophy covers just the sort of terrain that is a hallmark of anthropology as a contemporary discipline, namely the investigation of popular concepts used by ordinary language users. And, we might add, remembering Sartre, that such a cosmopolitan philosophy should explore popular concepts not as divorced from everyday practice, as "ideal type" cultural discourse, but rather as part of life, embedded within it. This embedding within practice even allows the philosophical anthropologist to examine how such concepts are critiqued, modified, indigenized, and reflected upon by their users.

Cosmopolitan Philosophical Anthropology and the Concept of "Hope"

In this second section of our chapter, we focus upon the concept of hope. The study of hope offers many difficulties to anthropology as well as to philosophy. Hope concerns imagined futures. Its direction is toward what may come to pass. This is not a future one can simply predict, but a future of "what if." To study hope, then, is to consider future time in the subjunctive mode. We will speak of hope not as simple optimism or faith in some "happy ending," but as something darker and morally demanding. Paradoxically, hope is on intimate terms with despair. It asks for more than life promises. It is poised for disappointment.

This existential paradox that has been developed in philosophical and literary texts takes cultural and structural root as it is shaped by particular local worlds. For the past fifteen years, one of the authors (Cheryl Mattingly), and her colleagues, have been carrying out field-work in Los Angeles among African-American families caring for children with serious and chronic medical conditions. This research has led to thinking about hope in increasingly complex ways. Hope is rarely a personal matter for the families in the study; rather, it is deeply interdependent. It connects very directly to their struggle to cultivate relations and build communities with others, to cultivate trust, even across social and political divides that may seem to make these tasks nearly impossible. Hope is a *practice* rather than merely an emotion, belief, or cultural model that members of a community simply enact, feel, or espouse.

For these families, hope emerges as a strenuous moral project. Even in the rare circumstances when the clinical problems can be more or less cured, the social situations in which many families live mean that the future may look exceedingly grim. Thus, cultivating a hopeful stance intimately involves an ongoing conversation with embittered despair. To hope is to be reminded of what is not, and what might never be. These families speak of the call to hope as a moral call, bound up in views of what it means to live a good life, to be a good person. Many of the families in our study have spoken repeatedly about working to have the "strength" to hope, even when times are hard.

How might we consider the perilous kinship of hope and despair as it emerges in the experiences of family members who both seek out and try to create *spaces of hope*, especially as connected to projects of personal and social transformation? And, how might this consideration illustrate cosmopolitan philosophical anthropology at work and enlarge our *conceptual* understanding of hope?

We are going to apply an Aristotelian-inspired theory of praxis (often called virtue ethics) developed in philosophy that emphasizes both the cultivation of virtue as an essential aspect of practice, and a kind of practical reasoning in which practical actors do not merely deliberate about what is most expedient or strategically useful, but talk about what might constitute the "best good" in the historically singular circumstances of their everyday lives. From this perspective the practical is always moral. And the moral is situated rather than universally dictated. It is also vulnerable in a host of ways—uncertain in its results because social interactions are always uncertain. Yet bringing this philosophical framework to bear in elucidating popular concepts and practices of hope raises the danger Sartre also noted: How are we to engage this vocabulary in a conversation with empirical investigations without becoming ideological? We address this danger in three ways.

First, we give some context to the concept of hope as it has developed within the cultural historical situation of African-Americans. Second, we contextualize the contemporary philosophical work on virtue ethics within current theoretical debates. To put it in dialectical terms: What is virtue ethics arguing *against*? Why this interest in excavating and revising moral schemes from Antiquity in European and Anglo-American philosophy? And why has this philosophical work been taken up, especially among some phenomenological anthropologists? How is it situated within contemporary debates in the social sciences? Obviously, within the confines of this chapter we can only be brief here, but hopefully this cultural historical glance at concepts and theoretical traditions will be suggestive. A third strategy for avoiding transforming everyday practices of hope into ideology is to examine, in some detail, how the popular concept of hope is not merely invoked, but recreated and critiqued by ordinary actors as part of their very practice of trying to create hope in their local circumstances.

Contextualizing Hope in the African-American Experience: Blues Hope

Why is hope so important for these African-American families? Why is it required? What kind of vision of reality does it offer? It has rarely seemed something as simple as delusion or denial. Even in cases where a child's diagnosis is not life-threatening or especially physically dangerous, the sheer chronicity of the situation has brought its own dangers. There are no simple solutions. Living with any significant disability, especially when coupled with poverty and racial stigma, can be grim work. From one view of reality (a "realistic" perspective), it is, in fact, cause for despair. And despair is precisely what families fight against. They do not see despair as realistic, but rather as having its own kind of delusion. A comforting delusion that nothing more is required, that the future is fated and they can simply "give up."

Their voices reflect a stance that has long been central for African-Americans. The idea of hope as a moral practice of survival and a battle against despair is embedded deep within African-American discourse and has been since the time of slavery. From a moral perspective, hope has always been a central concern, a stance meant to combat racism, poverty, stigma, and shame. Despite the pernicious continuity of political and economic conditions that continue to imperil a large segment of the African-American population (the bottom economic third are now comparatively as poor as they were over sixty years ago, before the battle for civil rights), the call to struggle against despair has historically been a primary theme. We can hear it voiced by African-American politicians, preachers, scholars, and artists. It has been an explicit concern voiced by the overwhelming majority of families in our study, from the poorest to the middle-class. Often families have spoken about this in highly personal terms, but equally often they have turned this personal determination to struggle against despair into public and political battles against injustice. Sometimes this move from the personal to the political sphere has meant that family members have begun to re-imagine their citizenship in ways that extend well beyond a political allegiance to fellow African-Americans.

Cornel West speaks of this as a "blues hope" that has arisen out of this ongoing press-back against the dangers of despair, around what West calls "the eclipse of hope," which he also equates with a kind of self-hate that plagues a group as highly stigmatized as African-Americans (West 2001: 9). The terrible danger is that hatred and despair turn inward, producing, for example, black-on-black violence, and black shame. Blues hope reveals itself in expressive culture through song, literature, and art, and especially through religious and political culture in the sermons and exhortations of prominent African-American ministers and leaders. But it is also present in the most ordinary, often religiously inflected, practices of African-American people trying to make their lives worth living, also morally, even against so many odds. Here is how West speaks of it: "Hope is inseparable from despair. Those of us who truly hope make despair a constant companion whom we out-wrestle every day owing to our commitment to justice, love, and hope. It is impossible to look honestly at our catastrophic conditions and not have some despair—it is a healthy sign of how deeply we care. Wisdom comes from wrestling with despair and not allowing despair to have the last word. That's why hope is always blood-stained and tear-soaked" (West 2008: 216).

"Hope" as Moral Practice: Dialectical Contextualizing in Contemporary Theory

To select "hope" as a topic and concept crucial to social practice says something about current theoretical debates. It puts us at odds with some of the most influential contemporary trends in anthropology and philosophy, especially those that have emerged out of linguistic, structuralist, and poststructuralist frameworks that have so consistently championed cultural or structural determinisms. Hope becomes a topic for scholars attempting to make room for the possibility of social and personal transformation. Hope has long been regarded with great suspicion in social theory. And perhaps nowhere has the skepticism been more clearly directed than to people's moralities, their beliefs about the good and the right, about individual responsibility and the cultivation of a self. Actors may have their hopes and dreams but these are not to be taken at face value. As David Harvey notes, Antonio Gramsci's famous call for a "pessimism of the intellect" has become a "battle cry" for those working in the cultural studies movement—a phrase turned "into a virtual law of human nature" (Harvey 2000: 7). Or, as Ernst Bloch has admitted, "Possibility has had a bad press" (Bloch 1986: 7). These scholars point out that it is a *stance of hope* that has been rejected here.

Why is this the case? One very powerful theoretical position that has long dominated social and philosophical thought is what Paul Ricoeur has called a "hermeneutics of suspicion." Charles Taylor has recently described this as a growing "moral imagination of unbelief" that arose in the nineteenth century, "accrediting a sense of reality as deep, systematic, as finding its mainsprings well below an immediately available surface" (Taylor 2007: 369). As part of this ethos, new kinds of critiques of personal and social life became possible: "the possibility of signifying another thing than what one believes was signified" (Ricoeur 1978: 215).

One could say that we contemporary social theorists have collectively become masters of suspicion. The poststructuralist influence, especially from Foucault's work, has enormously furthered this skeptical gaze within social theory. But it is important to say that Foucault's suspicion—one that continues to feed our sociological imagination—goes well beyond some idea that we are simply deluded about the structural forces that shape our lives, or that a deeper meaning to life eludes us as ordinary practical actors. Rather, he offers a much more powerfully destabilizing view, an analysis of social life and of truth itself that is intended to go *beyond* hermeneutics of any sort, suspicious or otherwise. Foucault challenges humanism itself in his insistence that meaning is not the point: that there is nothing "underneath" anything else, so to speak. What the Foucauldian-inspired genealogist uncovers is how truths, subjectivities, selves, and notions of meaning are produced in any historical period through various social practices that disguise their own power. That is, through forms of institutional governance, through the discourse of experts, through the training of bodies, through the organization of temporal and physical space, through a well-worn, invisible—to the common eye, at least, if not to the scholarly one—and immensely seductive "mobile army of metaphors," as Nietzsche would put it.

It is not just the idea of "meaning" that is rejected from a genealogical perspective, but also a host of other equally treasured concepts in the humanistic pantheon. Nikolas Rose (1998), following just such a Foucauldian line of thought, sees the kinship constructs of self, agency, morality, and the like as part of a "tired old humanism." He is cited here at some length because he offers such a usefully decisive condemnation of just those humanistic constructs that are called upon in developing our own consideration of hope: constructs that are also invoked by the families we write about. Rose points to poststructuralist writing that has finally exposed the "death of the self." He notes with approval the many theorists who have offered us "countless obituaries of the image of the human being that animated our philosophies and our ethics for so long: the universal subject, stable, unified, totalized, individualized, interiorized" (Rose 1998: 169). From Rose's point of view, this portrait has been so thoroughly demolished that it is simply untenable to hold onto it any longer. Even so, he notices that in everyday life this portrait flourishes more than ever as "regulatory practices seek to govern individuals in a way more tied to their 'selfhood' than ever before" (Rose 1998: 169).

In a whole range of practices, including medicine and health, "human beings are addressed, represented, and acted upon *as if they were selves* of a particular type: suffused with an individual subjectivity, motivated by anxieties and aspirations concerning their self-fulfillment, committed to finding their true identities and maximizing their authentic expressions in their lifestyles" (Rose 1998: 169–70). Equally in our political thinking, we "operate in terms of an image of each human being as the unified psychological focus of his or her biography" (Rose 1998: 170). Rose suggests that ordinary practices continue to be based upon these erroneous presumptions of an interior, coherent, agentive self, revealing how everyday persons are not only in the grip of this cultural mystification, but that such common-sense ideas about freedom and selfhood make a troublesome neo-liberal government possible.

This skeptical tradition that Rose represents and so beautifully elucidates here has been enormously fruitful in revealing the pervasive power of oppressive social structures, often emphasizing what it is that people on the ground are *not* seeing and *not* knowing, and especially how they are blind to the forces that constrain them. But why bother with this unmasking business if there is nothing like truth, or even meaning, to be discovered? Foucault puts it this way: "everything is dangerous," our primary theoretical task being that of pointing out the dangers of contemporary society. He argues for "a hyper- and pessimistic activism." Ethically speaking, the "choice we have to make every day is to determine which is the main danger," as he once remarked in an interview (Foucault 1983: 232).

Contextualizing Virtue Ethics

The popularity of virtue ethics can also be understood dialectically. It emerged as a response to, and challenge of, dominant deontological and utilitarian moral positions. Perhaps no one has stated the case for virtue ethics so clearly as Alasdair MacIntyre. But its popularity can also be attributed to concerns that point toward opening up new ways to consider the practical and the temporal from a phenomenological perspective.

Aristotelian ethics, or what is sometimes called Aristotle's "practical philosophy," has been important to both continental phenomenology and moral philosophy's Anglo-American virtue ethics. In the 1920s and 1930s, Heidegger introduced Aristotle to German philosophers in a whole new way, giving us a phenomenological Aristotle whose work had radical implications for understanding human experience (Brogan 2005; Hyland and Manoussakis 2006). Heidegger came to recognize that Aristotle was not simply the classic "classifier," as he had so often been characterized, but offered an avenue for grounding a practical ontology that wed hermeneutics and phenomenology to everyday practice and to a temporality of human becoming. In the tradition of continental philosophy, scholars within phenomenology and existentialism (notably Heidegger 1962; Arendt 1958; and Gadamer 1975) were instrumental in fostering a neo-Aristotelian revival that philosophers continue to develop in various ways. While Heidegger downplayed Aristotle's ethics, his "discovery" of the centrality of *becoming* and the *temporality* of being in Aristotle and pre-Socratic Antiquity paved the way for his students, including Hannah Arendt and Hans-Georg Gadamer, to take up these ideas in the context of Aristotle's ethics. Arendt, in particular, elucidates Greek Antiquity's conception of practical reasoning as related to moral concerns with *phronesis,* the cultivation of virtues, the human pursuit of the good life, and a portrait of the human condition as an experience of vulnerable temporality.

Neo-Aristotelian virtue ethics in Anglo-American philosophical traditions developed several decades after Heidegger's reintroduction of Aristotle to continental philosophy—around the middle of the twentieth century. There are many reasons for this "discovery" of Aristotle in ordinary language philosophy, moral philosophy, and philosophy of action. One is rooted not in a concern with ethics per se, but with an interest in promoting a picture of action that could counter the mechanistic explanations of human action then dominant within the social and historical sciences. Rather than subsuming actions under general laws, one could consider them in terms of intentions and consequences; a claim that presumed first-person agents who had reasons, desires, and some ends toward which they were fashioning their purposes. But it is in the work of such moral and political philosophers as MacIntyre, Taylor, Wiggins, Williams, Foote, Nussbaum, Murdoch, and Cavell that we find a strongly marked *first-person* tradition of *virtue ethics.* Beginning in the 1950s and 1960s, philosophers (such as Anscombe 1957; Winch 1958; Murdoch 1970) began to mount their own critiques of Enlightenment moral schemes, returning to Aristotelian virtue ethics for inspiration.

What Aristotle emphasized that has been taken up in both these first-person camps is a perspective that also belongs to the pre-Socratic Greek world: the notion that the essence of human existence is not so much in a quality or set of qualities of "being," but rather in a process, which is the process of becoming. Cultivating virtue is part of that be-coming, and action (with all its frailty) is at the center of things. For classical Greece, "to act in its general sense," as Arendt points out (and we emphasize above), "means to take an initiative, to begin … to set something into motion" (1958: 177). For Aristotle, this beginning was intimately tied to a "sense of an ending" because an action is always tied to a *telos*, "that-for-the-sake-of-which" (Knight 2007: 10). In his teleological account of action, Aristotle was concerned with potential-ity, as Cavell put it, with "the power to be attracted to a further self, or state of the self." This is an idea taken up by Heidegger, who speaks of "human existence … as essentially characterized by possibilities" (Cavell 2004: 352). This teleological picture of action does not accord with a means–ends utilitarianism, however. It is the *process of acting*, the *process of becoming* that is important. Put differently, the *action*, the *becoming*, is already an end in itself. Any linear or progressive picture of this teleological structure is further challenged because "becoming" even opens up the past. The past consists not only of what happened, but also of its unfulfilled possibilities (Baracchi 2006: 24).

Indigenizing Hope in Local Practice

We have already intimated why phenomenological and neo-Aristotelian virtue ethics as philosophical traditions that illuminate the moral as both *experienced* and connected to *cultivating character* are attractive in considering the situation of African-Americans struggling to cultivate hope. By contrast to skeptical or predetermined conceptual schemes, the African-American families, even those who are poor and living in exceedingly grim circumstances, struggle to hope even under the worst of conditions. They understand this as a *moral* struggle. And they do so with the view that their struggles are not simply about "coping" or "de-nial," but concern the possibility of social and personal transformation. To avoid reducing these struggles for hope into abstract philosophical schemes, we examine the practice of hope by turning to one particular historical event—a neighborhood vigil—and the actors that helped to create it.

The Neighborhood Park Vigil

Leroy was one of the boys recruited into the Boundary Crossing Re-search study in 1997 because of a congenital hip problem when he was

six years old. Through surgery and physical therapy his hip problem
was gradually diminished, and although he maintained some weakness, it was no longer apparent. He even went out for school football,
like his older brother Ralph had done before him. In his early teens
Leroy developed diabetes and was put on insulin to control it. Soon
after this new health problem arose, his mother went to prison. His
grandmother, who was very ill with breast cancer, could not take him
to his doctor's appointments. His diabetes, left untreated, grew worse.
When his mother was released from prison, she brought him back to
the doctors and the two of them went on a diet together. (She too suffers from diabetes.) In a few months his illness was under control and
he no longer needed medication. These two medical dramas during his
young life had apparently come to a happy conclusion. And then, quite
suddenly, everything changed.

In January 2008, at the age of sixteen, Leroy was murdered in front
of his house. Two young men in their early twenties wanted to take
his younger sister for a drive. She had gotten in the backseat of their
car when Leroy stormed out of the house (unarmed) and began arguing with them, and protectively trying to get his sister out. "She's too
young for you," he yelled. One of the men pulled out a gun and opened
fire. Leroy was shot nine times. He died two days later. Cheryl Mattingly
attended the funeral, where Leroy's older brother Ralph wept aloud at
the service, standing up and pleading with the audience, especially a
group of young men who lined the back of the church. "We have got to
stop the killing," he repeated over and over again. "This world is a cold,
cruel place," Leroy's best friend said in a poem she wrote and read
aloud at the service. The minister tried to reassure the audience that
Leroy was just "on loan," and that he was now in a better place. But the
misery in the room was palpable. Even the hymns of praise sounded
anguished. Yet despite its abysmal grief, the response of families like
Leroy's does not reflect the resigned despair that E. Valentine Daniel
(1996) documents among Sri Lankans, or that Nancy Scheper-Hughes
(1993) observes among destitute Brazilian mothers who have come to
accept the inevitable deaths of children "without weeping." Instead,
such despair is resisted, fought against. Leroy's extended family struggles to find ways for his death to serve as a kind of "witness," to call
out to others in the community to "stop the killing."

Here are a few lines from the lament spoken by Ralph, Leroy's older
brother, a young man in his late twenties. He is speaking at a candle-
light vigil just three days before Leroy's funeral, and two days after he
died in the hospital. This gathering of friends, relatives, and neighbors
takes place in a small, shabby park that is central to the black section

of his hometown (a township within Los Angeles County, located a few miles from the city itself). As usual, the park is populated with locals involved in numerous drug exchanges, or in drinking, talking, laughing, flirting, smoking crack. The mourners simply ignore this activity as they walk solemnly along, lit candles in hand, to gather in a circle around Ralph. Family members protectively surround Olga Solomon, the researcher in our study who filmed the vigil. Leroy's mother, Maureen, cautions a friend "I'm gonna stand with her. She don't want nobody to trip on her cause she videotaping. They don't know who she is." Leroy's family wants this moment documented and his mother directs friends to let others in the park know that Olga is videotaping by request. Participants in the vigil take their candles and place them on the ground near Ralph, at the center of the circle they have formed.

At the funeral many people will speak, whereas at this vigil Ralph is the only speaker. His words are addressed less to the women and children in the crowd than to the young men gathered around: men who, like himself, have been (or are) in gangs and have lived with violence. He speaks in a tone so angry and sad, so broken, that his words are difficult to listen to. His words, which at first seem fragmented, a torrent of despair, were, upon listening more carefully, a melody of rage and blame as well as a ferocious plea.

Many have argued that when great pain happens, there are no words to express it. There is a truth to that. But it is also true that poetry can arise at such moments: aesthetic creations that seem to be born from suffering itself. And so, in the face of the unjust death of his brother, Ralph abandons the casualness of ordinary speech. Instead, he offers a spontaneous prose poem, a hip-hop directive to the community to end the deaths and the killing. We have organized his words into stanzas to highlight the poetry of his language, the rhythms that bear down on the audience, so that even if—as he insists—no one understands, no one listens, he will speak, he will plead, he will confess, he will say the unsayable, he will say what must be said. Ralph offers us a stark portrait of that vanishingly thin line between hope and despair.

> I die.
> My Momma dies.
> Everybody dies niggah.
> My Grandma died.
> Ya'll don't know homie.
> All this shit, God, is fucked up niggah.
> We started the police trippin' on us niggah.
> Ya'll did it niggah, that's why ya'll gettin' it hard niggah.
> We did it.
> [I'm] one of the first niggah's on probation for gang shit, niggah.

> Ya'll don't understand niggah.
> They got us in a trap niggah.
> I've been in prison, back, everywhere.
> Ya'll going there too, keep doing that homie.
> I'm telling you.
> This shit fucked up.
> Ya'll don't understand homie.

Ralph begins to cry as he continues his anguished rap.

> Ya'll don't understand homie.
> No.
> Man, my little brother, man I got to deal with this thing all in my sleep
>   and everything.
> That's fucked up.
> Sixteen.
> No hope niggah.

Ralph shifts from this general lament and indictment of black-on-black violence to a graphic narration of the murder. He punctuates his narration with an enactment of where the bullets entered Leroy's body, pointing to this own body to illustrate. If these "homies" refuse to understand, he will compel their understanding, making them *feel* the entrance of the bullets, one by one. And he will admonish them to listen to their mothers and their grandmothers, to do whatever it takes to keep themselves safe. He refers to his brother through his affectionate nickname, "Man-Man."

> Ya'll gonna keep doing that stupid shit.
> And it took for *my little brother* to get shot for me to understand that this
>   shit is not stupid.
> It's not a game or nothin' homie.
> Ya'll got to understand this.
> Please understand this.
> I'm asking ya'll niggah.
> I don't ask people "please."
> I don't say "please homie," unless I really want you to do it.
> Please don't do that homie.
> He got shot nine times, niggah.
> Seven of the bullets stayed in his body, two of 'em went out.
> Man-Man fought.
> Ya'll got a lot to learn man.
> All that shit we been through, it ain't nothin' man.
> He fought on the [operating] table.
> He, he, got hit niggah, nine times.
> Five times right here. [Ralph points toward his chest.]
> Bam.
> Five times, one time right here. [Ralph points toward his wrist.]
> The niggah was running, he got hit in his ass niggah. [Ralph points to his
>   buttocks.]

He tried to get in the house, he got hit in his fucking liver.
One shot is all it took.
Liver, lungs, all that shit that's in your stomach.
One bullet hit that Man-Man, and went in there. [Ralph points to his stomach.]
You know why that happened?
Cause he ran.
He kept moving.
If he would've stayed still he probably would've lived.
He ran in the house, sat on the fucking couch man.
He fought hard.
He had three surgeries man.
He had three surgeries homie.
I don't know what it feel like to have no surgery.
He had three of 'em.
Man-Man went through all the surgeries.
They told us he was doing good.
Man-Man's heart started going down homie.
He just stopped fucking pumpin.
It slowly stopped pumping homie.

Ralph concludes the story of his brother's death by returning to his admonition to the crowd (and to himself) that black street violence has got to stop. For him, what emerges as especially unbearable is that his brother was an innocent victim. He wasn't meant for the streets. He was planning to become an engineer. Even white people cared about him. He was afraid to shoot a gun. He wasn't meant to be the one who got killed. Maybe Ralph and others might die—they lived by violence— but "Man-Man wasn't with that."

Tellin' ya'll, this is with all ya'll man.
Ya'll know Man-Man wasn't with that.
And he felt it. [The pain of violence.]
You know what I'm sayin'?
It's some of, you niggahs didn't even feel it, but Man-Man did homie.
That's how life go. God **show** us. You know what I'm saying.
Better than he can tell us.
And He tired of tellin' us.
He gonna keep showin' us and showin' us and showin' us until we get it right.
Look what that say niggah.
[Ralph points to a sign someone holds up high for everyone to see. It reads "WE MUST STOP KILLING US!"]
All you niggahs have probably seen this black car driving down the street with that [referring to the sign] on the side of the car niggah.
All you niggahs homie, been seeing **that** sign right there.
Niggah drive up and down the street in that black car.
And he serious.
We must stop killing us.
Two black niggahs just killed Man-Man, another black niggah.
And now we right here, I've gotta talk to ya'll.

> Man-Man wasn't half of the things that some of us was homie.
> You know that.
> He wasn't even **thinking** about **none** of that stuff.
> Niggah, Man-Man wanted to be an engineer homie.
> Ya'll don't even know the white people that came to my house that day niggah. [After Leroy died.]
> [Starting to sob] Gave cards for Man-Man.
> I fucked up homie!

Ralph breaks down, crying hard. He walks over to a man in the crowd and they put their arms around each other. He calls out to the crowd one last time:

> Fucked up my brother!

And with this, the vigil ends. Ralph's lament is not merely a piece of spontaneous poetry, not merely an expression of a quintessentially African-American cultural form. It is that, and it is something else besides. It is a form of moral deliberation. Ralph's lament raises such moral questions as: Who is to blame? Who can fix things? What can be hoped for? What can be done? How can this be bearable? What do we have to learn here? What have we not understood? What is required of us? How were we not just doing wrong but *seeing* wrong? What is it about our values and practices that leads us to this blindness? Why must we blame ourselves and not God, not even the "they's" who trap the disempowered?

The pondering over who is to blame is not, of course, a factual consideration (notably, Ralph never lays blame directly on the young man who actually shot Leroy), but a moral one. It is bound up not only with despair but also with hope, because it is about the possibility of agency, of social change. Ralph tells the others that only in coming to see more rightly, more wisely, will the community of "homies," his community, have any agency in turning the violence around. He lays blame to present moral lessons, where he sees that something can and must be learned. Here, many are culpable. Leroy and those who do not listen to their mamas. Himself for "fucking up." The "they" of the authorities, of a (white) social structure that "got us in a trap." More pervasively, the community of "homies" and "niggahs" who, like himself, have been blind, have refused to understand that violence is not "stupid." Stupid is too insipid a word for it. Stupid refuses the depth of despair that a truer, wiser gaze reveals. Violence is "not a game," but something much more heartbreaking. It must, at all costs, be stopped. "WE MUST STOP KILLING US" he reads aloud as a mourner holds up the sign high above his head for all to see.

Conclusion: Unmasking Spaces of Hope

How is this an example that could contribute to a cosmopolitan philosophy of anthropology? More specifically, how does drawing upon ethnography enlarge our *concept of hope*? In this conclusion, we point to several lessons that speak to both these questions. In doing so, it is important to note that the notion of "concept" comes to mean something rather different than our usual idea of what a concept might look like when we reflect on Ralph as a kind of philosopher. When "lay concepts" operate in everyday life, they need not be propositional, denotative, or even linguistic at all. Instead, they may appear in other ways, through the poetics of Ralph's speech, for example. Even more subtly, they may be articulated in the organization of material and social space, through bodily gesture, and a host of other cultural modes of expression. While it is well beyond the scope of this chapter, a further task is considering how we might need to reconceptualize Kant's lay concepts to incorporate this expanded sense of the term. We mention it here only to point toward an issue that deserves much more careful attention

The Singularities of Experience

First, we have brought people into the conversation whose everyday philosophy is not particularly visible. Marginalized by race and class, people like Ralph are not instances of Kant's "language users" so much as people whose voices have been brutally and systematically *suppressed* in public discourse. People like Ralph are ones whose actions are invisible from the perspective of dominant discourses and practices, having been dissolved into one great sea of subjugated victimhood. In offering this park confession, the point has not been to offer some kind of imitation of authentic indigenous meaning, some mirror of the "native's point of view." Even if this were possible (and of course it is not), the point of ethnography is not to textually mirror what others have said and done. Rather, what matters is unmasking the *profoundness* that lies beneath the surface of the ordinary. It concerns making visible the actions, commitments, and struggles of people in ways that are often disguised because, from an indigenous perspective, these are just everyday, just part of how life is, of what one does. This uncovering the drama of ordinary life is one of anthropology's most important unmasking tasks, and one of the primary ways in which it can contribute to philosophy. This means initially directing our gaze to the small moments of everyday life, the singularities of experience, trying to take the concerns and language of the actors themselves as a serious analytical starting point.

Everyday Practice, Self-Critique, and Narrative Re-Envisioning

Second, we have foregrounded the centrality of critique in the call for hope—an indigenous "hermeneutics of suspicion" in which Ralph calls into question ways of thinking and perceiving and valuing that have marked the perspective of the "homies," and in this manner contributed to the killing of his brother. He levels an unrelenting critical gaze on his own blindness and moral weakness, even though he was not, by any means, directly culpable for his brother's death. In the face of the kind of suffering Ralph's experience exposes, he suggests the need for himself and his fellow "homies" to imagine a new sort of life for themselves, or to become a different sort of people. He is propelled—at least for the moment—into a new, often unexpected and unwanted project of becoming. Furthermore, suffering can engender—and certainly does so, not only for him but for the families in this study—new or intensified *moral* responsibilities. These, too, may demand a transformative effort to reimagine not only what will happen, but what ought to happen, or how one ought to respond to pain and suffering. If we look at the dilemmas Ralph poses, we can see that he looks back upon earlier moments when he made certain kinds of decisions, or had a particular way of seeing things, that he later regarded with guilt, expressing a moral anxiety that he somehow lacked the sort of right thinking that would have enabled him to better understand the situations he was in, and the implications of this for his brother's safety and wellbeing. Without siding at all with his critical assessment of himself, it is important to consider such assessments not merely as the product of some subjectification (to the embodied enactment of a pre-reflective habitus or that which oppresses him), but in terms that dignify his own moral deliberations.

The Present (and Past) as Space of Possibility

A third lesson to be drawn is that hope emerges in this small park scene in a particularly underdetermined way. By looking closely at a particular event, we see life revealed not as a series of foregone conclusions, not as a "world of already realized ends," as Bourdieu has sometimes told us, but as contingent. Ernst Bloch argues that *only* when the past can be seen in its contingency (from the perspective of what might otherwise have been) can history provide a ground for action directed to *change* rather than repeating the past. He calls this imaginative access to the real the "principle of hope." As he explains, "Expectation, hope, intention towards possibility that has still not become: this is not only a basic feature of human consciousness, but, concretely corrected and grasped, a basic determination within objective reality as a whole" (1986: 7). This principle of hope reveals the "essence" of something that "is not-yet-being" (Bloch 1986: 343). From this stance, we discover that "The inheritance that is to be claimed from the past … is not a legacy of fixed tradition, but of undischarged hope-content." (Bloch 1986: xxvii). The "real," Bloch proclaims, is process—a process that is most importantly *unfinished*, as it mediates between present, unfinished past, and, above all, possible futures (1986: 196).

So one way to open up a conceptual space for enlarging our understanding of the practice of hope is to explore reality as a space of possibility. Obviously, there is a danger of romanticizing resistance or agency or possibility if one is not careful, thereby "blaming the victim" by overlooking the structural forces that conspire against those at the bottom of every social ladder. But the alternative is equally dangerous. If we treat social structures as pernicious containers that swallow up the actions, experiences, and concerns of all those caught within them, then we miss understanding life itself.

Note

Cheryl Mattingly would like to gratefully acknowledge support from the National Institutes of Child Health and Human Development, National Institutes of Health (RO1-HD38878) and Maternal and Child Health, Department of Health and Human Services. Funding from these agencies, particularly NIH, supported the ethnographic research upon which this chapter draws. The case presented here is also taken up, though in a different version, in Mattingly's book, *Moral Laboratories: Family Peril and the Struggle for a Good Life* (2014).

REFERENCES

Anscombe, Gertrude. 1957. *Intention.* Cambridge, MA: Harvard University Press.

Arendt, Hannah. 1958. *The Human Condition.* Chicago: University of Chicago Press.

Baracchi, Claudia. 2006. "Contributions to the Coming-to-Be of Greek Beginning: Heidegger's Inceptive Thinking." In *Heidegger and the Greeks: Interpretive Essays,* edited by Drew A. Hyland and John P. Manoussakis. Bloomington: Indiana University Press.

Bloch, Ernst. 1986. *The Principle of Hope,* vol. 1. Translated by Neville Plaice, Stephen Plaice, and Paul Knight. Cambridge, MA: The MIT Press.

Bourdieu, Pierre. 1997. *Pascalliam Meditations.* Translated by Robert Nice. Stanford, CA: Stanford University Press.

Brogan, Walter. 2005. *Heidegger and Aristotle: The Twofoldness of Being.* New York: SUNY Press.

Carrithers, Michael, Steven Collins, and Steven Lukes. 1985. *The Category of the Person: Anthropology, Philosophy, History.* Cambridge: Cambridge University Press.

Cavell, Stanley. 2004. *Cities of Words: Pedagogical Letters on a Register of the Moral Life.* Cambridge, MA: Harvard University Press.

Daniel, E. Valentine. 1996. *Charred Lullabies: Chapters in an Anthropography of Violence.* Princeton, NJ: Princeton University Press.

Foucault, Michel. 1983. "Afterword (1983): On the Genealogy of Ethics: An Overview of Work in Progess." In *Michel Foucault: Beyond Structuralism and Hermeneutics,* by Hubert L. Dreyfus and Paul Rabinow. Chicago: University of Chicago Press.

———. 2008. *Introduction to Kant's Anthropology.* Los Angeles: Semiotext(e).

Gadamer, Hans-Georg. 1975. *Truth and Method.* London: Continuum International Publishing Group.

Geertz, Clifford. 1973. "Thick Description: Toward an Interpretive Theory of Culture." In *The Interpretation of Cultures: Selected Essays.* New York: Basic Books.

Harvey, David. 2000. *Spaces of Hope.* Berkeley: University of California Press.

Heidegger, Martin. 1962. *Being and Time.* Translated by John Macquarrie and Edward Robinson. London: SCM Press.

———. 1997. *Phenomenological Interpretation of Kant's Critique of Pure Reason*. Bloomington: Indiana University Press.

Hyland, Drew A., and John P. Manoussakis, eds. 2006. *Heidegger and the Greeks: Interpretive Essays*. Bloomington: Indiana University Press.

Jensen, Uffe Juul, and Cheryl Mattingly, eds. 2009. *Narrative, Self and Social Practice*. Aarhus: Philiosophia Press.

Kant, Immanuel. 1998. *Critique of Pure Reason*. Cambridge: Cambridge University Press.

Knight, Kelvin. 2007. *Aristotelian Philosophy: Ethics and Politics from Aristotle to MacIntyre*. Cambridge: Polity Press.

Lukes, Steven. 1985. "Conclusion." In *The Category of the Person: Anthropology, Philosophy, History*, edited by Michael Carrithers, Steven Collins, and Steven Lukes. Cambridge: Cambridge University Press.

Mattingly, Cheryl. 2010. *The Paradox of Hope: Journeys Through a Clinical Borderland*. Berkeley: University of California Press.

———. 2014. *Moral Laboratories: Family Peril and the Struggle for a Good Life*. Berkeley: University of California Press.

Moody-Adams, Michele M. 1997. *Fieldwork in Familiar Places: Morality, Culture, and Philosophy*. Cambridge, MA: Harvard University Press.

Murdoch, Iris. 1970. *The Sovereignty of Good*. London: Ark Paperbacks.

Ricoeur, Paul. 1978. *The Philosophy of Paul Ricoeur: An Anthology of His Work*, edited by Charles Reagan and David Stewart. Boston: Beacon Press.

Rose, Nikolas. 1998. *Inventing Ourselves: Psychology, Power, and Personhood*. Cambridge: Cambridge University Press.

Ryle, Gilbert. 2009a. "Thinking and Reflecting." In *The Human Agent. Royal Institute of Philosophy Lectures* (1966–1967). London: MacMillan. Reprinted in *Collected Essays 1929–1968*, 479–83. London: Routledge.

Ryle, Gilbert. 2009b. "The Thinking of Thoughts: What is 'Le Penseur' doing?" University Lectures, 18, University of Saskatchewan. Reprinted in *Collected Essays 1929–1968*, 494–510. London: Routledge.

Sartre, Jean-Paul. 1963. *The Problem of Method*. London: Methuen.

Scheper-Hughes, Nancy. 1993. *Death Without Weeping: The Violence of Everyday Life in Brazil*. Berkeley: University of California Press.

Searle, John. 1995. *The Construction of Social Reality*. New York: Free Press.

Taylor, Charles. 2007. *A Secular Age*. Cambridge, MA: Belknap Press.

Theunissen, Michael. 1989. "Möglichkeiten des Philosophierens heute." *Sozialwissenschaftliche Literatur Rundschau* 19: 77–89.

West, Cornel. 2001. *Race Matters*. Boston: Beacon Press.

———. 2008. *Hope on a Tightrope*. Carlsbad, CA: Hay House Publishers.

Williams, Bernard. 1985. *Ethics and the Limits of Philosophy*. London: Fontana Press.

Wilson, Holly L. 2006. *Kant's Pragmatic Anthropology: Its Origin, Meaning, and Critical Significance*. New York: SUNY Press.

Winch, Peter. 1958. *The Idea of a Social Science and Its Relation to Philosophy*. London: Routledge and Kegan Paul.

Wittgenstein, Ludwig. 1967. "The Golden Bough." *Synthese* 17, no. 3: 233.

Dialogue Two

EXISTENTIAL ANTHROPOLOGY AND THE CATEGORY OF THE NEW

JOINT STATEMENT

Michael D. Jackson and Thomas S. Wentzer

Both chapters in this dialogue envisage an existential dimension that is likely to appeal to all human beings as such. We address the human desire to improve a given situation, and the suffering caused by not being able to do so. This gap between expectation and opportunity is experienced by a large segment of the world's population, often on a dramatic scale. Our point of departure is a shared interest in the simple but nevertheless astonishing fact that so many people, against all odds, continue to *hope*. What is more, they maintain their conviction of *being entitled* to hope—hope for the possibility of change, and for something new that will support their active participation in life rather than their passive endurance of circumstances into which they find themselves thrown. These two chapters analyze attitudes to life in the light of what Michael Jackson calls "the existential imperative." Critically echoing Kant's universal moral law, this imperative entails the desire "to live the world as if it were one's own" rather than abjectly or slavishly living a life decreed or decided by others. As the counterfactual "as if" indicates, conceiving of living according to the existential imperative often involves the suspension of received notions of where power lies, and what the situation actually is. In fact, it is the non-fulfillment of its condition that makes the imperative all the more urgent, given that the actual circumstances seem to prevent its fulfillment. It moreover expresses an intuitive sense of "natural justice" that combines the aforementioned desire with a tacit assumption that one is entitled to one's own share of the good life, even if this means seeking it elsewhere or from others who already possess it. It seems to be more convincing to speak of an existential dimension here rather than of an ethical demand (as, for instance, Løgstrup does) in any strict sense of the word, as it is not necessarily directed toward a real person or a political institution expected to answer or respond to it. It is a demand nonetheless, requiring from life an existence worth living.

The two chapters consider this issue from different angles. Jackson's approach to the study of human well-being reflects a long-held assumption that while philosophers have often asked the most probing questions about the human condition, ethnographic method offers one of the most edifying ways of actually exploring these questions. Wentzer's comments on the New raise both historical and existential questions that have a direct bearing on Jackson's ethnographic research. Accordingly, both chapters have been written from the standpoint of a shared intuition that human responsiveness and a historical search for "natural justice" are vital aspects of "existential anthropology." This phrase, which is Jackson's, indicates an approach rather than a discipline. It also points toward a new way to conceive of a *philosophical anthropology,* as it joins ethnographic and philosophical analysis in seeking to understand human existence. Such an approach might allow one to address "the human condition" without falling into unwarranted universalism or essentialism. It remains faithful to the innumerable differences in shaping a human life that has only this one formal requirement: to be lived.

THE REOPENING OF
THE GATE OF EFFORT
Existential Imperatives at
the Margins of a Globalized World

Michael D. Jackson

Nyendan bin to kile, an wa ta an segi
(The grass bends one way, then the other)[1]
—Kuranko adage

The title of my chapter is from the Arabic, *fatah al ijjihad*, and borrowed from Jean Duvignaud's (1970) anthropological classic, *Change
at Shebika: Report from a North African Village*. In this work, which
Duvignaud described as utopian because it was at once a work of the
sociological imagination and a description of the extravagant yearnings
of young Tunisian villagers in 1960–1966, we read of quandaries very
similar to those that dominate the thinking of many young people on
the margins of today's globalized world—the desire, amounting to an
ethical demand, that they receive an education, find paid work at home
or abroad, and yet be free to remain faithful to their own mores. Accordingly, the hope for a better future than farming or fishing goes hand
in hand with the despair at losing touch with the values of kinship
and community on which those traditional ways of life were based.
Failing to find utopia, they come up against the reality of what *does*
exist for them in the cities to which they migrate: closed doors, danger,
demoralization, and dead ends. All this implies that Knud Løgstrup's
assertions that "it is a characteristic of human life that we naturally trust
one another" and that "human life could hardly exist if it were otherwise" (1971: 8) reflect what may well be a *minima moralia* to which

Notes for this section begin on page 74.

most human beings aspire or pay lip-service. But this humanistic ethic, reflecting a sense that other human beings are similar to oneself (and that the other is oneself in other circumstances), runs up against hierarchical social orders in which worth is relative to birth, gender, age, class, and ethnicity. Though many migrants act *as if* they had a human right to move from places where life offered them very little to places that promised them life more abundant, these seemingly utopian societies often promulgate a morality and enact laws according to which the newcomer is owed nothing. The migrant often experiences this indifference to his or her situation as "violated trust."

The deeper problem is that life itself is the scarcest of all goods. Francis Fukuyama invokes Hegel's notion of human nature to argue that the conflict between great expectations and limited opportunity reflects not only a reasonable human desire to improve one's material fortunes but a struggle to be recognized as worthy of a better life (Fukuyama 1992: 145–46; 1995: 358). But comparative ethnography suggests that wealth and worth do not exhaust the range of existential goods of which the value is incalculable, and to which human beings aspire. For rich and poor alike, the search for money, work, love, happiness, power, presence, pleasure, knowledge, honor, and dignity all, in different contexts and at different times, betoken a struggle for life itself (Bourdieu 1977: 178). As such the struggles of migrants for new and improved lives echo the struggles of human beings everywhere to create and sustain fulfilling lives under conditions that are always falling short of their ideals, hopes, and dreams.

Exit Strategies

For several years now I have been documenting the lives of young men and women from Kuranko villages in Northern Sierra Leone and in southeast London, the heartland of the Sierra Leonean diaspora in the United Kingdom. My last trip to Sierra Leone took me back to the Kuranko village of Firawa, where I first did fieldwork in 1969. I was accompanied on this trip by a Kuranko friend now living in London and by my seventeen-year-old son, Joshua.

From our first day in Firawa, Joshua and I were waylaid by small boys begging us to give them money, help improve their lot, and even adopt them. The plea, "Take me with you … take me to America," became so familiar that Joshua asked me how he could respond without appearing unsympathetic and rude. Some of the appeals were written on scraps of paper torn from a school exercise book and folded to resemble an envelope—Ferenkay's letter, for instance, addressed simply to Mr. White Man.

Dear Sir,

I hope my letter will meet you in good condition of health. My main purpose of writing you this letter is just to inform you about my problem. Please sir I wanted to let you help me. Because my father here old. Than my mother his die. After that I don't have any body to help me about my problem. So please sir help me. So in that matter I wanted to go with you please sir. So when me and you go together to your living home; so I wanted let you help me to give me a job. Please sir take me like you children. Mr. White Man I don't have any responsibility about me. When you help me I will like that like my life purpose. I like to work with you sir please.

Just faithfully,
Sisay Ferenkay.

Born of a sense of desperation and isolation (all the notes Joshua and I received were from orphaned children or children with aging parents) these hopes for a utopia, far from Firawa, were as unrealistic as they were compelling. For why shouldn't I, a man of means, be able to move heaven and earth, and restore in some small measure the natural justice that seemed to have deserted the people of Firawa, just as God once turned a blind eye or slept while a brutal war ravaged their homeland?

More so than at any time in the past, villagers are demanding answers for why there is such radical inequality of wealth and power between those who govern their country and those who live in remote villages—and, by extension, between the first world and the third. Ferenkay's letter raises this ethical issue, at the same time as it implies a principle of natural justice whereby all people are entitled to the same due.

In his *Essai Sur Le Don* (1950), Marcel Mauss suggests that our most primitive sense of the ethical reflects the three obligations of gift-exchange, spelled out as the obligation to give, the obligation to receive, and the obligation to repay.[2] And it is to Mauss that we owe the insight that these basic modalities of exchange imply more than the trading of goods and services. Exchange is a "total social fact" with ethical and religious as well as material dimensions (Mauss 1954: 5). In other words, food, fertile farmland, money, blessings, honor, love, and recognition are all gifts of life, and exchange is, in effect, a way of distributing and redistributing the scarcest of all goods—life itself. But insofar as exchange presumes the possibility of equivalent value, it is ambiguous from the start. How can a material good be measured against a spiritual value? Does the plight of a refugee have the same moral claim on us as the plight of a citizen? Does an adult life have greater value than the life of an unborn child, or does the life of a sovereign take precedence over the life of a lesser mortal? And how can money indemnify a grieving family for the lost life of a loved one, or a verbal apology compensate for a death, or stolen lands and lost honor? Just as no economic calculus can unequivocally determine when a gift has been repaid, so no moral system can ever do complete justice to the particulars of real life human situations (Løgstrup 2007). Ethics defines a field of indeterminacy—of struggles and dilemmas that are born of human sociality itself, where partial and temporary agreements are all that is possible, where incompatible viewpoints are the norm, and where scarcity is a permanent condition.

Of all the contradictory viewpoints that define the human condition, none is more vexing than the contradiction between distributive and universal moralities. On the one hand, ethics reflects the interests of those in power, who argue that the life of society itself depends on their personal well-being, and therefore requires the subservience or sacrifice of lesser mortals. This is the distributive morality that makes worth relative to birth, wealth, citizenship, or power. On the other hand, human beings everywhere acknowledge a *minima moralia* grounded in a sense of sharing a common humanity. Among the Kuranko, this ethic is expressed in totemic myths that recount how an animal once saved the life of a clan ancestor who was lost, famished, or parched in a wilderness. In response to this act of altruism, the ancestor decrees that the animal will henceforth become a totem (*tane*, literally "prohibited thing"), to be respected and kept from harm. The totem later becomes adopted by clan allies, and over time a vast system of clan correspondences develops, encompassing the western Sudan, preventing the closure of each group, and promoting "an idea something like that of a humanity without frontiers" (Lévi-Strauss 1966: 166).[3] This idea also informs the social imaginaries of the young, who seek to escape the particular, confining world into which they were born and enter the global ecumene.

One way people rationalize inequality is to suppose that their impoverished or degraded status is the price they have paid for some ancestral or personal error. But it is also possible to argue that, having paid this heavy price, one now deserves to receive a share of the bounty that has accumulated elsewhere, in the hands of others.

On a rainy afternoon, many years ago, in the village of Fasewoia, I fell into a conversation with a group of elders. One old man asked me if I considered Kuranko to be my kinsmen. Mindful of the connotations of the Kuranko term *nakelinyorgonu* (literally "mother-one-partners")

I shook my head and said no. But the old man had used the term in a moral and tactical sense to imply "fellow human beings," and I was reproached: "Was I not aware that Africans and Europeans had the same ancestral parents, and that our grandfathers were brothers?"

According to the Fasewoia elders, the first people in the world were *bimba* Adama and *mama* Hawa—ancestor Adam and ancestress Eve. They had three sons. The eldest was the ancestor of the whites, the second the ancestors of the Arabs, and the third the ancestor of the blacks. The first two sons inherited book learning, but the last-born son—the ancestor of the blacks—inherited nothing.

It surprised me that the old men should imply that Africans were natively inferior to Europeans, and I asked them to explain why the last-born son was doomed to illiteracy.

"If you uproot a groundnut," I was told, "and inspect the root, isn't it always the case that some of the nuts are bad and some good?"[4]

When I returned to Firawa in 2009, I reminded the local Imam, Alhaji Hassan, of what I had been told. "I have heard that," Hassan said. "There were three calabashes. Allah put the book of inventions under one, the Qu'ran under another, and groundnuts under the third one. The ancestor of the blacks would have taken the Qu'ran or the book of inventions, but the ancestor of the whites tricked him into taking the groundnuts."[5]

Echoes of this leitmotif can be found throughout Africa, the assumption being that subsistence farming is an ignoble occupation that sustains the body but does not satisfy the soul or generate wealth. Indeed, it is a mark of inferiority, a curse, or the legacy of a dirty trick.[6] For example, Paul Riesman's conversations with RiimaayBe cultivators are reminiscent of Alhaji Hassan's view of things:

> Hoeing millet caused you shame, because you had to bend over in an unseemly posture. "Have you ever seen a merchant or a scholar, or any person who has other work, hoe a field?" asked one. "Why say agriculture is so important," he continued, "if everyone who possibly can do something else does so and stops raising millet?" "The Europeans lied to us," said another, "when they told us agriculture was honorable, for who ever sees them doing it? Anybody who hoes stays at the bottom. If you want to get ahead in the world the first thing you must do is abandon agriculture" (Riesman 1992: 64–65).

What interests me here, however, is that an old reading of inequality between Europeans and Africans, based on the assumption that Africans have only themselves to blame for being poor, has been supplanted by a new reading that emphasizes betrayal and injustice: Europeans had tricked Africans out of the technologies that defined modernity, and it was this *European* error that now gave Africans the moral right to demand justice and recompense.

All this reminded me strongly of Kenelm Burridge's description of a visit to the Melanesian island of Manam, during which local nobles revealed to the anthropologist their ancestral lore, contained in a "book" that was in fact a dusty collection of traditional objects made of turtleshell, hardwood, and stone. Taking the white man into their trust was but a prelude to asking him why the lore that made whites so wealthy and powerful had not been shared, and why the "message" Burridge supposedly carried, which "would straighten things out," had not been communicated with his younger Melanesian brothers. People were in tears as they spoke. But one impetuous young man did not mince words: "You see, this, the things you have seen [the ancestral lore], belong to us. They are ours, our own, and all we have. We think that white men have deceived us. So we are turning back to our ancestors. How is it that white men have so much and we have so little? We don't know. But we are trying to find out." The anthropologist's response? "There was little for me to say, little I could say" (Burridge 1960: 6).

Perhaps Burridge found himself in a predicament similar to mine. One is never quite sure how literally one is to interpret the overtures of others. Nor can one be sure how best to respond, given the extraordinary expectations and the impossible demands. Perhaps such complaints are symptomatic of the mimetic desire that afflicts all human beings to some degree—the craving to possess what others have, simply because one does not have these things oneself and experiences this lack as an injustice, an affront. In shrugging off the young Manam man's demands, did Burridge feel something akin to what I felt, reading Ferenkay's letter: that if the plea was left unanswered and the expectations not met, no great harm would be done, no grudge borne? For we address the powers that be—whether these be gods, chiefs, potential benefactors, or men of means—*both* in the hope that some good will come of it *and* in the knowledge that our petitions will probably come to nothing. Our imaginations lead us constantly to try it on—an expression that captures the sense that life is a gamble and an experiment. Ernst Bloch's "spirit of utopia" suggests that the human imagination works largely outside the constraints and constancies of time, place, and personhood. It occupies a no-place (*ou-topos*), making us creatures of wishful thinking who opportunistically seek some melioration in our circumstance while at the same time reconciling ourselves to our lot in the here and now, accepting the unlikelihood that our appeals will be heard or our wishes granted. But Bloch (2000: 167–71) also draws a distinction between "abstract" and "concrete" utopias, the first fantastic and unattainable, the second recognizing the limits to a person's aspirations. Hence the familiar rationalizations when our petitions fail, our gambles do not pay off, and our hopes are dashed—it's another day tomorrow, it was worth a try, I'll give it another go, someone's got to win. As Alain Badiou notes, hope does not necessarily encompass an expectation of improvement or justice; it is, in its most ontologically basic form, a kind of obstinacy, patience, or perseverance, warranted by the sense that one's subjectivity is ongoing rather than about to come to an end (Badiou 2003: 93).

The Spirit of Utopia

There was a full moon, and the village was bathed in its light. Sewa, Joshua, and I, along with some locals we hardly knew, were sitting around a courtyard fire when Musa Janneh came by for a chat. Musa, who was a small boy when my family lived in Firawa in 1979, had been a playmate of my daughter's. He remembered fetching water for us from the local stream, and my wife paying him for his good work. And he also remembered how my first wife, Pauline, fell ill and we had to carry her in an improvised litter from Firawa to the Seli river crossing, and take her to Kabala hospital.

"Have you never left Firawa?" I asked.

"I have gone away, but I have always come back."

"The kids all want to go to America," Joshua said.

"It is true. Everyone wants to go overseas or to America. People say America is very powerful. If you're serious you'll make money there."

"Why do they want to go to America? What do they hope to find there?" Joshua asked.

"Well, one person goes and does well, so others follow. One succeeds, and builds a fine house back in his village, so others want the same for themselves. Look at your friend Sewa Koroma. Look what he has done."

"And you?" I asked.

"My hands are empty. I have tried, but I did not find diamonds, I did not find work, I did not find a way of going abroad. So I am here. Farming."

A young man who had been sitting unobtrusively in the shadows stood up and pushed forward, toward the fire.

His name was Fasili Marah. He wanted to go "overseas." His father and mother were both dead. He wanted to go to America. Would I take him?

I was tired, and asked Sewa to explain to Fasili that he was asking the impossible.

"He cannot take you," Sewa said. "He says you need a visa, and it is almost impossible to get a visa. Besides, life is hard in America. America isn't paradise. Many people are poor there. They do menial work. Working long hours. And still they do not earn enough to cover the costs of a room or food. And when they get ill they cannot afford to go to a doctor."

Fasili was not dissuaded.

"I will do anything," he said. "I am ready."

I listened as Sewa talked to Fasili about the hardships he had endured in London.

"I know it is hard," Fasili said. "People have taken the little money I have saved, promising to put me in touch with a white man who can help me. When I went to see the white man all I got was a packet of biscuits."

"What do you want most?" I asked.

"Clothes," Fasili said. He had borrowed a pair of plastic sandals in order to come and see me. His shorts were held up by a broken belt, and he wore a T-shirt with a faded American Express Card logo printed on it.

"Only clothes?"

"Also a car. And money. Take me with you. I will be loyal. I will work hard. If I do not get abroad my life is at an end.

"You have no life here?"

"Our lives are in the hands of God. *Koe be altal' lon*, everything comes from God, everything is destined by God."[7]

"Everything? Did God take your parents? Did God make you an orphan? Did God decide you should be poor?"

I hated the unkindness of my questions. And I hated myself when I saw, in the light of the fire, that Fasili was crippled. His shin bones were grotesquely bowed, his feet splayed, his growth severely stunted.

"How old are you, Fasili?" I asked.

"I am twenty."

He had become crippled at age four. He fell from a bench. One minute he was normal, the next he was crippled. His mother told him it was witchcraft, though no witch ever confessed.

"But God is responsible for everything," Fasili assured me. "How we are punished, and how our destiny is made. God can make you rich one day and poor the next. You have to be patient. You have to accept that you must wait for God, and believe in God."

"But if the RUF [Revolutionary United Front] came and said you could get anything you wanted—clothes, money, a vehicle—would you go with them?"

"Yes, right away. Definitely."

I found it hard to reconcile this alarming admission—Fasili's readiness to seize an advantage without much thought for the repercussions—with his ethos of patience. But hadn't I been told that hunger gives no thought to the morrow, and that there is nothing more tenacious than hunger? And wasn't Fasili's hunger for a better life so great that moral scruples were an unaffordable luxury?

To change the subject I asked Fasili if he would tell us his favorite story.

Fasili did not need to be asked twice:

The animals formed a labor cooperative (*kere*) to dig a well. The hare (Fa San[8]) was asked to pitch in and help. But he pleaded sickness and said he could not work. The animals knew he was lying, and after they had dug their well they set the leopard to stand guard over it in case Fa San tried to take any of the water he had not earned the right to share. Sure enough, Fa San came to the well, bringing a sack of grasshoppers with him. "Heh," he said to the leopard, "don't you know these people are using you. They've got you standing guard over the well while they eat. Have they brought you any food? I don't think so. But here, see what I have brought you to eat." And Fa San gave the leopard the sack of grasshoppers and leapt into the water, which he spoiled by washing his dirty clothes in it. The animals, infuriated at having been tricked, set the bush cow to stand guard over the well, then lay in ambush in the bushes nearby. Fa San soon returned to the well with another sack of grasshoppers, confident he could fool the bush cow into letting him have access to the water. But the animals captured him, bound his wrists, and took him to a cotton tree where they intended to tie his legs together to stop him running away. But when the animals began tying Fa San's legs together, he cried out "Heh, that is not my leg, it's a root. You're not tying my legs, you're tying the roots together." And when the animals began tying their rope around a root, Fa San cried out, "Heh, that's not a root, that's my leg. Don't do that. You're tying my legs together." In this way, Fa San avoided having his legs bound, and was able to slip into a dark space among the roots of the great cotton tree and disappear. The animals now went to an old woman and asked how they might deal with Fa San. The old woman asked for food, and then told them what they needed to do. They should get their machetes and cut off his arms and legs. If he cries out, "You're killing me, you're killing me," this means that you are actually chopping the roots of the tree, but if he cries out "You're cutting the root, you're cutting the root" this means that you are cutting him. And so the animals succeeded in getting rid of the deceitful Fa San.

I was stunned by Fasili's story—for it was the first story of Fa San I had ever recorded (and I had, over the years, recorded scores of Kuranko trickster tales) in which Fa San gets his come-uppance. What is more, this violent turning of the tables was reminiscent of the RUF, who used machetes to sever the limbs of villagers who had allegedly betrayed them by voting for a government that enlisted the help of foreign forces to defeat the rebellion. And I did not have to think hard to recall the mango and cotton trees on whose long and buttressed roots the rebels laid the limbs of their terrified victims.

I was also mindful of the fact that the story Fasili had told us was the original of the trickster story that survived the Middle Passage and entered the New World as one of the so-called Brer Rabbit tales, many of which were collected by Joel Chandler Harris and first published in 1868 and 1869.

Regarding the story from the New World that most closely resembles the Kuranko tale (itself widely known throughout the Mande-speaking area of the West Sudan), Charles Long arrives at this arresting conclusion: "Brer Rabbit is not simply lazy and clever; it is clear that he feels that *he has something else to do*—that life cannot be dealt with in purely conventional terms" (Long 1986: 196; emphasis added). Although Long is interested in linking the trickster to the figure of the black preacher who "kept alive the possibility of another life" among an enslaved people, what struck me in talking to Fasili and other frustrated young men was the way they oscillated between a patient stoicism, declaring that one's fate was ultimately in the hands of God, and an impatient and urgent desire for transformation, dramatically conveyed by the alacrity with which Fasili said he would have no hesitation in joining the RUF if it would improve his lot.

"Were the rebels like Fa San?" I asked Fasili. "Did they use tricks to get their way?"

"Yes, all kinds of tricks."

Sewa knew them all. How the rebels would use all manner of cunning to cover their tracks, communicate with one another, and take their enemy by surprise. Identifying their comrades by taping red cellophane candy wrappers over their electric torches. Infiltrating towns, allaying suspicion, disguising their intentions, pretending one thing but doing another. But Sewa would not be alive had he not been able to beat them at their own game, outwitting them, making his escape. Not for nothing was he nicknamed Bonké, "slippery."

"Could you use the trickery of Fa San to get overseas?" I asked Fasili. "To get money?"

"No," Fasili said. "Trickery doesn't pay."

"And yet," I said, addressing Sewa, "you have used your wits, not only to escape the rebels when you were captured, but to get out of some tight corners in London."

Sewa agreed. But he had never broken the law, he said.

The line between social intelligence (*hankilime*) and trickery (*aliye*) was not, however, easy to draw. There was a gray zone—a zone of ethical ambiguity—in which it was difficult to decide whether trickery was justified in retaliation for being tricked, or simply your best chance of survival in a situation where the odds were stacked against you.

Sewa had always reminded me of Fa San. Quick-witted, playful, street-smart, smooth-talking, charismatic, and attractive to women, and he was not above using his wiles to beat a rap or secure an advantage. But he was not a scoundrel.[9] He honored his ancestors as a source of life to the same extent that he sought to create a life for himself that had no ancestral precedent. As such, Sewa and Fa San are both refractions of the classical figure of Hermes, who stands on the boundary between strange and familiar worlds: god of the roads, god of doors, god of trade and of craftsmanship, giver of good things. Hermes, whose power comes from his contact with strangers and strange places "on the other side" from whence he brings, through trade, theft, and barter, the very goods without which his own community will perish or pale into insignificance (Brown 1990: 32–45).

Clearly it is never easy to determine how far a person is justified in going in search of the "something else" of which Charles Long speaks— the lost portion that is owed to you, the stolen life-world for which you should be compensated, the life or livelihood that are you due as much as anyone else. For in securing a fair deal, or some form of natural justice, when does one draw the line between what is rightfully one's own and what is not? And as for those of us who live in the affluent West, who enjoy such privilege and power, when do we draw the line between what we feel we must give "to make a difference" or redress a historical wrong, and what we owe ourselves, what we must keep if we are to live. Such was the dilemma that Joshua and I experienced, trying to figure out how we could help people like Fasili in some small way without leaving ourselves with nothing, and the dilemma that Sewa experienced with even greater intensity as he struggled every day to meet his family obligations yet retain some semblance of the identity he had gained in London.

Well-being is never a settled state but a field of struggle. As with goodness and reasonableness, our difficulty in achieving wellness does not, however, diminish its hold over our imaginations, for it signifies a hope without which existence would be untenable—the hope that life, for ourselves and those we care about, holds more in store for us than less. Though it is rare to meet people who are completely and permanently satisfied with their lot, it is rarer to meet people who expect nothing of life, abjectly accepting the status quo, never imagining that their situations could or should be socially, spiritually, or materially improved. Because this sense that well-being remains elusive, transitory, and unevenly distributed is felt by the rich as well as the poor, and in all societies, I call it existential dissatisfaction. And it entails a perennial struggle to adjust our desire for more from life with the subjective and objective limits we come up against in reality. This yearning for more is highly variable, and may include a desire to be loved, to be a better person, to do a better job, to have a happy family, good health, long life, material prosperity, or greater control over one's fate and fortune. But common to all these aspirations is an existential need to feel that such goals are within one's grasp, that one's efforts will pay off, one's virtue be rewarded, one's needs be met. This is what constitutes our sense of natural justice. Life, however, seldom conforms to what we ask or demand of life, and it is universally the case that when we fail to fulfill our needs objectively we have recourse to subjective strategies of make-believe, imagination, and daydream. What fascinates me here is not so much the movement from reality to virtuality as the de-emphasis on trusting the people one expects something from or the situation one is in and placing one's trust in spirit entities, imaginary friends, supernatural allies, invented stories, and magical strategies that transform one's experience of one's situation, bolstering hope, reinforcing patience, lifting expectations. But my ethnographic work in Sierra Leone has taught me that people are always moving to and fro between real and magical strategies in an unceasing existential struggle to augment life and counteract its loss. Thus, fictional scenarios in which a disadvantaged orphan or junior wife places her hope in a djinn, encountered in dreams or in the bush, sets the scene, as it were, for attempts, like those of Ferenkay and Fasili, to go abroad or enlist the help of wealthy patrons, white men, or new religious leaders selling the prosperity gospel. In this way, the trust that ancestral blessings will be bestowed if one is patient and dutiful is transferred to God or Allah, just as distrust of corrupt rulers gives way to hope in the new regime—the ethical demand constantly finding someone or something on which to pin its hope of being met.

An Ethic of the Wish to Live Well

However one defines politics, it is so deeply rooted in our history and humanity that it is, in effect, "almost without origin." By this, Paul Ricoeur means "that there has always been politics before politics; before Caesar, there is another Caesar; before Alexander, there are potentates"

(Ricoeur 1998: 98). So it is with ethics: "Before the morality of norms, there is an ethic of the wish to live well" (Ricoeur 1998: 94). That is to say, before the advent of any particular cultural, cosmological, or philosophical ethics, ethics has existed. Not as a unified, normative body of maxims, obligations, duties, or categorical imperatives,[10] but as a set of recurring quandaries and questions, a sense of ethical anxiety or disquiet about the very possibility of achieving a good life, or of ever closing the gap between the ideals we espouse and the existential situations in which we find ourselves.[11] Although the origins of this proto-ethical sensibility cannot be pinned down, either in pre-historical or historical time, it is surely grounded in human sociality—in our awareness that our very existence is interwoven with the existence of others who are always there, as Sartre observes, even when physically absent, "in the form of some reminder, a letter lying on the desk, a lamp that someone made, a painting that someone else painted" (Sartre and Lévy 2007: 71). To this thought one might add Maurice Merleau-Ponty's observation that social existence means that we are never quite at one with ourselves. Our perspectives are never independent of each other; they have no definite limits; each "slips spontaneously into the other's," interweaving, merging, and in effect constituting "a common ground" that makes us "collaborators for each other in consummate reciprocity" (Merleau-Ponty 1962: 347, 353–54). This conception of intersubjectivity as a mutually constitutive process of give and take also suggests, as Sartre argues, that a meaningful life cannot consist simply in a passive or slavish submission to the world as one finds it. One must have some sense of being an actor whose speech and actions matter or make a difference to the way things are. For the Kuranko, custom is a given,[12] and when explaining why the world is constituted as it is, people typically fall back on such stock phrases as "That is how it happened" (*maiya ta ra nya na*), "That is how our ancestors let it happen" (*ma bimban' ya ta nya na*), or "That is what we encountered" (*maiya min ta ra*). Custom (*namui*) and law (*seria*) have been decided by others at other times. Nevertheless, the social order depends upon the capacities of the living to make that order viable. Moreover, the realization of this capacity to regenerate and generate the world often means going beyond what is given, if only because the given never appears as an abstract custom or law but as a particular problem that does not admit any one straightforward ethical or political solution. In other words, it is in the nature of life to continually interrupt and complicate the implementation of *any* system of abstract rules and to *appear* unprecedented. It is for this reason that I cannot agree with Knud Løgstrup that trust is natural, for in desperate and critical situations distrust may appear equally natural, and aspiring to a condition of intersubjective transparency and trust may be a luxury that those in extremis cannot contemplate, let alone afford. Rather, they pray, give us this day our daily bread, asking only that they receive their due—which is simply a small share of what the world has to offer: a respite from violence, food for a single meal, a chance to earn a few dollars, seed rice to make a farm.

Amputees' Camp, Freetown

Heaney with his Grauballe and
Tollund men might have focused on
the missing arm, its walnut burr and whorl
of skin from which I shrink, gone as far
as making their phantom pain
a metaphor for memory—the day
that they recall, slow-motion as in space,
a blunt machete sawing through a limb,
a screaming child, and all that followed
not in thought but flight.
We are voyeurs
whom bog-dark centuries keep safe.
Distant, these are not our kin.
He knows this best who has no words for it:
"They came at noon. By evening they were gone.
Twenty of us were dead, or bleeding
from our wounds. We were farmers.
What had we done to them?
We cannot forget, cannot forgive,
though life goes on."
The halter at the neck
is nothing they can use. No fingerprints
identify the enemy, divine a cause.
Images of ridge and river, grain or tar
make damn all difference.

Here is no "tribal, intimate revenge."
Only the matter of fact phrases:
"Seed rice is all we ask. With seeds we can begin again."

Notes

1. The *nyendan* grass is used for thatching. Here it is used as a metaphor for reciprocity. When you move through the grass it bends before you; but when you return through the grass it bends back the other way. Thus, greetings, goodwill, goods, and services move to and fro within a community, keeping the paths open, keeping relationships alive.

2. Sartre also begins his comments on ethics by saying that ethics is a reciprocal mode of consciousness, and therefore a consciousness of obligation (Sartre and Lévy 2007: 69–70).

3. Among the Akan of Ghana, the notion of "sympathetic impartiality" expresses a similar vision of *human* rights (see Wiredu 1996: 29–31).

4. For an extended, cross-cultural account of such stories, see Jackson (1998: 108–24).

5. According to a Limba narrative from northern Sierra Leone, Africans and Europeans were once brothers. That one became less advantaged than the other was a result of their father's favoritism. He wrote a book, containing instructions on how to make money, ships, and airplanes, intending to give it to his dark-skinned son. But his wife smuggled the book to her favorite son—the one with white skin. The dispossessed son ended up with a hoe and a basket of millet, rice, and groundnuts: "You see us, the black people, we are left in suffering. The unfairness of our birth makes us remain in suffering. That is why they want to send us to learn the writing of the Europeans. But our mother did not agree, she did not love us. She loved the white people. She gave them the book … Yesterday we were full brothers with them. We come from one descent, the same mother, the same father, but the unfairness of our birth, that is why we are different. We will not know what you know unless we learn from you" (Finnegan 1967: 263).

6. See Jackson (1998: 121).

7. Even though many Kuranko have embraced Islam, villagers tend to use the word "Altala" rather than Allah when referring to god.

8. *Fa San* (literally "Father Hare") may be translated "Mr. Hare," although in Kuranko stories hare—who is younger brother—is the trickster, while hyena—the elder brother—is the dupe.

9. In a compelling account of the ethical gray zone of the *favelas* of northeast Brazil, Nancy Scheper-Hughes describes the *jeitoso* "personality type" as "attractive, smooth, handy, sharp and a real operator" who can con people, beat the system, and even "get away with murder." Like the tactical ingenuity of the "rascals" of Papua New Guinea, the Brazilian trickster is amoral and opportunistic, with shallow loyalties and a thick skin (Scheper-Hughes 2008: 47).

10. I follow Sartre's and Merleau-Ponty's situated ethics, on the grounds that Kant's ethics was "too well-ordered to be true; to be, alas, too removed from human life—and death—; and probably even culpably remote, morally speaking, given the shattering realities of postwar Europe" (Williams 2000: viii). Thomas Schwarz Wentzer has also pointed out to me that Sartre and Ricoeur follow Hegel's discovery of the priority of an ethics inscribed in custom and shared routines, contrasting it with Kant's rationalist ethics and terming it *Sittlichkeit* rather than "morality."

11. I agree with Knud Løgstrup's view that ethics must be sought, not in basic moral laws—like Kant's categorical imperative—but in the "sovereign expressions of life" such as love, compassion, openness, and trust. Such virtues are subsumed in the Kuranko concept of *morgoye,* a term which connotes both personhood and magnanimity. But in focusing on lived situations rather than idealizations, ethnography reveals that these expressions are subject to the existential vagaries of human relations and do not reflect some essence—a natural disposition to trust others, or to show kindness and compassion.

12. The etymology of the term *namuge* or *namui* ("custom") is relevant here, for it literally means "mother-birth"; by extension, what is given, what is found, where you start from, as in the Kuranko adage, "Never forget the one who first filled your belly."

THE ETERNAL RECURRENCE
OF THE NEW

Thomas Schwarz Wentzer

Human power and weakness are nowhere more intimately attached than in the imagination. They can be phrased simultaneously in just two words, which begin a certain kind of sentence: "What if." With these words we try to invite other people to join us in our dreams, or to share our worries. We bracket the world and its usual course in order to conceive of a new world, a different world. In its wishful version, the what-if clause is omnipotent in the sense that it allows us to leave reality and its limitations behind, imagining a world where things are exactly the way we want them to be. Literally nothing lies outside the power of this imaginative capacity. In such a world there would be no wars, poverty, witchcraft, or injustice, or if there were, *we* would not be subjected to them. But the what-if clause is counterfactual. By its very nature, it reveals the factual powerlessness of its subject. We know that the world we hope for is not the world we actually inhabit. It expresses a fantasy, a daydream, a thought experiment at best; and the moment we stop dreaming, real life with its constraints and deprivations returns. Even so, for many of us it is the what-if that makes the real world and our existence become meaningful or charitable.

A person phrasing the what-if clause is not necessarily obliged to give evidence substantiating the likelihood of the concrete envisioned scenario. Under certain circumstances it would even be impolite to ask for such evidence; one would be refusing to join the outspoken invitation by insisting on a pledge guaranteeing its reality. The what-if clause does not (yet) determine those goals or ambitions that one wishes to pursue; it does not (yet) provide a plan or agenda for how to realize

Notes for this section begin on page 89.

them. Still, it has sufficient reason for its performance, an argument against the pertinence of social reality: Things *could* be different.

I take this thought as my basic starting point: *Things could be different.* This claim entitles us to enter "the what-if game" of the imagination, allowing us to anticipate a scenario that suits our dreams. This sentence might contain comfort and hope or warning and caution, depending on how one conceives of the future. Taken in its literal meaning, however, it is a claim about the present state of affairs. Hence, on the one hand, this basic thought states an ontological fact about the actual world, recalling the changeability of the conditions of our lives, even under the most restrictive or constant conditions. On the other hand, it is usually taken to refer to a possible world hidden in the actual. The what-if clause then becomes either a promise or a threat, depending on whether we hope or fear that things will be different. These two aspects—a person being *ontologically entitled* to conceive of a different world, and that person's *emotional stance* toward that new world in terms of either hope or fear—seem to be connected. This might indicate that there is a certain connection between our ontological vocabulary and our emotional states. It is this relation that lies at the center of my considerations, which elaborate on particular themes that are so richly developed in Michael Jackson's chapter. Boys like Sisay Ferenkay and a crippled man like Fasili utter their deeply rooted desire for a radical change, and yet they also express a somewhat stoic attitude toward their lot. They harbor both hope at the possibility of a future, and humility at their present fate. These attitudes display certain ontologies, that is, beliefs of how to think about temporality and change; they connect certain emotional attitudes—notably hope—to these beliefs. It is this connection that I wish to explore more extensively. I suspect that the ontology of change, meaning our capacities to conceptualize the historicity of the world and our existence, relies on our capacity to cope with its changeability. Moreover, I see this undertaking as having an agenda shared by both philosophy and anthropology; namely that of scrutinizing what kind of emotive and conceptual resources human beings bring into play in understanding and coping with a changing world (Jackson 2005; Lear 2006; Mattingly 2010). One way to express the experience of change is by focusing on what is new in it. The concept of novelty—taken here as a characteristic for anything that was not present before—is typically used to demarcate a certain situation and a person's approach to it. I will take this concept, the concept of "the New," arguably an aspect of any change or alteration, as the subject of the considerations that follow.

It might be helpful to emphasize that I am going to deal with novelty and the New using a phenomenological approach. That is, the suggestion presented here deals with the question: On what grounds do a mind, a person or organization, a population or people, members of a social group, or institutions, address a certain change or variation as new; or worded differently, when do they use the semantics of the New to articulate their situation? My claim is that only a historical being is able to experience something *as* new. Thus I defend an experiential account on novelty that seeks to pay due to the first-person perspective.

From a traditional, objectivist point of view one might try to scrutinize what novelty is by analyzing the concept of the New, its meaning and its reference, rather than by analyzing our emotional or affective stance toward it. However, one will soon realize that these problems that are, prima facie, different indeed are connected. The reality of the New actually *relies* on a certain existential mood or emotional stance toward it. In other words: Novelty always, and inherently, involves some sort of experiential involvement; it is tied to human experience. It is not until we experience something *as* new that we experience novelty. Exploring the New as a category of human experience is a way of contributing to an *existential anthropology* in the sense put forward by Jackson (2005; 2007) and by related approaches.

I hope that this idea can deepen our understanding of Ferenkay's and Fasili's actions and evaluations of their own situations. In what follows, I want to explore this idea in three steps. I will begin by examining a remark on the idea of the New in Western philosophical thinking, showing that novelty is tied to human historicity, and taking Seneca and Hegel as my key witnesses. However, as I am not interested in intellectual history here, I will then jump to my own life-world and the way I might experience or cope with novelty in light of the two semantic paradigms outlined so far. Finally, I will try to suggest a certain way to think about novelty and human existence from an existential–anthropology perspective.

The New: A Historical Category Throughout

Novelty is a historical category in a double sense. It is a *product of* history and secularization in as much as it *refers to* human secular history. Whereas in classical Ancient thinking the New and its synonyms did not gain any philosophical significance, it becomes important for Judaic and Christian religiosity and their prophecies. In these traditions, the New is no longer interpreted as being in opposition to that which is eternal and true, but brought into play as referring to the Messianic event as the ultimate goal of earthly existence hitherto. Seemingly coincidental processes are no longer regarded as random phenomena representing eternal laws or Platonic ideas, but gain (or lose) their significance in the perspective of future salvation. The New in this sense is tied to the future, not to contingency; it is opposed to the present, not to eternity. It signifies a world that is totally different, representing a new age as the last and ultimate age, at times in an apocalyptic prophecy. As a religious category, the new thus captures the meaning *of* history in its divine end (Jonas 1958). As a historical category, the new becomes part of the historical development itself, thus employing meaning *in* history (Löwith 1949; Blumenberg 1966).

The emergence of a historical understanding of the New in the development of Western thinking, from the Church Fathers to modernity, in fact mirrors the genesis of the idea of universal history as such. During this process the New, or novelty, has undergone its secularization—beginning with Saint Paul—developing from denoting the eschatological ultimate event of the resurrection of Christ, to becoming the promise of a human world as the goal of a secular world history. It took its time, but novelty has become a feature of the human in modernity that no longer belongs to the domain of the divine. This conceptual rearrangement was accompanied by a conception of the dimension of human destiny in terms of history, as seen in contrast to nature, fortune, or fate. Claiming novelty to be a historical category therefore means that it is due to modernity that we conceptualize historical events or changes with the category of the New. Consequently, only the modern mind can ask how to face the New, and ask what kind of emotional attitudes (anxiety or fear, hope, confidence or trust, and so on) we are entitled to display when envisaging novelty.

This remark does not imply a claim that earlier cultures, or non-Judeo-Christian cultures, did not, or do not, encounter novelty. Of course, as long as human beings have existed there have been, and will be, experiences of unexpected individual or collective joy and pain, the opportunity to seize a chance, and the need to adjust to new circumstances. But my claim is that doing this under the banner of novelty is fairly new, and is linked to the idea of modernity.

Let me call upon Seneca, a chief representative of Roman Stoicism, as a witness. In one of his letters to Lucilius he describes the despair of a man whose hometown, probably the most beautiful city in Gallium, accidentally burned to the ground in a single night. Seneca does not hesitate to tell his friend how he thinks experiences like these must be met:

> Nothing, whether public or private, is stable; the destinies of men, no
> less than those of cities, are in a whirl. ... Chance may tear you from your
> country or your country from you, or may banish you to the desert; this
> very place, where throngs are stifling, may become a desert. Let us place
> before our eyes in its entirety the nature of man's lot, and if we would not
> be overwhelmed, or even dazed, by those unwonted evils, as if they were
> novel, let us summon to our minds beforehand, not as great an evil as of-
> tentimes happens, but the very greatest evil that possibly can happen. We
> must reflect upon fortune fully and completely. ... Therefore let the mind
> be disciplined to understand and to endure its own lot, and let it have the
> knowledge that there is nothing which fortune does not dare—that she has
> the same jurisdiction over empires as over emperors, the same power over
> cities as over the citizens who dwell therein. We must not cry out at any of
> these calamities. Into such a world have we entered, and under such laws
> do we live (Seneca 1917–1925, vol. II, 435–43 [Epistle XCI]).

According to Seneca and his Stoicism, novelty—be it in the guise of
catastrophes, as described here, or events of unwarranted luck or happiness, as he describes elsewhere—has to be dismantled as just another
episode in the eternal circle of nature. There is nothing really new;
everything is under the law of fate or *fortuna*. In cases of unbearable
suffering or misfortune one should not lament nor despair. There is
nothing we can actually do to avoid or avert calamities. There is no hope
of either political or divine intervention, no request for social or technological solutions, as the modern mind would be inclined to demand.
Seneca knows of no ecclesial or human insurance company that might
help us avoid, or compensate us for, the worst of the damage. He rec-
ommends developing an unattached personal attitude and a state of
emotional independence, through gaining rational insight into the eternal conditions of human existence. At this stage, human intelligence
and skills are existentially useless. There is no appeal to a conception
of the human in terms of *homo faber* (Arendt 1958), which might give
cause to hope for improving the human lot. We are obliged to stick
to the economy of imaginative and experienced pains and pleasures,
which will ultimately lead to a leveling of the emotional balance. Nevertheless, we keep living and affirming our life according to nature and
its eternal laws.

Seneca obviously does not see reason or intelligence as something
that might constitute a sphere of actual human freedom in any modern
sense. According to him, our rational capacities free us from our inclination to seek pleasures and fulfill desires. We are thus not trapped in
the moment of lived experience, but are able to anticipate the future.
Notably, our mind has the potential to intellectually foresee unpleasant events. In times of change or devastation this provides us with
an important psychological resource. We should, as Seneca suggests,

simulate our misfortune and misery in advance. This will immunize us to our own emotional reactions, as we will have imagined the greatest conceivable pain in a sort of private gallery of horrors. It will help us to avoid breaking down when the real evil comes—since we will be prepared. Intellectual fantasy and imagination—Seneca's version of the what-if clause—become part of the Stoic strategy: to neglect the factual existence of novelty, to dismantle its false appearance and to downplay its existential significance. Seneca expects us to employ this strategy as a kind of emotional damage control, avoiding surprises (especially bad ones) and disappointment. According to Seneca, there is nothing really new; what appears to be new ("chance") is actually just the repetition of the usual, displaying the same law with its jurisdiction over cities and citizens, emperors and servants, a people and its constituent individuals.

And so we see that the Stoics have a natural conception of human existence and human agency that does not allow a substantial conception of the New as such. The freedom of imagination is best used when applied to build up a certain psychological state of emotional independence or indifference (*apatheia*). Real change, meaning the very concept of history and development, is not available within Stoic thinking. Hegel reflects on this in the introduction to his lectures on the *Philosophy of History*, when he writes:

> The changes that take place in Nature—how infinitely manifold soever they may be—exhibit only a perpetually self-repeating cycle; in Nature there happens "nothing new under the sun," and the multiform play of its phenomena so far induces a feeling of ennui; only in those changes which take place in the region of Spirit does anything new arise. This peculiarity in the world of mind has indicated in the case of man an altogether different destiny from that of merely natural objects—in which we find always one and the same stable character, to which all change reverts—namely, a real capacity for change, and that for the better—an impulse of *perfectibility* (Hegel 2001: 70).

Hegel thus refuses the universality of Stoic nature. The ontology of nature does not support the idea of real change, as this idea necessitates the possibility of something new. Without novelty, any change only perpetuates the eternal recurrence of the same, in a self-repeating cycle. One might therefore continue to talk about natural change and processes; after all, natural objects come and go, emerge and diminish. But these processes are subjected to the eternal laws of nature that do not alter or improve. Real change not only requires the changeability of its particular entities and events, but it also requires the alteration of the very standards and principles that pertain to or support these entities. If real change is to occur, we must conceive of an ontological domain that is capable of novelty. Such a demand transcends the realm of nature, moving toward the region of *spirit*. It is only in the region of spirit, that is, in history, that the New can arise.

Notice that in Hegel's version, the New is opposed to the predictability of cyclic repetition. Consequently, events and processes in the region of spirit are to be thought of as being open, providing an outcome that has not been there before. The impulse or motive of these real changes does not only rely on a drive toward indifferent mutability, but also depends on the human capacity to change for the better. This principle would not determine the concrete course of history; nor does it provide evaluative standards—"it is without scope or goal ... : the improved, more perfect, state of things toward which it professedly tends is altogether undetermined" (Hegel 2001: 70). It nonetheless displays the formal but mighty power of human development, namely the impulse of perfectibility.

The passage cited above entails an almost arrogant evaluation of natural change. Hegel declares its most substantial quality to be "boring." I take this remark to signify the experiential character of natural versus historical change. Natural change does not offer any chance to become actively involved; it is not something we can be engaged in. Historical change is rather different in character, as it does make a difference to those who experience it. In Hegel's view the concept of the New is tied to the experience of human subjectivity. It arises when people can change their lot for the better. Here change really *matters.* Events then gain significance; they mean something to someone, as they provide new ways of understanding. The "ennui" ascribed to nature is therefore not to be taken as an aesthetic predicate. Rather, it indicates the practical indifference and hollowness of natural change. "Spirit," the Hegelian notion that captures the logic of socio-cultural development, recognizes individual subjectivity, meaning the purposes and desires of human subjects who aim for something better.

To sum up: Hegel, my representative of modernity, unveils the eternal recurrence of the same as a principle of nature. He promotes the idea of historical perfectibility that supports the possibility of conceiving of the new. Although Hegel himself was rather reluctant toward "mere" hope, as it may lead to putting real change on hold for the sake of satisfying a hollow yearning, his version of the what-if clause endorses a semantics that was not conceivable to Seneca. It allows for promoting the sense of hoping for a new, and effectively better, world. The New as a historical category is tied to the idea of changing the world for the better. Allow me to rephrase this sentence in order to capture its modern significance even more precisely: The New as a historical category is tied to the idea of changing *my* world—my children's world, my people's world, or one of my other worlds—for the better.

Modern Stoics and the Semantics of Novelty

The outlines of Stoicism and Hegelian modernism that I have given above could serve as two different paradigms to deal with change and the challenge of the New. Because I am interested in the interface between individual experience and its conceptualization, I will not regard these paradigms as representing two epochs in the Western history of thought. I believe that both of them stand for modes of understanding change that remain available to us today. In fact, we are in need of both modes when conceptualizing our experience of a changeable world. How, then, do we actually refer to novelty? How do we conceptualize change, alteration, or development in everyday living?

Being a male member of a middle-class family, and an academic working in Denmark, the New comes to me in many flavors: a new friend, a new lover, a new child, a new idea, a new style, a new car, a new administration, a new age. What is more, not only do I meet novelty at every juncture in my daily living; I usually express novelty with a wide range of linguistic expressions, using not only the word "new." For instance: "a fresh start," "a second chance," "a surprising move," "a creative thought" "a revolutionary approach," "an innovative suggestion," "a new beginning." In all these expressions, I refer to novelty. But note that in these phrases novelty is ascribed to something that I might actively do or initiate. Moreover, the changes that are implied in these activities are usually met with approval. Innovation, freshness, creativity—these are plus-words denoting novelty, precisely because what is new in them originates from the initiative that is mine, that is, from a subject and its sphere of action. These plus-words indicate something I can do, changeability under my command (see Husserl 2000: 277ff.).

But what if I become the victim of an unexpected crisis? A disease? A crash on Wall Street? An evil spell? A civil war? An earthquake? These events surely entail the need to adjust our behavior to new circumstances. But they are hostile events, which disturb or destroy our pursuit of the plans we made, endangering our social or even our physical lives. Hence, we do not celebrate the new that they bring, for two reasons: (1) These events seem to put an end to some or all efforts of our agency. They seemingly do not imply any future to come; rather, they ultimately finish what we have so far accomplished. (2) The changes

implied descend upon us, as events beyond our control. Instead of being subjects, we find ourselves subjected. There is nothing fresh, innovative, or creative about realizing that the design of one's life is being
ended, whatever the real outcome of a crisis proves itself to be.

Taking these personal observations into account, we can now see
the relevance of the Stoic and the Hegelian worldviews, not insofar
as they might refer to two different epochs in Western thought about
human destiny, but as representing two existential attitudes toward the
changeability of our existence. The point I am making here is an observation about when we actually respond to something new *as new.*
The same response is not accorded to any and every change. Only those
changes that we experience as possibly enriching our lives are articulated using the semantics of novelty and its expressions. Although it
would be legitimate for us to refer to any event whatsoever as new, provided it changed our recent circumstances, we only seem to explicitly
articulate novelty if it comes across as the opening of an opportunity
for us. We have to comprehend the change and its outcome as being at
our disposal, as being ours—and only then do we tend to describe its
process using the vocabulary of novelty. Novelty, then, is not a property
or a quality in and of itself; it does not have an independent, objective reality. We employ the concept of novelty relative to the degree to
which we consider ourselves to be agents, or experiencing subjects. *We
are "Moderns" when we act, but Stoics when we suffer.*

It is a peculiar feature of human life that, when seen in the light of
later developments, the very same event that initially was an item of
suffering or loss proves to be the beginning of a positive story. When
thinking back on a crisis that nearly destroyed us years ago, we may
later realize that those new circumstances actually opened opportunities we would not have had without the initial crisis. So it is, that when
we are in control of the situation once again, we might refer to the initial event in terms of novelty, as a new beginning or starting point. We
then comprehend the initial crisis or catastrophe not as the end of our
doings, but as a beginning of a new period in our lives, which contains
new possibilities. At this point we have succeeded in transforming the
event that was an ending into the initial moment of an active beginning.[1] This transformation is typically achieved by means of narrative
strategies. We regain the future, that which is to come, as our own time,
which initially seemed to have been taken from us. We re-establish
ownership over our lifetime through experiencing the new *as new.*[2]
As this shows, once again: Novelty is bound to a person's capacity to
conceive of himself or herself in terms of open possibilities and active
participation in life.

It may sound trivial, but I consider it substantial to mention that the New is always new *to someone.* The New is thus a phenomenon in the phenomenological sense of the word: *Something* is given *as* something *new* to *someone* (Husserl 1998: 126ff.). As such, any phenomenon has an addressee, is given and directed to someone, and thus tied to some person's experience. To experience something or someone *as new* does not mean to identify an objective property of the natural world. The experience of the New is not just the process of becoming acquainted with something one has not met before. It means to reflect, and to integrate the world in one's own horizon of understanding, and vice versa. And so, understanding something as new entails the need to revisit the old and the familiar in light of one's new experience.

Consider the temporal dimension that is essentially connected to any talk about things new. The New implies temporality, given that novelty divides the continuous flow of time into a before and an after. This does not refer to physical time, however, but to someone's—an individual's, a family's, a people's, a nation's—historical time, and of the future that awaits them. So strictly speaking, when referring to something as "new," one is not qualifying a certain object recently acquired. One is qualifying one's own lifetime, one's way of being-in-the-world, which has changed through the entrance of the new item or event. Novelty therefore refers to people's historical time or their lifetime, which may take a turn it would not have taken in the days before a certain event occurred. In this sense, novelty changes one's world.

Any potential change in someone's life could, in principle, be recognized as new in the manner just described, whether it be a result of important personal decisions (marriage or emigration, for instance), of external events (such as disease or an unexpected promotion), or of minor episodes that other people hardly seem to notice (discovering that first silver-white hair). Any event could, in principle, be the one that marks day zero in my personal biography, dividing my life into a period before and a period after the event in question. This possibility provides the conditions necessary to underpin the logic of fashion, trends, and the advertising industry, since such campaigns usually promise to design a different personality or lifestyle that can be achieved simply by buying a particular lipstick, shampoo, or cell phone. Just a single order, and consumers will be in a position to shape their future lives according to their dreams.

In this case, the what-if clause provides an imaginative doorway to a new lifetime. In its wishful, strong, existentialist version it articulates the hope of a new life under new circumstances, providing that the antecedent clause is fulfilled. That is what the letters written by Sisay

Ferenkay and other children in Sierra Leone, addressed to Mr. White-Man, were about: Take me with you and everything will change. The existential demand that Jackson has identified in these letters, in his conversations with Fasili and his version of Kuranko trickster tales, relies on the conviction that one has the right to demand the possibility of experiencing the New, meaning the right to experience the event of a new beginning. Phrased in a Marxist vocabulary, it denotes the request of an end to alienation and the beginning of a life in dignity, with social as well as economic wealth. Or, worked into the matrix of this chapter, it demands the transformation from being a creature subjected to the logic of Stoic nature (including social structures of violence and suppression) into being the subject of one's own history. Note that by presenting this angle on the what-if clause, I am not saying anything about a person's chances of really improving his or her lot, even if the antecedent clause is fulfilled. As Jackson in fact tried to explain to Fasili, the actual conditions of living in the United States might be as hard, or even worse, than in Fasili's homeland. This is to say that the content of the what-if clause might very well be ideologically "misguided" and its actual fulfillment harmful. It may well be that what the person thought would be the initial beginning of getting a grip on their own share of life, turns out to be just another episode in the chain of suppression and structural violence. But from the perspective of the first person, that is, from the point of view of Sisay and Fasili, these objections miss the heart of their request. They are articulating their existential entitlement to each live their life as if it were their own—no matter what the conditions would actually be like that might do justice to this demand.

Let me summarize my considerations so far: As such, there is nothing new, were it not new to someone, capable of changing someone's life with respect to their future lifetime. The New is thus not a quality present in objective mutability, or in processes that emulate nature, but a historical moment given in subjective experience. The New is real only as a mode of experiencing significant possible change. Experiencing novelty means to expect to gain or regain the ownership of one's future lifetime as a resource that can be shaped according to one's own—individual or collective—desires or needs. In short: The New is an experiential, not a physical feature; it denotes a historical, not a chronological category. It is a modern thought in so far as it is tied to the idea of an opportunity opened to a subject, allowing that subject to gain a grip on its future. *Things could be different*—as they entail the possibility of novelty.

Hope and the Human Condition

Exploring the concept of novelty might help us exemplify what philo-sophical, in the sense existential, anthropology could mean, as indicated in my introductory remarks. Novelty and the experience of the New have been almost universally ignored in traditional philosophy. Two of the rare exceptions that remedy this sin of omission are Hannah Arendt and Ernst Bloch. Both are antipodes to any Stoic worldview because, in different ways, they celebrate the human capacity to bring about some-thing that was not there before. In this sense, the Heideggerian neo-Aristotelism of Arendt and Bloch's neo-Marxist aestheticism both point in the same direction. Being born, in the sense Arendt understands it, means to be the individualized promise of being one of a kind, and a person who might make a difference. Bloch even tried to develop a certain sense for the New: the "anticipatory sense" vis à vis the future, which discovers possibilities that lie open in any given situation. Natal-ity, the capability to be forgiven or to grant forgiveness (Arendt 1958), and the principle of hope (Bloch 1986) are two contributions to a phil-osophical anthropology that approaches human beings—not by what they essentially are with regard to an asserted human nature, but by what every particular individual could come to be. They are thus an-thropologies of the possible.

What is more, both Arendt and Bloch are aware of the emotional side of human future orientation. Hope, fear, pleasant anticipation—these emotional attitudes all have a future orientation. They are intentional in the sense that a person is hoping for, in fear of, or looking forward to *something.* They may well be unintended, since they may come to us against our will. One is struck by them, rather than intending to exercise them. They are nevertheless directed at something. And this "something" refers to an event to come; an event that will impact the person's current situation. The person emotionally foresees a change of circumstances; willingly or not, that person is facing the future and its potential gift or danger, its joy or despair. According to Bloch, *hope* is the appropriate state of mind or emotional stance for *novelty. The Principle of Hope,* Bloch's most comprehensive philosophical work, was written at a time that many regarded as being beyond remedy. Bloch responds to his time by developing a theory that may do justice, at least conceptually, to what he takes to be a universal human trait: the dream of a better life, in a better future. *The Principle of Hope* defends the atti-tude of thinking about the future in other terms than those of fear and anxiety, in other terms than as the eternal recurrence of the same. From an ontological perspective, it insists on recalling the fact that the world as we know it could be different. From an anthropological perspective, it declares hope to be the most human of all our states of mind, and the one that distinguishes the human being from all other animals (Bloch 1986, vol. 1: 83). Its philosophical agenda is, at once, very simple and yet all-encompassing. It legitimates the right to expect and to pursue a future that is worth wishing for.

Bloch's line of argument does not build upon empirical findings in a scientifically satisfactory way. The material is both very broad and very selective at the same time. It acknowledges phenomena of individual daydreaming, modes of curiosity, a person's desire for a homeland, a mother's wishes for her children, the somehow vague but nonetheless concrete anticipation of a reality that one would appreciate rather than abide. *The Principle of Hope* unfolds this one thought: Human beings have the capacity to anticipate a world that could be their own. It is already in the mere possessing of this capacity—and not with the much later potential fulfillment of its anticipated content—that human beings transcend the understanding of reality as being the realm of brute facts. It is this capacity that allows us to see a "concrete utopia," which means seeing opportunities and possibilities rather than factual constraints. This, in turn, makes space for revision and novelty, including the revision of our conceptual capacities, which we use to understand ourselves and the world we live in (see Lear 2006 for a similar approach). In that sense, Bloch's whole approach is an elaboration on the what-if clause.

One could, perhaps, object that the whole line of argument in this chapter disregards the findings of structuralist and postmodern approaches. It could seem naïve to maintain a Western, modern paradigm that is somehow bound to the idea of subjectivity and an autonomous human subject. Even so, I suspect that the predominant focus on institutions, structures, semiotic systems, and power—following first Lévi-Strauss and de Saussure, and later Foucault, Bourdieu, and others—underestimates the reality of a life lived in the first-person perspective, and hence tend to ignore the legitimacy of a methodological approach that tries to capture life as lived experience. The "modernism" addressed in this chapter is not to be understood as a political or sociological program, but rather as a paradigm that acknowledges the experiential dimension of human life. In that sense, existentialism is a part of modernism.

It follows, then, that my existentialist approach to the question of the New reads as follows: Novelty belongs to human existence. The New is a feature of the human, and a historical category. It has its origins in the experience of change that entails the promise, or at least the possibility, of a better life. It refers to a future, a time to come, which is expected to be someone's, entailing possibilities of agency and realization in both an individual and a collective perspective. Its emotional attitude might most appropriately be described in terms of hope. It is ontologically authorized by the indeterminacy or openness of our life-world, which is underdetermined enough to harbor the eternal recurrence of the new. And with this version of the Nietzschean phrase, we can venture to articulate the formal nature of what it means to experience something as new: It means always and ever seeing oneself in the light of new possibilities. Framed within a terminology that is familiar to a hermeneutical approach (Heidegger 1962), I would say that novelty is an "existential" of any human's being-in-the-world.

Notes

1. This description draws heavily on Gadamer's (1960) hermeneutical concept of "experience."
2. For a general theory on how narrativity constitutes human time and temporality, see Ricoeur (1984–1988, esp. 1988). The therapeutic use of narrative strategies is documented extensively, for instance in Mattingly (1998), Mattingly and Lawlor (2001), and Coulehan (2003).

JOINT AFTERWORD

Michael D. Jackson and Thomas S. Wentzer

That our face-to-face and emailed exchanges of ideas, and critical feedback on each other's work-in-progress, proved both personally and intellectually edifying is a testament, we like to think, to the value of bringing ethnographic and philosophical perspectives into conversation. While the first draws on raw material from, as well as direct experience in, contemporary life-worlds, the second exploits historical sources and critical theory to interrogate that data from a detached point of view. This is not to imply that such detachment secures scientific objectivity; nor is it intended to privilege any Western tradition of thought over any other. Rather, it serves as a strategy for placing seemingly incompatible or radically different modes of experience on a par, and exploring the possibility of overcoming the classical antinomy of thought and being. Indeed, it is our refusal to separate concept and existence, and "to demonstrate that the concept is a living thing, a creation, a process, an event, and, as such, not divorced from existence" (Badiou 2012: lxi) that accounts for our interest in existentialism.

A common concern, as well as a shared conviction, is tied to the alleged universality of existential thinking, most strikingly when we address *the* human in particular human beings. Existential anthropology, be it engaged through fieldwork-based or phenomenological analysis (or in some combination of these), does in fact postulate some universal aspects of human existence as such, and we confess it to be pivotal to highlight its formal and indeterminate, but nevertheless crucial, significance for social theory. At the same time, however, we acknowledge the limitations of any tool—material or conceptual—in securing the ends to which it is applied, be this interpreting the world, changing the world, or renegotiating our relationship with the world.

Notes for this section begin on page 94.

In stressing the non-identity of words and worlds, thought and be-ing, Adorno's negative dialectics reminds us that concepts never fully cover or contain our life experiences (Adorno 1973: 5, 8). In our dia-logue, we have squared anthropological and philosophical perspectives to elucidate how actual people understand the existential constraints of their lives. This has given rise to several questions concerning how to conceptualize this understanding. First is the question of modernity, which arises because it has been common in Western thinking to deal with the desire to improve one's lot in terms of historical progression, established by technological progress, moral improvement, and politi-cal autonomy achieved by virtue of an ever-growing emancipation from religious and feudal authorities. This view, however, obviously turns a blind eye to premodern or non-Western societies. Does the Enlight-enment's emphasis on the human as the measure of all things imply an eclipse, not only of God's omniscience but of the Ancestral as the ultimate source of truth and value? Does the Enlightenment mark an epistemological break between societies without history and societ-ies within history; between revealed truth and empirically established truth; between primitive irrationality and modern rationality? Echoing Horkheimer's and Adorno's *Dialectic of Enlightenment,* one should rather assume these distinctions to be intellectual simplifications that gave warrant to Europe's mercantile, missionary, and mercenary ex-ploitation of the non-European world. There is abundant ethnographic evidence in support of the view that while the *experience* of novelty and natality are universal, ideology or anxiety may lead us to downplay or deny the New, conjuring an image of the social as an ahistorical and transcendent reality that one must dutifully replicate and respect gen-eration after generation.[1] But if the concept of a premodern society that admits nothing new is largely illusory, so too is the modern concept of a society that is wholly open to the future. These extremes are never en-countered in reality. Ethnohistorical and archaeological research shows that societies that represent themselves as unchanging have undergone radical changes over time,[2] while societies that see their history as a series of radical epistemological or technological disjunctions forget the extent to which their members remain constrained by familial struc-tures, developmental processes, and existential limits that are common to all humanity. Wentzer's invitation to address the "interface between individual experience and conceptualization" not only frees us from the kinds of epochal or absolute distinctions between *types* of societies or *types* of human being that have underwritten centuries of colonial and social violence; it broaches questions as to how human beings, whatever their historical or cultural situations, struggle to create lives that are worth living.

This interest informs Jackson's recent monograph, *Life Within Limits: Well-being in a World of Want*. Kuranko would readily identify with Seneca's stoicism as he exhorts his friend to accept unavoidable misfortunes, ungovernable forces, and irremediable afflictions. Although often fatalistic in retrospect, however, Kuranko do not live as if their lives were entirely predetermined, or their fates wholly in the hands of others, for the course of one's life depends on external forces and internal dispositions, on the actions of others, and on one's own actions based on those actions. And even when action fails, there is always the possibility, through ritual, narrative, and the imagination, of making circumstances appear less oppressive than they actually are. In their fascination with what people do in order to make life fulfilling, both chapters raise the question of hope—that sense of things forthcoming, of newness or possibility, without which life slips out of one's own hands and falls into other-directedness, repetition, endurance, and routine. Just as poverty and illness are never simply objective conditions, because they are always conditioned by how people actually live them, so newness, as Wentzer argues, is always subject to interpretation as the necessary condition for experiencing something *as new*. As an experiential category, novelty ultimately belongs to one's own temporal existence, and not to things or events of the world. The experience of newness moreover displays novelty as a dialectical concept necessarily bound to the old. Revolutionary action, for instance, may be inspired by this sense of hope and newness; but it is not necessarily identical with it. As Hannah Arendt (1965 36–37) observes, even the French Revolution—the archetype of modern forms of irreversible social transformation—was, in its earliest stages, driven by a reversionary zeal seeking to restore an ideal of justice that had existed in the past. As for hope, Ernst Bloch (1986) reminds us that although hope is not necessarily tied to ideas of a better future, it may take the form of longing for a lost world, a lost love, or a missed opportunity.

For these reasons, Jackson refuses to reduce the longings of contemporary Sierra Leonean youth to modernity or globalization, for the longings that now attach to the pursuit of wealth in distant lands, fantasies of marriages made for love, or freedom from the constraints of parents and elders, also include the hope of continuity with their ancestral past or sustained contacts with natal villages. Moreover, such longings predated contact with Europe, finding expression in imagined alliances with djinns, journeys into the wilderness in search of fame and fortune, or magical transformations leading to fabulous elsewheres. For all the emphasis placed on the ancestral order, individual experience has never been entirely constrained by that order. Rather than speak of deviations from tradition, one should see these experiments in life in the light of an existential imperative common to all human beings: to live the world as if it were one's own; to feel that one may act to the same extent that one is acted upon; to experience one's life at the same time as being the same as other lives and being unique, being new. There are always "two existential attitudes toward the changeability of our existence," as Wentzer argues, that balance our past with the future to come. These are not to be reified as different social formations or different forms of humanity. These attitudes must be recognized as being present, and creating tension, in all of us: to be open to the world and to others, yet wary of the world and of others who may be our undoing; to look to the world and to others (including forebears and the powers that be) for our livelihoods and our welfare, yet look to ourselves as the final arbiters of our own fate; to have regard for the old, for we are shaped by what has been, yet to know that each person who is born opens his or her eyes upon the world as though it were new, as though it were theirs, and as though they had a claim on it and rights in it not because of their particular birthright but because they are human like everyone else.

This returns us to the question of hope—that sense that one may become other, or more, than one presently is or was fated to be. For Gabriel Marcel (1962: 53), hope is the feeling that time is not closed to us, a sentiment echoed by Pierre Bourdieu (2000: 216–18), for whom hope is the belief that our social investment in the world will pay off, if not immediately, then at some time in the future. For Arendt (1958: 178), hope is synonymous with the appearance of the New, which has the character of "startling unexpectedness"—something that is "inherent in all beginnings and all origins" and occurs despite "the overwhelming odds of statistical laws and their probability, which for all practical, everyday purposes amounts to certainty." This sense of promise and potential transformation that Marcel (1962) refers to as "enthusiasm for living" (*l'entrain de la vie*), Bourdieu (2000: 206–45) as "the forthcoming,"[3] Arendt as "natality," and Bloch as "the spirit of utopia" finds expression in millennial dreams and revolutionary ardor as much as in the quotidian pleasure of an excursion to somewhere new, the anticipation of a lottery draw, a sporting contest, the denouement of a mystery novel, a child's Christmas, or the impatient excitement with which one counts the days before a vacation, prepares for a new departure, or awaits the return of an absent lover or friend. Like Arendt, Bloch makes pregnancy a metaphor for this yearning for the new, this heightened anticipation of what will surprise us, take us out of ourselves, or give us a new lease of life. Yet, he argues, all such aspirations have their origin in a sense that something is missing (Bloch 1986 1–17) in our lives, and that there is more to life than what exists for us in the here and now. Because it is notoriously difficult to pin down exactly what it is we lack, or what will complete us, our imaginations wander from one thing to another as though searching for a mislaid article. At times we imagine that the lost object was once in our possession—a loving family, an organic community, an Edenic homeland, a perfect relationship. It was there before we realized what we had; it slipped from our grasp or was stolen, leaving us to hope that it might be restored to us, as well as to dread that it is irrecoverable. At times we imagine that what we need lies ahead, promised or owed but as yet undelivered, unrevealed, or unpaid, not yet born. In this yearning for what is missing, but that we regard as rightfully ours, lies our sense of *natural justice.* But as Bloch observes as he discusses these questions with Theodor W. Adorno, our sense of what is possible is always tempered by a sense of impossibility and danger. Accordingly, hope is never the same as confidence, since one who hopes is haunted by the sense that he is hoping for the impossible, that his hope is, deep down, a hope for life everlasting or absolute security, and that he knows, equally deep down, that he is bound to die. Because hope always comes with fear and anxiety in tow, we tell ourselves to be careful what we wish for, since experience teaches us that the fulfillment of a dream often leads to disappointment. But behind all this inner anguish over what will make life more rather than less fulfilling lies a sense of existential dissatisfaction that exists in all people, in all societies, regardless of their histories, social identities, or levels of prosperity. If there is any one thing that is not new under the sun, it is this.

Notes

1. Mircea Eliade (1965) spoke of this attitude, which he considered typical of so-called Archaic societies, as "the terror of history."
2. Bruno David (2002) presents such a case with respect to Australian Aboriginal societies, presumed to be among the most unchanged in the world.
3. See also Jackson (2005).

REFERENCES

Adorno, Theodor. 1973. *Negative Dialectics.* Translated by E. B. Ashton. New York: Seabury Press.

Arendt, Hannah. 1958. *The Human Condition.* Chicago: University of Chicago Press.

———. 1965. *On Revolution.* Harmondsworth: Penguin.

Badiou, Alain. 2003. *Saint Paul: The Foundation of Universalism.* Translated by Ray Brassier. Stanford, CA: Stanford University Press.

———. 2012. *The Adventure of French Philosophy.* Translated by Bruno Bosteels. London: Verso.

Bloch, Ernst. 1986. *The Principle of Hope,* 3 vols. Translated by Neville Plaice, Stephen Plaice, and Paul Knight. Cambridge, MA: MIT Press.

———. 2000. *The Spirit of Utopia.* Translated by Anthony A. Nassar. Stanford, CA: Stanford University Press.

Blumenberg, Hans. 1966. *Die Legitimität der Neuzeit.* Frankfurt: Suhrkamp.

Bourdieu, Pierre. 1977. *Outline of a Theory of Practice.* Cambridge: Cambridge University Press.

———. 2000. *Pascalian Meditations.* Translated by Richard Nice. Cambridge: Polity Press.

Brown, Norman O. 1990. *Hermes the Thief: The Evolution of a Myth.* Great Barrington, MA: Lindisfarne Press.

Burridge, Kenelm. 1960. *Mambu: A Melanesian Millennium.* Princeton, NJ: Princeton University Press.

Coulehan, Jack. 2003. "Metaphor and Medicine: Narrative in Clinical Practice." *Yale Journal of Biology and Medicine* 76: 87–95.

Duvignaud, Jean. 1970. *Change at Shebika: Report from a North African Village.* New York: Vintage.

Finnegan, Ruth. 1967. *Limba Stories and Story-Telling.* Oxford: Clarendon Press.

Fukuyama, Francis. 1992. *The End of History and the Last Man.* New York: Free Press.

———. 1995. *Trust: The Social Virtues and the Creation of Prosperity.* New York: Free Press.

Gadamer, Hans-Georg. 1960. *Wahrheit und Methode: Grundzüge einer philosophischen Hermeneutik.* Tübingen: Mohr/Siebeck.

Hegel, Georg Wilhelm Friedrich. 2001. *The Philosophy of History.* Translated by J. Sibree Kitchener. Ontario: Batoche Books.

Heidegger, Martin. 1962. *Being and Time.* Translated by John Macquarrie and Edward Robinson. San Francisco: Harper & Row.

Husserl, Edmund. 1998. *Ideas Pertaining to a Pure Phenomenology and Phenomenological Philosophy: First Book.* Translated by Fred Kersten. Dordrecht: Kluwer.

———. 2000. *Ideas Pertaining to a Pure Phenomenology and Phenomenological Philosophy: Second Book.* Translated by Richard Rojcewicz and André Schuwer. Dordrecht: Kluwer.

Jackson, Michael. 1998. *Minima Ethnographica: Intersubjectivity and the Anthropological Project.* Chicago: University of Chicago Press.

———. 2005. *Existential Anthropology: Events, Exigencies, and Effects.* Oxford: Berghahn Books.

———. 2007. *Excursions.* Durham, NC: Duke University Press.

———. 2011. *Life Within Limits: Well-being in a World of Want.* Durham, NC: Duke University Press.

Jonas, Hans. 1958. *The Gnostic Religion: The Message of the Alien God and the Beginnings of Christianity.* Boston: Beacon Press.

Lear, Jonathan. 2006. *Radical Hope: Ethics in the Face of Cultural Devastation.* Cambridge, MA: Harvard University Press.

Lévi-Strauss, Claude. 1966. *The Savage Mind.* London: Weidenfeld and Nicolson.

Long, Charles. 1986. *Significations: Signs, Symbols, and Images in the Interpretation of Religion.* Aurora, CO: The Davies Group, Publishers.

Løgstrup, Knud E. 1971. *The Ethical Demand.* Foreword by James M. Gustafson. Translated by Theodor I. Jensen. Philadelphia: Fortress Press.

———. 2007. *Beyond the Ethical Demand.* Notre Dame, IN: University of Notre Dame Press.

Löwith, Karl. 1949. *Meaning in History: The Theological Implications of the Philosophy of History.* Chicago: University of Chicago Press.

Marcel, Gabriel. 1962. *Homo Viator: Introduction to a Metaphysic of Hope.* Translated by Emma Craufurd. New York: Harper.

Mattingly, Cheryl. 1998. *Healing Dramas and Clinical Plots: The Narrative Structure of Experience.* Cambridge: Cambridge University Press.

———. 2010. *The Paradox of Hope: Journeys Through a Clinical Borderland.* Berkeley: University of California Press.

Mattingly, Cheryl, and Mary Lawlor. 2001. "The Fragility of Healing." *Ethos* 29, no. 1: 30–57.

Mauss, Marcel. 1954. *The Gift.* Translated by Ian Cunnison. London: Cohen and West.

Merleau-Ponty, Maurice. 1962. *Phenomenology of Perception.* Translated by Colin Smith. London: Routledge and Kegan Paul.

Ricoeur, Paul. 1984–1988. *Time and Narrative,* 3 vols. Translated by Kathleen McLaughlin and David Pellauer. Chicago: University of Chicago Press.

———. 1998. *Critique and Conviction: Conversations with François Azouvi and Marc de Launay.* New York: Columbia University Press.

Riesman, Paul. 1992. *First Find Your Child a Good Mother: The Construction Of Self in Two African Communities.* New Brunswick, NJ: Rutgers University Press.

Sartre, Jean-Paul, and Benny Lévy. 2007. *Hope Now: The 1980 Interviews.* Translated by Adrian van der Hoven. Chicago: University of Chicago Press.

Scheper-Hughes, Nancy. 2008. "A Talent for Life: Reflections on Human Vulnerability and Resilience." *Ethnos* 73, no. 1: 25–56.

Seneca. 1917–1925. *Epistulae (Moral Epistles)* 3 vols. Translated by Richard M. Gummere. Loeb Classical Library. Cambridge, MA: Harvard University Press.

Weiner, James F. 2001. *Tree, Leaf, Talk: A Heideggerian Anthropology.* Oxford: Berghahn Books.

Williams, Forrest. 2000. Preface to *An Investigation of Jean-Paul Sartre's Posthumously Published Notebooks for an Ethics,* by Gail Evelyn Linsenbard. Lampeter, UK: The Edwin Mellen Press.

Wiredu, Kwasi. 1996. *Cultural Universals and Particulars: An African Perspective.* Bloomington: Indiana University Press.

Dialogue Three

INTENTIONAL TRUST IN UGANDA

JOINT STATEMENT

Esther Oluffa Pedersen and Lotte Meinert

A shared curiosity about and interest in understanding *trust and distrust* as features of social interaction makes up the basis of our collaboration. Our understandings of the phenomenon of trust and distrust have gained significantly from the process of discussing and writing together. The questions that an anthropologist poses to a philosopher are simply different from the discussions sparked within philosophical contexts and vice versa. The conclusions that philosophy reaches often have a welcome verve and generalizing power that is seldom reached in empirically grounded ethnographic discussions. On the other hand complex ethnographic data challenge generalizing philosophical statements and taken seriously within philosophy it enriches the philosophical theorizing with the diversities of the human life-world.

Ideas about what can be taken to pose an academic challenge differs in our disciplines: Does Ugandan distrust challenge Løgstrup's theory of trust or does Løgstrup's perspective on trust challenge our perspective on Ugandan realities? In a philosophical wording it concerns theoretical considerations about the ontological status of the human life-world prior to and underlying the empirical evidence. So where philosophers tend to argue about the proper ontological framework anthropologists will point to the evidence from fieldwork studies. In this context we want to underline that neither of these positions in their pure form are adequate if the aim is to enlarge theoretically sound understandings of real human life.

The conclusions and level of verve dared by a philosopher are challenging, sometimes provoking, but also highly liberating for an anthropologist—in ways that merit some scrutiny. Philosophers dare to generalize at levels that most anthropologists are not comfortable and familiar with. When the philosopher proposes a conclusion about human beings (in general) or writes "we" (about all humans) the anthropologist gets dizzy and worried that complexity, nuance, difference, and context all get conflated into indifference, where there in fact may be difference. On the other hand the anthropologist's detailed nitty-gritty knowledge and material gets invigorated and lifted to another level by being asked some of the "big" questions from philosophy and being urged to make further-reaching conclusions. Sometimes anthropologists cannot see the forest for the trees—or cannot see The Human Being for people— having a philosopher by the side may help see contours that are not usually foregrounded in anthropology. A philosopher willing to take in evidence from the field gains tremendously from the anthropologist's exclamations of cautions with regard to generalization. The anthropologist is often able to point at the blind angle of the-taken-for-granted of philosophy and thus launch a critical scrutiny of ontological assumptions within philosophy.

In our case the provocation from across the disciplinary borders of anthropology and philosophy has forced both of us to rethink some of our concepts and preconceived understandings. Pedersen's conception of interpersonal trust and distrust was challenged and shaped by the discussions with Meinert and the ensuing conception has worked as a framework for Meinert's interpretation of her fieldwork, raising new questions. The reality of distrust in Uganda has not changed as such due to our collaboration, yet, the questions asked by the anthropologist during periods of fieldwork have no doubt been influenced by conversations with the philosopher and thus a common perspective has been formed. All philosophers who try to develop philosophical theory concerning the social world with the aim of being able to say something that could be of interest outside of the philosophical community should wish for the opportunity to collaborate with an anthropologist.

The two chapters ensuing from our collaboration can be read independently of each other. We have, however, been engaged in fervent discussions and, as noted above, the conception of interpersonal trust that Pedersen puts forward here is highly indebted to the counter arguments and friendly criticism of Meinert. The attempts by Meinert to generalize about distrust have no doubt been generated by the gentle, but firm push forward by Pedersen. We have been meeting and sending our chapters back and forth learning, wondering, commenting, and discussing content and intent. In our chapters we highlight the importance of recognizing and theorizing distrust and trust as a continuum. This goes for academic collaboration as well. Our collaboration has only been possible because of a common trust in the interdisciplinary discussion as enlarging the understanding of the social world by questioning presuppositions of philosophers and anthropologists alike. At the same time some level of distrust in and critical distance to the other discipline's methods and limitations is productive in provoking further insights.

Pedersen offers a general conception of interpersonal trust and distrust alike. She argues that both trust and distrust may be internalized as the backbone reaction of individuals and only by reflecting on the internalized patterns of reaction may individuals be able to alter this. Meinert opens her chapter by rendering apparent that war, betrayal, and lack of law and order often are common and ordinary living conditions for humans. Therefore distrust ought not to be understood as derivate from an original state of trust. Meinert analyzes how two young Ugandan men strive to trust in spite of the prevailing distrust. Thereby the distinction between prima facie and reflective trust/distrust worked out by Pedersen is put at work in the analysis.

AN OUTLINE OF INTERPERSONAL TRUST AND DISTRUST

Esther Oluffa Pedersen

The main idea behind the interpretation of interpersonal trust and distrust put forward here is that any attempt to understand the social phenomenon of trust needs to pay attention to three characteristics. Firstly, whether a person trusts or distrusts others and whether she herself is trustworthy or untrustworthy depends for a large degree on her personal life story. She may be prone to either trust or distrust most people because of her past experiences and social interaction. Similarly, she will be inclined to act trustworthy or untrustworthy depending on how others have reacted on her past actions, that is, whether they have accepted and perhaps even sanctioned untrustworthy behavior or only supported what seemed to be trustworthy actions. An agent's trust or distrust toward others relies to a considerable degree on social conditioning stemming from upbringing and social experiences that play out behind the agent's back.

Secondly, trust or distrust between agents develops, changes and evolves over time. A trust relationship has a history in the straightforward sense of time simply passing by. But it also has a temporal quality in the sense that each individual agent gains new insights and information about herself and the other participating agents, changes her aspirations for the future and reinterprets her own past and her relationship to the other agents. Thus, the horizon of expectations toward oneself and the other agents in a trust relationship that continues over time may change significantly and thereby change the possibilities of successful concerted actions. Conversions of the individual agent's horizon of expectations can be world-shattering in the sense that the individual's judgments of the trustworthiness or untrustworthiness of intimates as well as distant acquaintances and strangers may be turned upside down. A wonderful example hereof is portrayed in the fieldwork of Lotte Meinert in Northern Uganda (this volume). Becoming a father has altered Oloya's horizon of expectations. His aspiration to be a conscientious father makes the importance of trust, the problems of distrust as well as who to trust, vital. In a sense he has grown more distrusting because he assesses the risk of being deceived as a higher stake than ever when it concerns his young child. But in another sense he is more acutely aware of the need of trust relations for his family to prosper and he endeavors to create such within his new small family. His horizon of expectations has changed radically from when he was young and on his own to now where he is a father with responsibilities toward his child.

Thirdly, trust relationships are social and culturally embedded in the sense that their development is a result of the social cooperation between two or more agents in a concrete social reality. Although each agent may decide to trust or distrust it is neither possible for the individual agent to determine the reaction of others nor to shape the social reality in which he engages with them. Whether trust or distrust emerges between agents cannot be controlled singlehandedly by anyone. The social settings of, for example, Danish suburbia or Northern Ugandan villages deserted during the civil war affect the prospects of thriving trust between agents differently. Just as no individual can change the social setting by will neither can he decide whether the individuals with whom he interacts will turn out to trust him and be trustworthy themselves or rather distrusting and untrustworthy. Norms concerning the value of trust are established in social groups as a result of collective estimations of what is proper, secure, or worthwhile and how trust is valued depends largely on the social group and its dynamics.

As a consequence of these three general characteristics of trust relationships it is necessary to view interpersonal trust between agents as an emerging occurrence that arises as a mixture of willing action and social conditioning. To encompass these complex qualities of trust as a social phenomenon I outline a theoretical framework that takes seriously how interpersonal trust arises as a consequence of individual actions and choices and furthermore is shaped by the emerging development of social cooperation in concrete social situations. The development of a trust relationship, therefore, is both an individual endeavor and a social occurrence larger than any individual choices. In what follows this double aspect of interpersonal trust being formed by individual actions *and* emerging out of social situations and concerted actions that are beyond the control of the individuals will be elaborated through (1) the concepts of prima facie and reflective trust/distrust that relate to the individual's decisions to trust or distrust others and (2) the concept of a locus of trust which concerns the fact that relationships of trust always take place in a social situation that contains various preconditions pertaining to societal order and collective worldviews.

Prima Facie and Reflective Trust/Distrust

The term "prima facie trust" covers the immediate position of either trust or distrust that an individual agent expresses in the actual meeting with others. Thus prima facie trust should not be taken to mean that all agents immediately or primordially meet others with an attitude of trust. Rather, prima facie trust is framed as a generic concept that includes the agent's immediate trust reaction, let it be an expression of trust or distrust in a given situation. The term "prima facie"—literately meaning "at first sight"—suggests that actions of trust or distrust mostly take place without further deliberation and consideration as to whether the other is truly trustworthy or untrustworthy. In everyday life we engage with each other and cooperate in concerted actions directly without asking ourselves whether such engagement and cooperation is warranted.

The measurements of high and low degrees of social trust that social scientists conduct (see www.worldvaluessurvey.org; Sønderskov 2008; Putnam 2000; Fukuyama 1995) provide generalized pictures of prima facie trust and distrust in different social groups. Thus there is a palpable difference between Danes and Ugandans as social groups with the Danes scoring very high on social trust and Ugandans scoring low. Generalizing we may say that the prima facie attitude of Danes tends toward high trust where the prima facie attitude of Ugandans leans toward distrust. The variations in score results indicate that interpersonal trust thrives or deteriorates under the different conditions of living in different nations. The measurements of high and low social trust thus suggest that trust between people requires social stability and predictability to prosper. However, if we content ourselves to such measurements as indicators of interpersonal trust the phenomenon of trust will be reduced to a broad generalization of behavior and expectations. The first-person perspective of the engaged agent pondering whether to trust somebody cannot be captured by the statistics of the social scientists. The measurement of social trust provides at best a snapshot of the overall conditions under which interpersonal trust or distrust endures. It provides us with a generalized understanding of the experiential background and implicit expectations of different social groups.

The difference in the experiential background of individuals points to a very important aspect of trust, namely that the prima facie trust of different agents depends to a large degree on which sort of predictability the agent has internalized. Prima facie trust pertains to the individual's relations to intimates as well as the larger social environment of the society. Experiences of support as well as experiences of disaffection shape the horizon of predictability from which the agent implicitly views every new social situation, the first being positive the second negative. You learn to expect that other people will be either reliable or unreliable. There is a close connection between the prima facie attitude of trust or distrust and the expectations you bring along from your past experience of similar situations. Attitudes of prima facie trust can be compared to attitudes of confidence and reliance. Acting in everyday life we rely on each other to behave "normal" in traffic situations, while shopping, riding public transportation, small talking, etc. This is what Harold Garfinkel calls "the constitutive order of things" (Garfinkel 1963: 190) that covers the constitutive expectancies in everyday situations. These presupposed expectancies are on pair with what we as a matter of simple reliance expect of everyday life. As Garfinkel notes, "The operativeness of these constitutive expectancies … in everyday situations thereby serves as an important condition of stable features of concerted actions" (Garfinkel 1963: 200). The routines of everyday life count as the background horizon for each individual agent's prima facie attitudes of either trust or distrust toward others. This implies that reliance upon simple routines of everyday life is a crucial element of the individual's prima facie trust/distrust.

Reliance and Trust as a Deliberate Choice

Where the implicit normativity of everyday situations is made explicit for theoretical scrutiny it becomes clear that trust and reliance in everyday life are intimately connected. The impulse of a positive prima facie trust toward others is evidence of a concerted social setting where there is high predictability of successful social interaction. If this order is knocked over the normal expectancies will no longer prevail and what in the ordinary setting was simply a matter of reliance becomes an acute question of whether we will trust others in the unfamiliar situation. This might be the case for the individual stranger in a new cultural and social setting (see Schuetz 1944) or for the whole community in a state of social upheaval where it suddenly becomes a matter of intentional trust to walk the streets. Thus what in a familiar situation was simply a matter of reliance may in a large array of different unfamiliar situations become a matter of reflective trust, that is, a question of whether the individual agent is willing and ready to take the risk to trust others.

If human beings were only capable of prima facie trust we might run trust and reliance together and argue that the ability to display trust toward others is a causal effect of the social environment, upbringing, and past experiences of the agent. Thus human beings would be well described as Bayesian agents as is done in game theoretical modulations of trust such as Russell Hardin's (see Hardin 1993: 507–8). But the obvious problems with such explanations is firstly that we thereby lose any sense of trust being something willed and secondly that all experiences count the same. The game theoretical approach has difficulties explaining what happens when a person on the background of a seminal experience decides to either stop or begin trusting. To avoid such difficulties and to underline that human agency cannot be explained as a calculus of predictability Niklas Luhmann (1973) and Annette Baier (1986) exclude reliance, confidence, and predictability from their definition of trust. Instead they understand trust as a willed risk or an acceptance of vulnerability to accentuate that the agent believes the risk is worthwhile and hopes the other will act benevolent toward her. Their theories of trust thus highlight trust as a deliberate choice.

I invoke the differentiation of prima facie trust/distrust from reflective trust/distrust to disclose the insights and limits of both approaches. The understandings of trust as social conditioning and trust as deliberate choice are partially right in the sense that, depending on the situation, we humans react as conditioned agents of past experience or we enact a vision of a future state of affairs by taking the risk to trust others. But both approaches are also erroneous insofar as the perspectives of either conditioned reliance or willed trust behavior is taken to be the exclusive and universal explanation of the human capacity to trust. The objective of the differentiation between prima facie and reflective trust is to give an explanation of trust actions, attitudes, and beliefs as unfolding in a continuum that stretches from the conditioned reliance in the routines of everyday life to the willed engagement of trust in others where the agent is acutely aware of the risk he takes by involving himself in a trust relationship. Depicting individual trust actions, attitudes, and beliefs as such a continuum draws attention to how the individual's trust/distrust in others depends upon social conditioning as well as individual choice (see Pedersen 2010).

Specific emphasis is placed on the shift from prima facie to reflective trust/distrust because it marks a gestalt shift between the engaged interaction in prima facie trust that resemble conditioned social reactions and the distanced deliberation of reflective trust where the individual judges the rightfulness of her prima facie trust. Once the agent has posed the question of whether trust is warranted she cannot simply re-engage in the immediacy of social interaction. She is compelled to justify to herself that her trust or distrust toward others befits the situation. And she will see past situations in light of her reflections upon the reasonableness of her past trust or distrust. If, for example, she discovers that her husband who she trusted unconditionally has been adulterous she will view their common life in a new light that exposes her trust in him as unwarranted. The new knowledge of his infidelity seems to rearrange and reinterpret her life with him and thus her horizon of expectations is shattered. Suspicion as to whether this and that in the past were revelations of his adultery makes her past life story unwarranted and shaky. Reflective trust entails unrest where all actions, attitudes, and beliefs are signs to be interpreted: Did I act naively supporting our separate holidays? Was I credulous when I trusted him? When he came home late from work was it *really* because he was with the mistress? Thus reflective trust compels the individual to continue to interpret her life situation until she is able to endorse an interpretation of it as warranted. Going back to prima facie trust indicates that a new horizon of expectations has been formed. This might involve new reflective standards for trust and distrust and thus that the individual has established a revised interpretation of her life and her social roles. It might also mean that the individual has given up on reflective endorsement and basically incorporated that intimates can turn out untrustworthy and that is something to be endured. If the latter is the case her prima facie attitude will have become more distrusting but short of reflective reasoning as to why.

Roads from Prima Facie to Reflective Trust/Distrust

Whereas some kind of prima facie trust or distrust toward the world is learned from social life experience and therefore is *given* to the individual, acts of reflective trust or distrust are *chosen* by the individual. The shift from prima facie to reflective trust or distrust involves a shift in attitude toward the other. Trusting or distrusting reflectively entails deliberating on what one is doing and rejecting or endorsing one's motives and actions as adequate responses to other people and situations. Such deliberation forces itself upon the individual as an experience and acknowledgment of breaches in the expected. The outbreak of a civil war as occurred in Northern Uganda represents a most dramatic and collective breach in the routines of everyday life (see Meinert's chapter for elaboration).

The highly complicated situation of a society suffering under prolonged civil war includes that almost all elements of the constitutive order of social life have been erupted turning the predictability of events into a predictable unpredictability. This makes, on the one hand, trust even between peers and friends a risky business. Whether to expose yourself in trust becomes something to consider before engaging in social interaction. A filter of reflection as to whether it is worth the risk and whether the other actually is trustworthy inserts itself in between the performance of interactions that under friendly circumstances would be routines. Thus the situation of civil war places the individual agents under circumstances where questions of reflective trust arise. For example, do I dare trust my son who has returned from captivity in the rebel army? On the other hand, even predictable unpredictability is some kind of social order that enables social interaction to take place. Therefore a new prima facie trust may transpire and supersede the original. What at one point was a result of reflection as to whether someone could be trusted can turn into a new set of default actions, attitudes, and beliefs toward the other; a prima facie *distrust*.

In more peaceful surroundings the individual will also experience breaches in what she expected from others. Social interaction is never a straightforward realization of any individual's expectations. Every individual meets others and the world with an outlook of prima facie trust or distrust that affects her interpretation of what causes and motives lay behind events. But breaches in an individual's expectations may stem from different sources. They can be the result of mere coincidences and mistakes, manifestations of deliberate deceit, or something in between. To take notice of a breach as a breach and not something to be excused or to be expected is a special act because it involves questioning one's prima facie approach of either trust or distrust toward others. It is also remarkable because it instantiates the perspective of reflective trust as the individual asks for justifications of her own actions, attitudes, and beliefs in comparison with what she supposes are the motives of others. Thereby the individual is separated and distanced from her immediate engagement in the praxis of social action by her examination of whether some action, attitude, or belief warrants trust or not.

It is only through the reflective evaluation of one's trust in others that the individual agent acquires a distanced view of her trust behavior. When a bystander evaluates the behavior of engaged agents he will commonly—as a third-person observer—think that some are guileless and others much too suspicious. But acting out of prima facie trust/distrust the agents do not reflectively assess their own behavior. What seems apparent from the third-person perspective may be entirely covered from the engaged first-person point of view. Once an agent performs a shift from prima facie to reflective trust or distrust she commences to call the features in her social reality that she took for granted into question and thereby she initiates reflection on their grounds. The distanced observer is from the outset judging and evaluating the motives and reasons of the observed agents. The engaged agent, in contrast, only estimates her own behavior as she intentionally reflects on her reasons to either trust or distrust. I disapprove of Luhmann's and Baier's focus on calculation of risks and acceptance of vulnerability in ordinary trust behavior because they thereby predominantly give attention to the distanced deliberation of reflective trust/distrust and tend to misrepresent the engaged praxis of prima facie trust/distrust. Luhmann and Baier seem to build their theories of trust on the third-person perspective of the observer of social interaction thus discounting the first-person point of view that is absorbed in praxis.

The Interplay between Prima Facie and Reflective Trust

The perspective of a distanced reflection upon the justification of one's own actions is like a third-person perspective upon one's life. It enables the individual to interpret and pass judgment on the rightfulness of her actions, attitudes, and beliefs as well as on those of others. Thereby the perspective of reflective trust creates the space and distance necessary for the individual to reconsider or change her prima facie trust or distrust. As a default attitude, however, it is unattainable. When engaged in living one's life the individual cannot maintain a distanced third-person view on her own doing. Resuming to social interactions implies resuming to a variant of prima facie trust. The perspective of reflective trust opens a room for evaluation of motives and causes in past and future social interaction. But whether the individual is able to put the insights of reflection into operation in lived life depends on her strength of will as well as on the social situation. Nevertheless, the original immediacy of prima facie trust/distrust is broken as the individual gains a reflective awareness of her impulsive ways of action. Whether she restores the old pattern of prima facie trust or tries to establish a new version of prima facie trust it will be colored by reflection.

The shift between prima facie and reflective trust is best described as interplay between reflection and action. The reflective judgments and the immediate actions shape each other in the sense that much reflec-

tion is accomplished while acting and much action is informed by reflection. But that does not mean that reflection and action naturally
cultivate each other. Most often it is a result of great efforts when the individual achieves to make his prima facie actions, attitudes, and beliefs
of either trust or distrust fit with his reflective deliberations. Changing
habits and behavior according to what one intellectually finds right
is never easy. But the individual may also find himself in a situation
where his reflective judgments as to why he has reason to trust or
distrust turn out to be inadequate because the immediate interaction
with people discloses a different reality. The match between reflective
endorsement of who and why to trust/distrust and the concrete and engaged conducts of the individual acting from prima facie trust/distrust
is difficult to attain. Decisive is, however, that once the perspective of
reflective trust is operative the guileless immediacy of prima facie trust
cracks up leaving the individual with the potential to searchingly assess
his own actions, attitudes, and beliefs.

The post-war situation in Northern Uganda illustrates powerfully
how external forces affect reflective deliberations over personal relationships and thus influence the basis of the individual's reflective trust/
distrust toward others. If, for example, your mother left you and your
siblings in the middle of the war and you want to know if this was an
act of crude egoism or harsh necessity—as is the case of Peter in Northern Uganda (see Meinert's chapter)—the answers you find will depend
on how you evaluate the dangers of the war zone that your mother was
facing. If you believe that fleeing Uganda was the only way for her to
stay alive she can be excused as a mother for deserting her children.
On the other hand, if you consider her flight from Uganda and her
children to be based in her lack of consideration and her wish to make
the most profitable outcome for herself you discount her as a caring
mother. Peter is facing exactly these kinds of considerations. Whether
he concludes that her fleeing Uganda was a betrayal or a matter of her
survival his judgment of his mother is molded by the information about
life under the civil war that he receives from others and cannot control.
Even though the story of Peter is highly dramatic and more obviously
linked up with contemporary social history than the life story of many
others we all depend on information and evaluations received from
others to interpret and understand our social position and social relationships. This fact about trust accentuates that whether to trust or not
is not an insulated decision of the individual. Rather trust emerges as a
social phenomenon among humans. Exactly the social setting of trust
is elaborated through the concept of a locus of trust.

The Locus of Trust

The concept of a locus of trust presents a modeling of the concrete situation where interpersonal trust/distrust between two or more agents takes place. The locus of trust focuses on the emergence of trust/distrust between agents. It is a third-person perspective analyzing trust as a social occurrence. Focus is on what influences the interaction of either trustful or distrusting behavior between individuals. Discussions with Meinert about trust in Northern Uganda made it apparent to me that who, what, and under which circumstances we trust can be very different and that a theoretical framework that purports to be comprehensive is required to take these differences into account. It is, for example, not unusual in Northern Uganda to say that you do not trust your home village. Among Ugandans attribution of agency to places is widespread. In the ears of many Western academics it sounds like a false ascription of intentionality to the inert. However, if the analysis of interpersonal trust limits the standards of who and what can be trusted to a Western scientific or any other restrictive definition the result is that a large range of expressions of trust will be ruled out as nonsensical even though they function effortlessly in the context. The concept of a locus of trust is developed as a descriptive model that renounces on normative evaluations of who and what it is sagacious and foolish to trust. Thus the locus of trust differs significantly from the distinction between prima facie and reflective trust/distrust. The latter concerns how an individual reflects on and attempts to justify her trust behavior. It is an analysis of a normative aspect of trust/distrust. The former, on the other hand, relates to the social conditions and the development of these as individuals interact by trusting/distrusting each other. However, the two perspectives complete each other seeing the locus of trust as a kind of spelling out of the conditions of prima facie trust/distrust. This I shall return to in the concluding remarks.

The locus of trust should be understood as an attempt to model the concrete time, space, and context of the unfolding of interpersonal trust. It constitutes a field of interaction depicted as a co-ordinate system with two axes. The horizontal axis represents the social order and the vertical axis represents the worldviews or ideology. This field develops and takes shape in accordance with how the interacting individuals give content to the trust diagram. On the horizontal axis the left side is reserved for the *conventions of social action.* It includes patterns of behavior and conventions such as eating and dressing manners, ways of greeting different people, use of language, etc. These differ in different

social groups and thus it is important to depict the conventions of social action of all participating individuals in order to estimate whether
there is a pronounced familiarity between the participants, or whether
they are estranged from each other with regard to conventions of social
action. If an outline of the conventions of social action for each individual is recorded, different groupings between the individuals will
come to the fore. The right side contains the *institutions and social
structure.* The institutions refer to the socio-political environment of
the individual. Thus, the political institutions of the constitutive monarchy in Denmark shape a Dane. Danish political institutions are stable
and have endured for a long time. In Uganda the civil war has given
rise to a complex range of political institutions with an unstable form.
The national government, the NGOs, and the rebel army are all political centers of power. The individual may not be able to assess clearly
who exercise legitimate authority and who exercise de facto physical/
economic/communicational power. Thus trusting each other under the
auspices of the Danish and the Ugandan political institutions is something very different. Besides the political institutions the social structure influences the particular position in society of an individual. How
this position is defined differs in social groups. It includes the relative
wealth/poverty of the individual measured as social, economic, and
cultural capital (see Bourdieu 1990).

The vertical axis is divided in a similar manner. The top part en-
closes the *collective worldviews.* It pertains to the belief systems or *Wel-
tanschauungen* that an individual is influenced by. Thus one person
may be an atheist and believe that the political power ought to belong
to the working class but is usurped by the rich and the mighty, another
may believe in traditional ancestor worship mixed with Christianity and
think that the political power belongs to the great men of great families. Differences and similarities in the belief systems that individuals
partake in enables or foils that they meet each other with prima facie
trust. Thus, if individuals immediately sense that they rely on greatly
different worldviews this will often give rise to prima facie suspicion
between them. Likewise if a group of individuals is conscious that the
members share worldviews they will be more likely to meet each other
with prima facie trust. The lower part of the vertical axis concerns *ways
of behaving toward nature and social entities.* Here the more concrete
action is depicted. Thus a worshipper of ancestors will act with great
reverence toward places where she believes that spirits of ancestors
hide. A person who believes that physics fully explains the world does
not regard places as carriers of meaning. However, if that person is also
a bit influenced by traditional values he might think that the cemetery

is an exception. To place trust in one's car is an example of a sort of trust behavior that would be ruled out by many definitions of trust as nonsensical. Nevertheless, many do behave toward their cars as though they were more or less trustworthy and willful agents. It is important to be able to analyze and discuss how different ascriptions of agency influence the interaction of individuals. Indeed, I want to argue that much prima facie trust between individuals stems from the immediate recognition of one self in the actions of the other and some attitudes of prima facie distrust originate from the stereotyped understandings of others that act and believe differently from the individual and what she knows as customary. The individual holding strange worldviews and acting in unfamiliar ways seems unpredictable.

Depicting the locus of trust between individuals or groups of individuals in the study of interpersonal trust implies drawing together the relevant information about all agents participating and asserting where and when the trust relationship takes place. All individuals engaging in a particular trust relationship contribute with their particular variant of both axes. The *locus* of trust is the interface of all participating agents' individual positions with regard to (1) conventions of social actions, (2) institutions and social structure, (3) collective world views, and (4) ways of behaving toward nature and social entities in concrete time and place. It is important to note the concrete time and place to be able to understand how the agent's understanding of self and others may be reinforced or enfeebled during the concrete trust relationship. The agent's attitude of prima facie trust/distrust toward others will vary greatly depending on whether she interacts in a familiar social setting with likeminded or she is placed in an unfamiliar setting and required to interact with people with different mindsets. Thus it is important to observe whether all, only some or none of the participating agents see themselves as interacting in their everyday social environment. Having the advantage of a recognizable social setting includes a higher likelihood of being able to predict the actions of the other participating agents. The hypothesis is that analyzing these aspects will enable the understanding of concrete possibilities and difficulties of meeting each other with prima facie trust.

Even though it may not be possible to obtain precise information about all four dimensions for all participating agents, the effort to try to depict the variations and similarities of these background assumptions does give a first approximation of whether the situation furthers interpersonal trust or distrust. A guiding hypothesis may be that in situations where individuals share conventions of social action they may easily interact, but whether this interaction is permeated by prima facie distrust or trust will only show as the interaction is analyzed. Thus developing a depiction of the locus of trust does not in itself provide an answer to the question of whether agents meet each other with prima facie trust or distrust, but it offers important background information to understand different forms of interpersonal trust between agents in different situations.

Concluding Remarks

With the double perspective of the distinction between prima facie and reflective trust/distrust, on the one hand, and the concept and model of a locus of trust, on the other hand, I have sketched a theoretical framework for understanding and analyzing trust behavior. An important aspect of this framework is that it clearly distinguishes between the normative or evaluative qualities of interpersonal trust that are central to the distinction between prima facie and reflective trust/distrust, and the descriptive or sociological context of the formation and development of trust behavior illustrated through the model of a locus of trust. The double perspective offers a way to understand how the individuals and the social context are interdependent. Individuals are interdependent upon each other in developing interpersonal trust. This is true with regard to the important role that the individual's personal life story plays for the individual's disposition to either trust or distrust other people. It also pertains to the emergent quality of trust; it can never be established at the will of any singular individual. Interpersonal trust develops, grows and endures in the social interaction which all participating agents can wish to shape in one direction or the other but only accomplish to influence if they cooperate and agree on the direction. Individuals, so is the postulate of the concept of a locus of trust, are products of their social context in the sense that an individual is who he is by taking part in a social world that consists of conventions of behavior, speculative worldviews, social institutions, and ways to deal with the human, cultural, and natural environment. As individuals meet in interpersonal trust/distrust they produce and restructure that same social context. In effect individuals are formed by the social world and forming the social world concurrently. Interpersonal trust/distrust discloses this reciprocated interdependence between individuals as individuals and the social setting in which they interact.

Reflective trust as a capacity to evaluate whether the trust/distrust shown others and their trustworthiness are warranted endows all agents with the option of changing their own mind and thereby changing the way they meet other people. It is this capacity to willingly trust or distrust others that makes it possible for the individual to alter his horizon of expectations and when employed collectively enables social groups to transform the default attitude of prima facie trust—either establishing or eroding high trust. The distinction between prima facie and reflective trust discloses how interpersonal trust regardless of the importance of social conditioning also is a dynamic and open occurrence.

Tricky Trust

Distrust as a Starting Point and Trust as a Social Achievement in Uganda

Lotte Meinert

You never know
what is in another person's heart
—Peter, nineteen years old, Northern Uganda 2011

The Danish philosopher Knud E. Løgstrup argued that it is basic to human life that we meet each other with natural trust. We do not distrust other people unless we have a reason to, and we do not anticipate that another person will lie before we have an experience of this other person lying (Løgstrup 1997; see also Jackson in this volume). Løgstrup (1997) regarded trust as fundamental to the human condition and wrote that it takes extraordinary circumstances for us to meet other human beings with mistrust; situations such as war, betrayal, and the breakdown of law and order. Based on ethnographic findings from Northern Uganda, I suggest that trust is much trickier, and that the order of things may very well be the other way around: that trust is unfolded over time with distrust as the starting point.

In some ways the specific historical situation in Uganda that I deal with in this chapter is extraordinary, in that it concerns the possible ending of one the longest-lasting violent conflicts on the African continent. Yet oscillating violent conflict situations are, in fact, both common and chronic in large parts of the world (Vigh 2006; World Development Report 2011), and so it seems to have been throughout history and in prehistoric times (Vandkilde 2003; Otto et al. 2006; Gar 2006).

Notes for this section begin on page 133.

We could therefore argue that conflict situations, not only large-scale wars but also conflicts on a smaller scale (betrayal, legal conflicts), can be considered as characteristic of much human life. This raises questions about the universality of the conditions for trust—conditions like peace—as the starting point from which we should basically understand and theorize social interaction as argued by Løgstrup.

In this chapter I explore the seemingly paradoxical reliance on distrust in everyday life in Northern Uganda, and how distrust is taken for granted and produces possibilities. Trust—in personal relations, institutions, truths, and places—is less familiar here, and something people may achieve in specific relations and institutions over time. From this perspective, trust is a willed action—intentional trust in the words of Pedersen—rather than a natural given, and as I would put it: Trust is a tricky social achievement that people may encourage themselves and each other to work toward, even while reminding themselves that there is great instability and unpredictability in who and what can actually be trusted, and under which circumstances. Consequently, trusting in Northern Uganda remains a tricky, open-ended endeavor.

Before I proceed to unfold my argument based on the Ugandan ethnography, allow me to address three problems I have with Løgstrup's basic assumptions. The first is that war, betrayal, and the breakdown of law and order are not extraordinary circumstances, but actually make up the normal, ordinary framework of many people's lives (Das 2007), as indeed they have done at multiple points in history (Vandkilde 2003; Otto et al. 2006; Gar 2006). Secondly, concrete examples from around the world and down through history show that most often there is no clear distinction between times of peace and times of war, and no definite borders between peaceful and conflicted regions. On the contrary, there are connections and networks that reach beyond national and geographical boundaries and into pasts and futures. The third problem—which is of a more fundamental nature—is Løgstrup's basic ontological assumption that trust is the elementary and universal foundation of human interaction.

Could it possibly be the other way around? That we normally meet each other with distrust and only trust each other when we have reason to trust? Numerous geographically widespread anthropological examples show how distrust, suspicion, ambiguity, deception, and doubt form social assumptions on which actions are based, both in intimate relations and in dealings with strangers (Evans-Prichard 1937; Gluckman 1972; Douglas 1992; Geshiere 1997; Viveiros de Castro 1992; Højer 2004; Willerslev 2004; Nielsen 2010; Corsín Jiménez 2011).[1] There may be situations when we are half-aware and half-in-doubt as to whether others are telling the truth, and we kind of know that nobody can be telling the whole truth—given that truth is always contingent upon a particular perspective. We may convince ourselves and others to trust because we believe it is good or even necessary to do so, but this may rather be conceptualized as something achieved socially, often as a moral project, and not as a natural or existential given.

Exploring Distrust

With this in mind, I will seek to understand how distrust works as a social dynamic, and how it produces a social reality in Northern Uganda. I also explore how trust is unfolded over time, and is strived toward as a social, reflective achievement. Distrust plays an important role in the process of building intentional trust, as we will see in the examples from Uganda. Distrust and suspicion may be what people expect in social relations, because this is how everyday life works, and these are the things people can rely on. Trust is the unusual exception that would be considered unwise to follow as a general strategy. In situations of social instability—which may, in fact, characterize more of the human condition than situations of social stability—distrust may be the starting point for most social interaction, and trust may be something that people strive toward and perhaps temporarily, or never, succeed in achieving.

This approach to distrust and trust has been developed through an interplay between my fieldwork in Northern Uganda and conversations with Esther Oluffa Pedersen, and readings of Løgstrup and the work of other philosophers and anthropologists. Based, among other things, on our conversations, Esther Oluffa Pedersen has formulated an outline of interpersonal trust and distrust as a continuum between prima facie trust and reflective trust/distrust, which stretches between the conditioned reliance in the "taken-for-granted" world, and the willed and reflective engagement of trust in others. The ethnography from Uganda has helped to develop, challenge, refine, and qualify these ideas, which find some resonance with Niklas Luhmann's ideas about distrust and trust as social systems that increase and reduce social complexity, and trust as a risk to be taken, not given (Luhmann 1979). However, my attention is focused on the complexities and potentials that distrust creates in social worlds, and on how trust may emerge over time.

I draw upon long-term and episodic fieldwork that I have done in Uganda since 1993. This specific study was carried out during periods of fieldwork in Northern Uganda from 2008 to 2011 among a small group of young Acholi men and their families.[2] I have repeatedly visited these young men at their workplaces and "hang-outs," had conversations with them, gotten to know their families and friends, shared meals, followed their production of music and videos, and interviewed them.

When "Peace Broke Out"

In Northern Uganda people jokingly say that "peace broke out" in 2008. This peace was preceded by twenty-two years of fluctuating armed conflict, intertwined with the conflicts in Sudan and Congo, between the rebel Lord's Resistance Army (LRA) and the government of Uganda. The rebel army recruited their fighters mainly by abducting children and young people and training them as soldiers. The conflict forced about one million people to move to Internally Displaced People's (IDP) camps, where they were supposed to be guarded by the national army. But often the situation was the opposite: The government's soldiers were located in the middle of the camps while the refugees acted as a human shield against the rebels (Dolan 2010). People mention this military "human-shield" strategy as yet another sign that you can seldom trust even those who are supposed to protect you. Both the Ugandan national army and the rebel LRA committed crimes, but the media had a tendency to mainly report on rebel violence, contributing to a distorted image of the conflict as a black-and-white story with no nuances or ambiguities. Some young and older people actually joined the rebel group voluntarily, and some of the "child soldiers" and "sex slaves" who escaped from the rebels later decided to return to the LRA, where they found life better. These perspectives are, however, less loudly broadcasted (Finnström 2008; Lanken, personal communication; Dolan 2010). In other words, the lines between good and bad, perpetrators and victims, were blurred and ever-changing during this conflict, as indeed they are in most conflicts.

After two years of protracted peace negotiations, which kept breaking down due to mutual distrust between the parties but which, at the same time, created income for some and possibilities for others, an agreement between the LRA and the government of Uganda to cease hostilities was signed in 2008. The rebels left Uganda more or less peacefully, but they continued the patterns of violence and abduction in Congo, Sudan, and the Central African Republic. Skeptics suspected that the rebels were simply regrouping in order to strike back in Uganda, as they had done several times before. However, the President of Uganda, Yoweri Museveni, decided to declare the area officially peaceful in 2009.

A substantial consequence of this decision was the closing of the food-rations support from the World Food Programme in the refugee camps, compelling people to return to their long-lost villages in the bush to resume subsistence farming for survival. Some, perhaps especially the older generation, had been longing to go back to village life, because this was what they knew as "normal life." Yet the only sort of normality that many young people knew was the semi-urban camp life. They regarded the bush and the village as an ambivalent, wild, and unknown place. They had never had the experience of being entrusted with animals or a piece of land by their older kin, as used to be the practice in Acholiland and Luoland (see Shipton 2007 on entrustment in Kenyan Luoland). On the one hand, there seemed to be a strong cultural myth about village life: "original life" as harmonious and good, pulling people toward their original homes. On the other hand, remaining landmines in the hinterlands literally made every step toward the "old homes" a dangerous and "unheimlich" affair, creating fear and doubt. There had been landmine-clearing programs, but now and then people would still stumble across landmines and unexploded bombs. They could not even rely on something as basic as the ground they walked on, because it might explode under their feet. But there was little else to do when their survival depended on farming, besides be careful when stepping into "cleared" land and hoping that a landmine would not suddenly go off. Many also feared the evil spirits (*cen*) of people who had been killed during the conflict in the villages and the bush, and who had not been properly buried. People reminded each other that when they came across a body in the bush, they must show their intention to bury the remains and lay the soul of the deceased to rest by picking a leaf from a tree and throwing it on the body, saying "I am not the one who killed you" (Finnström 2008: 88). Otherwise the evil spirit of the deceased might attack the person intruding on its peace.

In areas of major massacres or particularly "bad deaths," where the *cen* were powerful and disturbing, clan leaders, sometimes with the support from NGOs, would organize rituals to cleanse the land. It was obvious that people only dared to go to the old villages and fields if others went there too. Daring and trusting under these circumstances appeared to be a radically *social* endeavor; not really something individuals decided to do on their own, but a momentum and an atmosphere that had to be built up collectively for individuals and families to dare to start moving. "Big people" (powerful rich men) went early (and in fact they often sent, and sometimes paid, relatives who were under their wings) to get hold of more land. This land-grabbing by "big people," and by smaller people as well, ignited an outbreak of land disputes. Actually, about one-third of the families we followed in Awach sub-county (total population: 19,234) reported that they were involved in land conflicts with someone (Kaducu et al., forthcoming), reminding us that "peace breaking out" is a serious joke, and that conflicts, such as the war in Northern Uganda, are seldom solved and ended, but often transmute into other, related conflicts.

Some people stayed behind in the de-camped, semi-urban areas, reasoning: "We are still studying the situation," or "We don't trust this peace yet," or "At least here we know our steps." The majority of those in the former camps were women, who mainly stayed on because they did not have the human link—a husband—to get access to land in the old villages (Whyte et al. 2013). Others remained, or only went to their villages half-heartedly, because their dead had been buried in the old camp and they felt insecure about leaving the place before they could afford to perform the necessary rituals, exhume the body, and return it to the village (Meinert and Whyte 2013). A good number of young people stayed behind hoping that, and trying to find out whether, an urban future had more to offer than a future in rural farming. The young men I describe in this chapter belong to this last category. These young men had little or no experience of village life before or during the 22-year-long conflict, and they did not share any romantic ideals about farming as representing the original, good life. One of the young men had been abducted from his village, and he did not hesitate to articulate that he did not "trust that place" and did not have high hopes for a future there. What is more, intergenerational relations had been seriously damaged during the conflict, partly because often the children and young people were the one's who were abducted or joined the rebels, and were sometimes even forced to kill or mutilate members of their own families to prevent them from returning home. Parents recount the horror of not being able to trust their own children as a particularly destructive form of social torture (Dolan 2010). Paradoxically, this intergenerational distrust also created a certain degree of freedom and new possibilities for the younger generation (and the older), because it made them stop expecting support from each other.

Most of the young men I came to know had left school because they, or their parents, could not afford the school fees. Others were still in school, at least part time. They met their friends and girlfriends at the video shop and taught themselves IT, filming, and editing skills. Meanwhile, they hoped to meet someone who would offer them a "real job" or a music contract, or pay their school fees so they could return to school. In the next section I will present two young men and their music, which they let me hear during the time we spent in the video shop.

Peter: Changing Versions—Changing Expectations

I first met Peter when he was sixteen. He had told me about his life in the urban camp. We had done a sort of life-history interview, and so I have to admit that, naively, I thought I had a fairly good idea about his past and who he was.

One evening, about a year later, Peter, his friend Oloya, and a small group of young men and I were seated in the video shop. An extremely violent war film entitled *Unisoldier*, playing at the back of the room, occasionally attracted our attention. The young men were exited because they had finished recording their latest song (*Hope 4 da New*, which I discuss below). They were burning it onto CDs that would also include their other songs and videos.

One of the videos Peter had made was called *Hardship*, and it caught my eye. This video begins with a scene cut and pasted from the film *Blood Diamond*, in which young children have their hands chopped off by soldiers from a rebel army. The film and music continue with scenes from Peter's everyday life: on the road, in the field, at the homestead; footage of girls dancing traditional Acholi dances, and of Peter himself and other young men dancing. The lyrics go like this:

HARDSHIP

Verse
I have suffered in this world
And can't stay in the world today
Staying away from my clan mates
They took me as a slave
I have to rent a place to plant crops
For sure the world is spoilt today

Chorus
It is difficult to stay with people who are not your clan mates
It is hard to stay away from your clan mates
Let me go back to my clan mates
From there they will not let me suffer like this

Verse
The people of Lamogi have come
They are going back to their land
All the Acholi are raising orphans back home
Look!! The people of Otici today
Have gone back to stay at their land
To stay in harmony
Look!! The people of Palaro are now going back to their land
Which means peace has come

Chorus
It is difficult to stay with people who are not your clan mates
It is hard to stay away from your clan mates
Let me go back to my clan mates
From there they will not let me suffer like this

Peter explained that he wrote and recorded this song because people needed encouragement to feel safe about going back home. When they know that others are going, they will also get the courage to go, he said. He was not going back himself, however. I asked him why he had included the hand-chopping scenes from the film *Blood Diamond*, which led to the following exchange:

Peter: "Because it was like that."

Lotte: "But you did not experience that?"

Peter: "I did. I was in the bush for two years." [He glanced nervously at the other young men in the video shop to see their reaction and quickly added] "But I did not kill anyone!"

Lotte: "OK, you didn't tell that part earlier [in the life-history interview we had done previously]."

Peter: "I did not tell anyone yet. I study people before I tell [laughing]."

He then quietly narrated to us how he was seven years old and playing with his mother when rebels came and asked her to let them have the boy. She cried, but agreed. Peter spent two years in the bush with the rebels. It was a tough life, he said, but the rebels did not beat him because he was still young, and they carried him on their backs when he was tired. He learned "everything about guns in Sudan," and he saw lots of killing and mutilation. It *was* like *Blood Diamond*, he said. But he did not kill anyone, as he reminded us again and again. The rebels enjoyed watching him dance; dancing was his job. "I could really entertain them with dancing. But they did not know my heart," Peter said. After two years he recognized that he and the rebel group were close to his home, and during an attack he managed to escape and hid in his mother's house. Peter's mother was happy to see him alive, but she refused to take him to one of the many NGOs specializing in the reintegration of child soldiers. She told him not to trust those NGOs: "They inject medicine in children to make them look healthy and fat, but after some time the children commit suicide or simply die." Peter regretted that his mother deprived him of the chance to have his school fees paid, and to get other benefits from the NGO projects. He did not believe that the NGOs mistreated children, but even so he asked me: "Do you think so?"

After the session at the video shop and hearing Peter's new version of his life story, my rather naive expectations to life stories as being "true," and my sense of "knowing people," changed. Trusting the stories I had from Peter and the other young men became trickier. Did I know Peter better now because he had confided in me, and in the others, sharing sensitive information about his former life? Perhaps, but doubt crept in. Having been cheated by his first version, I realized that one cannot ever really know in this scenario when, or whether, others are telling their real story. Sometimes they even seem to have lost track of the truth themselves. And what a person tells, to whom, where, when, and how depends on the circumstances, and will continue to do so.

Two years later, Peter was listening to interviews we had done for another project and commenting on the stories of two abductees: "I believe one of them, and I don't believe the other. Never believe what people tell you right away! They may be making up stories for you because they think they will get something out of that." I thought about Peter's earlier stories and versions and realized that I had already given up on the quest to find out what was really true. Determining which version was true was not really the point. The trick was to expect distrust, and then possibly, and carefully, to unfold a sense of trust over time; trust which might, however, later revert to distrust.

In his song Peter says that he wants to go back to his home in the village, and be with his clan mates. The lyrics assume that life will be easier there, that young people will be given land, that a person can trust his clan mates, because this is the ideal. The song also mentions that in the bush with the rebels, it was the clan mates—Peter's own people—those he was supposed to be able to trust, who kept him as a slave. When I asked him if we could go and visit his home in the village, he immediately refused: "I don't trust that place. Maybe next time." Having caught on to the trick, I could not help but suspect that Peter did not want me to go there because I would find out other versions of his story than he wished.

During the session in the video shop, Peter's friends listened intently to Peter's account of his past with the rebels. Later they told me they had no idea he had been in the bush, and that they were surprised to hear of it. But it struck me how they were not surprised at being surprised. They expected, and took for granted, that others do not necessarily tell the truth about their past and themselves. Telling the truth would be naive, and even dangerous in some cases. "I study people before I tell," Peter had said. I was astonished to see how easily they accepted the news that Peter had been with the rebels, and how there was no awkwardness at their having been deceived into thinking otherwise. Their horizon of expectations was not being shattered in any way. This is what they experienced and expected all the time: You expect distrust unless you have a reason to trust. Likewise for me: Over the years since I had first met these young men, I had experienced many surprises, and gradually my horizon of expectations had changed.

Other anthropologists working in this area and other "chronic conflict" zones have written insightfully about lying, telling half-truths, changing versions of stories, and telling multi-layered stories (Utas 2003; Lanken personal communication) Peter Metcalf has extensively discussed lies in anthropology in his book *They lie, we lie* (2002), which deals with the lies told to anthropologists by our informants during fieldwork and the lies told by anthropologists to our informants and in our writings. What I find interesting for our discussion of prima facie distrust is that discovering a lie among the young men in Northern Uganda was not considered to be particularly embarrassing, because it was taken for granted that one does not tell the truth, but always gives a version of things that fits the audience, the situation, and one's own purpose. Trusting or blindly believing what someone recounts would be considered naive. Being able to tell different versions of a story on the right occasions is wise, and sometimes even a matter of survival. "Other versions" may be resources that lie dormant in the social fabric of life. They may be historically untrue, but they are potentially useful.

The fact that Peter knows that one should not expect trust and truth does not mean that he has come to terms with this as an ideal, or an end-point. He struggles to trust his friends, his siblings, and his neighbors, and over the years Peter keeps returning to questions about his mother's decisions during and after the war, and about her disappearance into Sudan. Peter asked and almost seemed haunted by questions about motherhood in general, and about his own mother's actions in particular: How can a mother give her child away to the rebels like my mother did? How can a mother refuse to take her child to school? How can a mother leave her children and stay in Sudan? Peter reasoned that maybe his mother did not have much of a choice with the rebels. She may have known that she had to give up the boy in order for both of them to survive. But when he returned, why did she not tell him this? And why did she not want to take him to the NGOs, who would have let him attend school? Was she hiding something from him? Was she right about the NGOs doing bad things to children? He had seen other former child soldiers benefitting greatly from NGO projects. When his mother left her children to go to Sudan, was she actually planning to make a lot of money to sustain the family? Or did she go there to meet a man she had fallen in love with? Peter seems to be trying to deal with a sensation of breached trust. He attempts to take into account that the situation of actual and possible threats influenced his mother's decisions. He is trying to convince—or deceive—himself that there are, or should be, certain relations that one can trust, even if there are aggravating circumstances. Peter is left pondering the questions of who you can trust, and under what circumstances.

Oloya: But Now That I Am a Father . . .

Oloya was—I believe—twenty years old when I first met him in 2008. He was wearing hip-hop clothes, had dreadlocks, and appeared to be very laid-back as he hung around in the video shop with the other young men. Oloya had lost his mother when he was two years old and was raised by his maternal aunt until he was six. One day his father picked him up and told him: "You don't belong here (with your mother's family)." According to the patrilineal and virilocal ideals, children belong to their father's clan, and they should live with, and receive a piece of land from, their paternal clan when they grow up. It was an abrupt change in Oloya's life when he had to move in with his father's family, which he hardly knew, and was taken to school in a neighboring district (where he did not speak the language) to avoid abduction by the rebels. After Oloya's father died, he had to stop going to school because no one could pay his school fees. Oloya had no real job, but he eked out a living by producing his music and videos and helping others do the same, earning some money but barely making ends meet. His family had a piece of land in the village, said Oloya, but he did not want to go there and be a farmer. His paternal uncles were living in the village at that point, and Oloya did not know whether they would share the land with him. He indicated, while shaking his head, that he did not trust them. Nor was he interested in having a rural future, but felt more attracted to moving on with his music career at the time.

The following year, Oloya introduced me to his girlfriend—Lucy—and told me how he was trying to convince her to marry him. The next time I met Oloya he was happy, and worried. Lucy was pregnant and her family wanted him to pay bride wealth, including a fine (*luc*) for having gotten Lucy pregnant before he had officially declared his plans of marriage to Lucy's family, as was proper according to Acholi custom. Oloya asked his uncles to help him pay the bride wealth, but they declined. Oloya, who had been hopeful, was disappointed, but not surprised. "You never know who you can count on until you really need their help," he explained. His uncles were supposed to help Oloya pay the bride wealth, according to Acholi ideals, but the reality of the situation was different.

The following year the couple's baby was born, and Oloya's perspective changed. He cut off his dreadlocks, struggled to find employment, and succeeded in getting a job in a photo and printing shop to earn money. He still wanted to play his music, but explained that now he was a father and had to be responsible, because others depended on him. Lucy encouraged Oloya to contact his uncles and get a piece of land in the village so they would have a home to return to. She felt that living in town in a rented house was too unstable, now that they had a child to take care of and a future that was not just their own. In this vulnerable situation Oloya seemed more open to the idea, and realized that he had to rely on and establish some kind of trust relationship with his uncles.

During this time Oloya and his friend recorded a song in one of the small music studios in town. Mixing reggae and hip-hop rhythms, English and Acholi lyrics, they pictured hoping and trusting as hard work, but as a kind of moral and social obligation, no matter how tricky it may be.

HOPE 4 DA NEW

Chorus
Why 's so hard to trust somebody?
I wanna know my people
Why 's so tricky to trust somebody?
Say it be your best friend
Why 's so hard to hope for the new?
I wanna know my people
Yeah, yeah …
I wanna know my people

Verse (translated from the Acholi original)
I was asking myself
Why the future is not known
But I could not get the answer
'Cause the world's so tricky
And full of prediction

Verse
Truth's one thing
We have to practice
And enforce in this world
Belief in oneself
Is what we have to do
In order to hope for the new

Let's be having the same focus
Let's be having the same goal
Then we can trust each other
Oh yeah, Mama

Hope for the new
Hope for the new, my people

Verse (translated from the Acholi original)
I want you to understand this
You shouldn't undermine people
You shouldn't be arrogant to other people
You should have love in life
You should have truth among others
You should learn to listen to each other in life
We need to be friendly
We need to know God
We should be faithful in life
We should learn to forgive one another

Chorus
Why's so hard to trust somebody?
I wanna know my people
Why 's so tricky to trust somebody?
Say it be your best friend
Why 's so hard to hope for the new?
I wanna know my people
Yeah, yeah …
I wanna know my people

Verse
Peace broke out
But fighting over land
Is what we have to stop
Elders! Children are dying
But why can't you see?
Truth, truth, truth
Where is your hiding place?
We need to go back home
But fighting over land

Verse
On the other hand
Husbands and wives
HIV has no cure
Both of you have to trust
Mummy, Daddy
Boys, boys, boys
Defilement is a tricky case
You have to be so careful
Brothers, sisters.

Coming to Terms with Trust

The basic premise of this song is what Esther Oluffa Pedersen terms "social prima facie distrust": People are used to distrusting, and they take it for granted after decades of civil war and unrest. Oloya's song is, in itself, an act of social reflective trust, in which the singers question what has happened to trust, and attempt to evoke reflection among their audience about the difficulties in trusting. At the same time there is a moral imperative and an expression of necessity in the song: "You should ... we need to ... we have to ... trust," which sounds like someone trying to persuade themselves and others to do so because there is no other option—although it is something they instinctively know is risky.

When they sing: "Truth's one thing we have to practice and enforce in this world," it clearly indicates how they see trust and trustworthiness as contingent upon truth, which, in a context where distrust and lying are the norm, is something that needs to be built over time in social practice. This suggests that truth is a reflection of trust that must be produced socially out of distrust. Truth does not have objective qualities, but has to be practiced as a temporal and willed phenomenon.

For Oloya, *Hope 4 da New* also marks a change in his personal perspective. He used to be more cynical about not trusting other people. He did not trust that his uncles would give him land, and indeed they did not help him pay the bride wealth, but in his new situation as a father he cannot afford to be laid-back and critical. He engages himself in public reflection from a more vulnerable position, realizing that he is dependent on being able to trust others. Esther Oluffa Pedersen points out how trust and distrust evolve over time and have a temporal quality, in the sense that individuals gain insight into themselves and others over time, and their horizons of expectations change accordingly. For Oloya, the temporal transformation is quite sudden with his shift in position in the kinship and family hierarchy, which obviously influences his horizon of expectations.

Esther Oluffa Pedersen also reminds us in her chapter that trust relationships are always embedded in social and cultural contexts. An individual agent may decide to trust or distrust another person, but whether trust or distrust emerges between the involved parties cannot be controlled singlehandedly by anyone. The social situation is saturated with a kind of inertia, and with norms about what is proper, secure, and worthwhile. Oloya knows that he cannot influence his relationship to the uncles in any remarkable way, but he tries with his song to create social reflection upon the norms and inertia that frame their relationship.

Both Peter's and Oloya's struggles with and questions about trust, and their more reflective songs about trust, point to the continuum that Esther Oluffa Pedersen sketches in her outline of interpersonal trust between willed action and social conditioning: Their stories emphasize that willed action is not only an individual endeavor, but to a large extent a social achievement, which embodies the potential to influence the conditioning of a situation or, in Pedersen's words, the locus of trust.

Conclusion: Trickiness

Peter's changing stories and Oloya's changing perspectives, their songs and questions, raise far more issues than I can sum up here, but they do point to certain phenomena that I encounter again and again in Northern Uganda, namely that distrust is taken for granted in a matter-of-fact way, and that people do not expect to be told the truth. Expecting to be told the truth would be naive. Trusting is a struggle, a tricky but necessary moral project, and a willed action.

Three issues seem clear, based on this exploration of social worlds in Northern Uganda: One is that truth is contingent upon trust; a second is that trust may develop through interpersonal processes of mistrust; and a third is the social productivity of distrust. Distrust makes many possible versions of reality lie dormant, and in this way opens possibilities and disassembles. Trust, on the other hand, closes, connects, and assembles.

The experience that "things are not always what they seem to be" is a theme that runs strongly through African ethnography (for instance in Evans-Prichard 1937; Gluckman 1972; Geshiere 1997; Whyte 1997), fables, and myths (Jackson 1982 and in this volume). Even so, there seem to be examples from all over the world describing how "the tricky" works. Højer writes about the anti-social contract in Mongolia: "The premise for relating to each other seemed fundamentally insecure. Indeed one could be a witch and there would be no way to know for sure because relations were based on an idiom of deceit; things were not necessarily what they seemed to be.... The only thing known for sure was that someone was not to be trusted, because relationships were cast in an idiom of distrust" (Højer 2004:49).

Willerslev argues that among the Yukaghir in Siberia, deceit, ambiguity, hiddenness, and seduction are central aspects of life and people manage the unity of their social world through the administration of its disunity or division (Willerslev 2004). Viveiros de Castro, with his studies of Amazonian Indians, has taught us the trickiness of perspectives, enemies, and selves (1992). Corsín Jiménez points out with material from various places, including contemporary Europe, that distrust is necessary, and also thrives and is part of most social worlds: "We need divisions and disruptures to know what unites and integrates. We need the occult to know why some things are worth making visible. We need a realm that lies *after trust* to make trust meaningful. There is, in a sense, no trust in society except in an "after-trusting" mode" (Corsín Jiménez 2011: 193). Likewise, we may say that there is no trust in society except in an "after-distrusting mode," or rather, that processes between trust and distrust oscillate and are conditioned and willed. Trust is unfolded and created in specific situations over time through interpersonal processes of distrust and doubt.

Trust is a social achievement, not an ontological starting point as Løgstrup suggested, because as Peter reminded us in the opening quote: "We cannot know for sure what is in another person's heart." *If* there is a starting point, it is a tricky one.

Notes

My warm thanks to the young men in Gulu who have shared *versions of* their lives and stories with me. I am also grateful to Anne Line Dalsgård, Morten Nielsen, Esther Oluffa Pedersen, the Trustland researchers, and the African Seminars group at Johns Hopkins University for their stimulating comments on this chapter.

1. "Silent trade" is a phenomenon known in many parts of the world, particularly West Africa. The principle is that people trade with others without meeting or exchanging words. One party simply leaves their goods at a designated spot and trusts—yes, trusts—that the other party will do the same. Yet interestingly, they do not trust direct interaction with the other party.
2. The study is part of a collaborative and comparative project on youth and futurity in Brazil, Denmark, Georgia, and Uganda, involving Anne Line Dalsgård, Susanne Højlund, and Martin Demant Frederiksen and funded by the Research Council for Culture and Communication (FKK) from 2008 to 2011. The focus on young musicians in Uganda came about because we were looking for innovative strategies among marginalized youth, to develop ideas that went beyond theories of social reproduction and social inheritance. Their songs and videos caught my attention because they are such appealing and intense ways of expression for these young men, who as a group are otherwise not very articulate. Apart from this specific research project with the young men, I base my reflections on seven years of living and doing fieldwork in other parts of Uganda, stretching from 1993 to 2011. I also draw upon research done as part of a project funded by the Danish Council for Development Research (FFU) entitled "Changing Human Security: Recovery after armed conflict in Northern Uganda." This includes an ethnographic study of forgiveness (Ovuga et al 2011), the return process (Whyte et al. 2013), and a demographic cohort study of about 19,000 inhabitants in Awach sub-county in the Gulu district (Kaducu et al., forthcoming).

REFERENCES

Baier, Annette. 1986. "Trust and Anti-Trust." *Journal of Ethics* 96, no. 2: 231–60.

Bourdieu, Pierre. 1990. *The Logic of Practice*. Translated by Richard Nice. Cambridge: Polity Press.

Corsín Jiménez, Alberto. 2011. "An Anthropology of Trust." *Anthropological Theory* 11, no. 2: 177–96.

Das, Veena. 2007. *Life and Words: Violence and the Descent Into the Ordinary*. Berkeley: University of California Press.

Dolan, Chris. 2010. *Social Torture: The Case of Northern Uganda, 1986–2006*. New York: Berghahn Books.

Douglas, Mary. 1992. *Risk and Blame: Essays in Cultural Theory*. London: Routledge.

Evans-Pritchard, Edward Evan. 1937. *Witchcraft, Oracles and Magic Among the Azande*. Oxford: Clarendon Press.

Finnström, Sverker. 2008. *Living with Bad Surroundings: War, History, and Everyday Moments in Northern Uganda*. Durham, NC: Duke University Press.

Fukuyama, Francis. 1995. *Trust: The Social Virtues and the Creation of Prosperity*. New York: The Free Press Paperbacks.

Gar, Azar. 2006. *War in Human Civilisation*. New York: Oxford University Press.

Garfinkel, Harold. 1963. "A Conception of, and Experiments with, 'Trust' as a Condition of Stable Concerted Actions." In *Motivation and Social Interaction*, edited by O. J. Harvey. New York: Ronald Press.

Geshiere, Peter. 1997. *The Modernity of Witchcraft: Politics and the Occult in Postcolonial Africa*. Charlottesville: University Press of Virginia.

Gluckman, Max. 1972. "Moral crises: Magical and Secular Solutions. The Marett Lectures, 1964 and 1965." In *The Allocation of Responsibility*, edited by Max Gluckman. Manchester: Manchester University Press.

Hardin, Russell. 1993. "The Street-Level Epistemology of Trust." *Politics and Society* 21, no. 4: 505–29.

Højer, Lars. 2004. "The Anti-Social Contract: Enmity and Suspicion in Northern Mongolia." *Cambridge Anthropology* 24, no. 3: 41–63.

Jackson, Michael. 1982. *Allegories from the Wilderness: Ethics and Ambiguity in Kuranko Narratives.* Bloomington: Indiana University Press.

Kaducu, Ocaka Felix, Emilio Ovuga, Lotte Meinert, Susan Whyte, Ceasar Okumu, and Morten Sodeman. Forthcoming. "Demographic Characteristics of a Post-Conflict Rural Population: Findings from Awach Demographic Surveillance System (DSS) Site in Northern Uganda." Submitted to *The Journal of Demography.*

Luhmann, Niklas. 1973. *Vertraue: Ein Mechanismus der Reduktion Sozialer Komplexität.* Stuttgart: Ferdinand Enke Verlag.

———. 1979. *Trust and Power: Two Works by Niklas Luhmann.* Chichester, UK: John Wiley and Sons.

Løgstrup, Knud E. 1997. *The Ethical Demand.* Translated by Theodor I. Jensen and Gary Puckering, revised by Hans Fink and Alasdair MacIntyre. Notre Dame, IN: University of Notre Dame Press.

Meinert, Lotte, and Susan R. Whyte. 2013. "Creating the New Times: Reburials after War in Uganda." In *Taming Time, Timing Death,* edited by Dorthe R. Christensen and Rane Willerslev. Farnham, UK: Ashgate Publishing.

Metcalf, Peter. 2002. *They Lie, We Lie: Getting on with Anthropology.* London: Routledge.

Nielsen, Morten. 2010. "Contrapuntal Cosmopolitanism: Distantiation as Docial Relatedness Among House-builders in Maputo, Mozambique." *Social Anthropology* 18, no. 4: 396–402.

Otto, Ton, Henrik Thrane, and Helle Vandkilde. 2006. *Warfare and Society: Archaeological and Social Anthropological Perspectives.* Aarhus: Aarhus University Press.

Ovuga, Emilio, Julaina Obika, Susan R. Whyte, and Lotte Meinert. 2011. "Attainment of Positive Mental Health through Forgiveness in Northern Uganda." *African Journal of Traumatic Stress* 2, no. 2: 71–79.

Pedersen, Esther Oluffa. 2009. *Die Mythosphilosophie Ernst Casssirers: Zur Bedeutung des Mythos in der Auseinandersetzung mit der Kantischen Erkenntnistheorie und in der Sphäre der modernen Politik.* Würzburg: Königshausen & Neumann.

———. 2010. "A Two-Level Theory of Trust." *Balkan Journal of Philosophy* 2, no. 1: 47–56.

Putnam, Robert. 2000. *Bowling Alone: The Collapse and Revival of American Community.* New York: Simon & Schuster.

Schuetz, Alfred. 1944. "The Stranger: An Essay in Social Psychology." *American Journal of Sociology* 49, no. 6: 499–507.

Seligman, Adam. 1997. *The Problem of Trust.* Princeton, NJ: Princeton University Press.

Shipton, Parker. 2007. *The Nature of Entrustment: Intimacy, Exchange, and the Sacred in Africa.* New Haven, CT: Yale University Press.

Sønderskov, Kim M. 2008. *Making Cooperation Work: Generalized Social Trust and Large-N Collective Action.* Aarhus: Politica.

Utas, Mats. 2003. *Sweet Battlefields: Youth and the Liberian Civil War.* PhD diss., Uppsala University.

Vandkilde, Helle. 2003. "Commemorative Tales: Archaeological Responses to Modern Myth, Politics, and War." *World Archaeology* 35, no. 1: 126–44.

Vigh, Henrik. 2006. *Navigating Terrains of War: Youth and Soldiering in Guinea-Bissau.* New York: Berghahn Books.

Viveiros de Castro, Eduardo. 1992. *From the Enemy's Point of View.* Chicago: University of Chicago Press.

Whyte, Susan R. 1997. *Questioning Misfortune.* Cambridge: Cambridge University Press.

Whyte, Susan R., Sulaiman Babiiha, Rebecca Mukyala, and Lotte Meinert. 2013. "Remaining Internally Displaced: Missing Links to Human Security in Northern Uganda." *Journal of Refugee Studies* 26: 283–301.

Willerslev, Rane. 2004. "Not animal, Not *Not*-animal: Hunting, Imitation and Empathetic Knowledge Among the Siberian Yukaghirs." *Journal of the Royal Anthropological Institute* 10: 629–52.

World Development Report. 2011. *Conflict, Security and Development.* World Bank: Available at http://web.worldbank.org/WBSITE/EXTERNAL/ EXTDEC/EXTRESEARCH/EXTWDRS/0,,contentMDK:23256432 ~ pagePK: 478093 ~ piPK:477627 ~ theSitePK:477624,00.html.

TRUST, AMBIGUITY, AND INDONESIAN MODERNITY

JOINT STATEMENT

Sune Liisberg and Nils Bubandt

This dialogue centers on the relationship between trust and ambiguity. Ambiguity, we both suggest, represents a challenge to trusting behavior. Both chapters seek to address the same overall questions: How is trust possible in uncertain conditions? What kinds of paradoxes go into trust when trust itself is being eroded by the exigencies of existential life-worlds or political power? How, inversely, do existential life-worlds and political power interpellate each other—call each other into existence—through the ambiguities of trust? Indonesia and Sartre are strikingly apposite—and in some ways similar—places to begin an inquiry into the ambiguities and paradoxes of trust, because both the philosophy of Sartre and the modern politics of Indonesia, as we have come to realize, entail an engagement with the problem of inauthenticity. Indonesian politics, as Nils Bubandt demonstrates, has since independence from Dutch colonialism in 1949 cultivated a public climate of ambivalent authenticity, in which people place a striking amount of trust in a political system they perceive to be inauthentic. The philosophy of Jean-Paul Sartre, as Sune Liisberg highlights, addresses the notion of inauthenticity, i.e. self-deception, as an emphatic demonstration of the inherent nothingness and ambiguity implied in our conscious existence. Identifying it as a perpetual threat to every human project, Sartre at the same time conceives self-deception as a strategy mainly motivated by the conflictual nature of our social relations. In line with Sartre's analysis, and on the basis of empirical findings in psychological research, Liisberg suggests a conception of trust as a benign form of self-deception by which we cope with the ambiguities of social life.

Inauthenticity haunts, as the two chapters show, trust at the individual, existential level as well as at the political and social level. At the individual level, as Liisberg argues, the deliberate cultivation of positive ideas about the other is the condition of trust, but involves also a form of self-deception. Only people who are able to consistently undertake this kind of self-deception can trust other people amidst the ambiguity that everyday life and social interaction entail. Indonesian people could be said to be hyper-tolerant of ambiguity in this sense because they, as Bubandt demonstrates, trust the political power that they know to be inauthentic.

Interdisciplinary dialogue of the kind this anthology pursues also requires a high degree of ambiguity tolerance. The knowledge interests of philosophy and anthropology for instance differ greatly: Philosophers frequently aim to establish general truths about human understanding and life, while anthropologists tend to use ethnography to take aim at the Western provincialism of such general truths. This, at least, was the disciplinary difference that we found ourselves up against: Liisberg anchors his contribution in empirical psychological research about the concept of ambiguity (in)tolerance as the basis for his rather universalizing philosophical ambition, in which he endeavors to understand how ambiguity relates to trust. Bubandt's chapter, on the other hand, insists on the importance of context for such an understanding. Bubandt substantiates his view with an analysis of (in)authenticity and trust in contemporary Indonesian politics. So the overall difference is this: Bubandt wants to use Indonesia as a "counter-ethnography" against common, Western and philosophical assumptions about authenticity and trust, while Liisberg seeks to demonstrate how concepts drawn from psychology and existential philosophy captures the Indonesian case as well. In Liisberg's reading, ambiguity is a condition of the human existential realm, whereas Bubandt suggests that ambiguity may have a variety of different political and ontological histories. We leave it to the reader to decide which, if either, perspective holds the most truth.

In that sense the following two chapters are a dialogue without a common conclusion. Instead, it proceeds purposely by allowing two complementary perspectives to meet. We do so in our chapters by making shorter or longer digressions that contain meta-reflections about how our individual exposition speaks to the other. A format we came up with over coffee and cake (exchange of sugar and stimulants being one of those means through which humans have always sought to deliberately cultivate the kind of conviviality in which they could foster positive ideas about each other), it seemed to us the best way to allow the strength of each disciplinary approach to be maintained without dialogue being lost. So regardless of whether ambiguity is best conceived as a universal analytical category, or should be seen to be lodged within and shaped by specific political ontologies, both of our chapters share the same point of departure: We are both concerned with the categories of authenticity/inauthenticity (or self-deception) and how they relate to trust/distrust.

TRUST IN AN
AGE OF INAUTHENTICITY
Power and Indonesian Modernity

Nils Bubandt

One of my favorite media quotes comes from *Miami Vice*, the 1980s television series starring Don Johnson and Philip Michael Thomas. They play two fashion-conscious police detectives, Sonny Crockett and Rico Tubbs, who see their share of the shady side of human behavior in the Florida underworld. But their experiences are nothing compared to those of their lieutenant, Martin Castillo, who has a past as a drug-enforcement agent in war-torn Vietnam in the 1970s. Often, during an interlude between shootouts and car chases, the lieutenant tells horrific stories from the Vietnam War's heart of darkness that shock even the seasoned detectives. In response to one particularly outrageous story from the tropical jungle, the two Miami detectives respond: "But that's crazy!" "No," the pockmarked sergeant retorts in his distinctively hoarse voice: "It's not crazy; it's Southeast Asia."

To suggest that Southeast Asia is a "place apart"—a site of otherness, let alone a site of madness—is clearly problematic, even Orientalist (Said 1995). I will nevertheless venture to suggest a part of Southeast Asia, specifically Indonesia, as a counter-example; a kind of counter-ethnography to the theme of trust and novelty. If trust, in conventional social theory, is bound to authenticity and a belief in systems of expertise and generalized exchange guaranteed by the state, how then does trust (in people, in power, in truth) look in a political environment where the practices, rationality, and ideological goals of the state are seen as fundamentally inauthentic? How is trust possible in a political world where it is not the past that vouchsafes the authenticity of power; but rather power that guarantees, if always in inauthentic ways, the authenticity of the past by what it promises to be in the future? In Indonesia, three decades of highly rationalist, but also oppressive, authoritarian rule have produced just such a paradoxical kind of trust within inauthenticity. In Indonesia, I argue, the trust that people place in the state exists in ambivalent tension with a popular sense that the signs and signatures of the state are inherently inauthentic. People, in short, trust an inherently inauthentic state. The endemic sense of inauthenticity is predicated on the claim of state power being not the result but the producer of temporal authenticity. The result is an inversion of the relationship between power and authenticity that dominates Western notions of power. It is not power that needs to prove itself authentic, but power that is ascribed the ability to shape the authentic. This ascription is, however, not stable. Rather, it is accompanied by a popular social reading of power that is characterized by both dissimulation and a fundamental wariness of trust as the basis of social cohesion. Within this ambivalent relationship between trust and distrust, power nevertheless operates effectively in Indonesia. Arguably, it does so exactly through its reliance on a popular trust in power in the face of power's fundamental inauthenticity.

A Counter-Ethnography of Trust

This chapter is interested in the same topic that also runs through the chapter by Sune Liisberg—namely, the topic of ambiguity. My particular interest lies in exploring the social life of ambiguity and, by implication, in inquiring into its social, political, and historical variability. This entails focusing on the social and political "conditions of possibility" of ambiguity itself: How does ambiguity come to be experienced and conceptualized in a particular manner by the way reality presents itself to human beings through particular discursive and institutional means? If my suggestion is correct, and political power in Indonesia is indeed effective because of (rather than in spite of) the fact that it is inherently inauthentic, the analysis of this chapter raises the question whether it makes sense to say that politics may be premised on "bad faith" or "self-deception." Self-deception (*mauvaise foi*), as discussed by Liisberg, is a term by which Jean-Paul Sartre wishes to denote something that is universal to conscious human existence; namely, a particular self-negation of oneself, a denial of some aspect of one's being that is essential to the production of a certain reality about oneself, one's own self-making. According to Sartre, "the nature of consciousness simultaneously is to be what it is not and not to be what it is" (Sartre 1956: 116). A similar paradox I suggest—at the level of political rather than existential epistemology—afflicts the authority of contemporary power in Indonesia. The legitimacy of power is not based on the premise that it needs to prove itself authentic to be legitimate. Rather, power is legitimate by definition and produces authenticity. But this authenticity is always-already inauthentic. What might this mean for people's trust in power?

Based on two examples—theme parks and forgeries—I will explore how trust fails, and how it works, in Indonesia through a mutual state-society cultivation of inauthenticity rather than through a stable trust in the authenticity of power. I think the social and political life of trust in Indonesia might suggest that ideas of trust and distrust, which are often treated as universal problematics for the moral foundation of society, for its social cohesion, and for the legitimacy of the modern state (Fukuyama 1995; Hardin 2006; Uslaner 2002), may in fact be peculiar to Euro-American modernity (and possibly even to only a certain perception of this version of modernity). This, in turn, would entail that seemingly universal predicaments involved in "trusting the new" are related to one particular epistemology and ontology of trust and novelty within modernity. In a world of multiple modernities (Eisenstadt 2002; Gaonkar 2001; Knauft 2002), ideas of the new and the predicaments of trust, I argue, come in a variety of modern forms, and not all of them look the same. I consequently take the Indonesian political imagination, with its ambiguities of (dis)trust and (in)authenticity, not as a foil for an exotic Southeast Asian tradition that challenges modern conceptions. Rather, I suggest that Indonesian political modernity is producing and produced by an alternative political epistemology and ontology of (dis)trust and novelty that is related to its political history, its postcolonial genealogy, and its place in the contemporary global political economy.

Conventional Stories of Trust?

According to conventional social theory, the predicament of trust and the new could, I think, be formulated as follows: The modern world is changing rapidly. This is necessary, even inevitable, but change is not necessarily good. In the modern world, all that is solid melts into air (Berman 1982). The iron laws of change are inescapable. But they are also morally ambivalent. On the one hand, we moderns need to trust in the new as a slayer of the old and the stagnant. The new and better society of modernity will produce equality, brotherhood, and freedom, a political community within which free and authentic human beings can develop. On the other hand, there is also, within modernity's account of itself, a sense of suspicion, a distrust of the new. This ambivalent attitude toward the new runs through all the great classical social theories, from Simmel and Durkheim to Marx and Weber (Sayer 1991). The past is stagnant and unfair, but also social and intimate in a way that modernity is not. The future harbors emancipation, technological solutions, clean air and hygiene, but the future is also characterized by forms of alienation and abstraction that threaten to destroy the social. Trust, it would appear, is under pressure in the conditions of modernity and its inexorable demand for constant change. Social cohesion, once guaranteed by tradition, is in modernity being undermined by new technologies, new forms of politics, and new formations of capitalism (Hardin 2006; Putnam 2000; Tilly 2005). Trusting the new therefore constitutes a particular dilemma in this representation of modernity: One needs to trust, but one cannot. A contemporary version of this model is that of Anthony Giddens and Ulrich Beck, in which post-traditional modernity has abandoned trust in tradition and replaced it with trust in new, de-territorialized systems: the systems of expert knowledge and money (Beck and Lash 1994; Giddens 1990, 1991). This trust is full of ontological uncertainty, however, unlike the supposed certainty that traditional society bestowed upon human beings (this is a representation of traditional society that in my experience is, itself, an Orientalist myth about traditional society [see Argyrou 2000 and Bubandt 2014a], but that is another matter).

One could say that Euro-American modernity, in its classical form and according to its dominant self-account, is a future-oriented project of transcending the present and establishing the new (Habermas 1987; Kumar 1995). The new is associated with utopian betterment and emancipation, but also with alienation and the tragic decay of the socially authentic. At the same time that modernity destroys traditional authenticity, it is, however, also associated with a new form of authenticity, an authenticity that comes not from tradition but emerges from within the individual itself. Modern authenticity is associated with the inner, psychological space of the individual and takes the place of the imagined social authenticity of the past (Heelas 2008; Rose 1998; Taylor 1991; Trilling 1972). In this nexus between social transformation and possessive individualism one finds many of the central aporias of modern life as we conventionally think about it, and as social theory presents it to us. Marshall Berman poses this, our central problem of being modern, as one of being torn between our desire to be rooted in a stable and coherent personal and social past, and our insatiable desire for growth—not merely for economic growth but for growth in experience, in pleasure, in knowledge, in sensibility—growth that destroys both the physical and social landscapes of our past, and our emotional links with those lost worlds (Berman 1982: 35).

Governmentality and modern biopower hinges on this desire for social betterment and individual improvement (Dean 1999; Foucault 1991; Rose 1999). Acting sincerely and speaking the truth about oneself is one aspect of this new politics of life. The other is that we expect sincerity and authenticity of power itself. Power (and here, as before, I suppose I am speaking with Michel Foucault) is held accountable for its authenticity. For this reason, change (toward the new) is only justified when power appears sincere about it—when the new speaks the truth about itself (Foucault 1980, 1991). This is what we expect, but at the same time we suspect that those in power are not entirely sincere. It is precisely the role of democratic checks-and-balances, the tripartition of power, the media as the fourth estate, and so on, to expose and undermine power when it is not sincere. That is why modern trust in the new is both inevitable and full of ambivalence, and why it is a matter of such concern that trust in democratic government appears to be in decline (Hetherington 2007; Nye 1997). We have to trust power, and yet we cannot. Such would be my characterization of a central aporia of Euro-American modernity (Derrida 2005). The account is all too brief, and a caricature of Western modernity no doubt. But still, I would contend, it is not entirely wrong. It is against this version of modern trust in the new that Indonesian modernity presents a different, and to my mind illuminating, set of aporias or impossibilities and a different way of dealing with trust, novelty, authenticity, and power.

Indonesia is the world's most populous Muslim nation. It has an estimated population of 245 million, 86 percent of whom are Muslim. The country achieved independence from Holland in 1949. Its first leader, President Sukarno, was a flamboyant and charismatic leader whose attempt to navigate a single, secular supertanker bearing a cargo of combined nationalism, Islam, and socialism shipwrecked on the rocky shores of Cold War politics. Ousted in a 1966 coup that was accompanied by a genocidal purge of several hundred thousand suspected communists, Sukarno was replaced by Suharto. In opposition to the "Old Order" (*Orde Lama*) that it replaced, Suharto's New Order regime (*Orde Baru*) was technocratic, centralist, and modernist. Supported by, or at least accepted by, most Western powers as a necessary bulwark against Southeast Asian communism, the New Order combined ideological repression with the promise of economic progress; a promise that finally cracked with the financial crisis in 1997. Since 1998, Indonesia has embarked on an experiment with democracy; an experiment that has been marred by endemic corruption, patrimonialism, and recurrent violent conflict between the country's ethnic and religious constituencies.

Across and throughout these periods of experimenting with socialism, authoritarianism, and democracy, a recognizable conception of power weaves its way. In Indonesia, state power is accepted as a fact of life, and strong leadership is a frequently expressed expectation. But this basic acceptance of power is not associated with a basic trust in its authenticity. If it makes any sense at all to talk about how a quarter of a billion people relate to power (and it probably does not), one could say that people in Indonesia accept power as a matter of fact, but they do not expect to trust it. The facticity of power combined with its dissociation from fidelity generates a different set of predicaments with power in modern Indonesia than those that haunt modernity in the Western tradition (see Bubandt 2014b for an elaboration of this argument). I would like to pursue these predicaments through two brief ethnographic examples: theme parks and forgeries.

Example 1: Theme Parks

John Pemberton argues that New Order rule, a term that labels the authoritarian rule between 1966 and 1998 of President Suharto, was based on a peculiar form of authenticity (Pemberton 1994). Pemberton describes this relation between power and authenticity by analyzing *Taman Mini Indonesia Indah*—the Miniature Theme Park of Beautiful Indonesia—or Taman Mini, for short, a national theme park on the outskirts of the Indonesian capital, Jakarta. A theme park built to celebrate the Indonesian nation, to make it visible to its citizens, Taman Mini was the brainchild of Ibu Thien, President Suharto's wife, who conceived the idea after a trip to Disneyland. Built in the 1970s and still a popular excursion destination from many Jakartans, the 174-hectare park is an eclectic collection of kitsch and reconstructed copies of ethnic architecture and attire from around the archipelago. The centerpiece of the park is a set of twenty-seven pavilions that represent the cultures of the twenty-seven provinces, which made up the nation until 1998—the year the New Order collapsed, and the provincial map of Indonesia was redrawn to reflect a new political agenda of decentralization and democracy. Intended to be a visible manifestation of the state slogan "Unity in Diversity," the park is a state-authorized, authentic display of the New Order nation; a site where the state is present through representation. Visitors to the park can get a glimpse of this state perspective, in its geographical entirety, by taking a cable-car ride over the park's central lake. The artificial islands in this lake have been shaped into a large-scale map modeling the Indonesian archipelago, allowing viewers to see the nation as the state sees it, and represents it in iconic form (see Anderson 1992; Scott 1998).

The authenticity of the park and its exhibits, however, is based neither on historical antiquity, nor on claims to being original. On the contrary, most artifacts in the park are copies, miniatures, or composites. The pavilions that are intended to exhibit the cultural architecture of peoples from Sumatra to Papua, for instance, are actually composite houses that fuse various forms of architecture from the province in question, and which are assembled into a whole as imagined by the mainly Javanese and Balinese builders who were contracted to construct the pavilions. As Pemberton and others have argued, the pavilions do not represent an attempt to reconstruct an original culture at all. Rather, they construct deliberately artificial, but emblematic, icons of domesticated culture that fitted neatly in with the New Order state's political ideals, and that aligned cultural difference to coincide with the provincial borders set by the state (Pemberton 1994; Acciaioli 1985; Errington 1998): One province, one culture. Such was the political ideal of New Order "unity in diversity"; evidence of a political domestication of culture that reduces cultural identity to politically innocuous, and commercially marketable, aesthetic forms.

In line with this premise, artifacts at the park's museum were not original pieces, and there was no pretense of originality or authenticity. In fact, quite the opposite claim was made: The pieces are authentic precisely *because* they are new. As the Indonesian First Lady declared soon after the opening of the park: "We may call it a museum now because someday everything in it will be antique" (Pemberton 1994: 256). In other words, authenticity is not claimed to exist because of history, but because of an imagined future. The theme park in this way is an example of how the political present bestows authenticity because it, in the future, will be an authentic past. Authenticity is an effect of political power, not vice versa.

This view of history and culture as phenomena that only achieve authenticity through political power is part of a broader political epistemology in the modernism of Suharto's New Order Indonesia. New Order rule began after Suharto had deposed Sukarno, the first president of Indonesia, in 1967, eradicating his predecessor's power base, which consisted of the largest Communist Party in the world, in a massacre of suspected communists that led to the death of perhaps 500,000 people (Cribb 2001). This coup set up a sharp historical juncture between the

"New Order" (*Orde Baru*) and the rule of Sukarno, renamed as the "Old Order" (*Orde Lama*). The new regime was authenticated by its ability to assume power, inauthenticating the previous regime as "old" in the process. The association of novelty with authenticity did not mean that the New Order was divorced from the past. Rather, it made the past possible, improved it in fact. Thus, Suharto's consistent claim was that the New Order rectified and brought to fruition a project that had failed during the Old Order. As in the theme park, historical chronology was unimportant to this claim. Pemberton shows that while Suharto saw himself as a reincarnation of a Javanese king from the mythical Maja-pahit Empire, the authenticity of this reincarnation was greater than that of the original king. In a sense, then, the New Order was older and more original than the past it replaced (Pemberton 1994: 257). The result is a political idea about "original newness" that lies, paradoxically, "beyond the postmodern"—the title of Pemberton's article. Power does not need historical authenticity to be morally just. Instead, it is power that makes historical authenticity (and by extension moral legitimacy) possible in the first place. Authenticity, as seen by the state, is, in other words, not a fading quality of the past; rather, it is a future potential enabled by power (see also Anderson 1990b). Made to serve a particular political function during the New Order, this peculiar historiography continues to characterize notions of power and politics in contemporary and democratic Indonesia (see Bubandt 2014b).

While in many ways hegemonic, this state vision of political authenticity is, however, also constantly challenged in Indonesia. In fact, people roundly suspect the state-sanctioned authenticity of power of being wrong and of hiding a fundamental inauthenticity. Naïve trust of the "authentically new" that state power offers is therefore not an option. The upshot of this is a particular relation to state power: People accept power but do not trust its authenticity. State-society relations are therefore not, as in Euro-American modernity, about seeking a basis on which to trust the authenticity of state power and of revealing its occasional lapses into insincerity. Power in Indonesia, rather, is an expression of a kind of modernity in which power is accepted and expected, even though it is inherently inauthentic. Modernity without stable authenticity is not—I think—restricted to Indonesia. It is a feature in many postcolonial nations regarded as failed states. They are not necessarily failed states, I would hasten to add, because they are too weak, but equally often because they are too strong (Yurchak 2006). And even this is too narrow a statement. In fact, I will cast the net even wider and suggest that inauthenticity and "bad faith" (*mauvaise foi*) are general features in modern politics, authoritarian or not, in ways that are not encompassed by the Euro-modern portrayal of the relationship between temporality and authenticity.

(In)authenticity as the Basis for Rational Politics

In her analysis of the Pentagon papers about the Vietnam War published by the New York Times in 1971, Hannah Arendt concludes that modern political deception presupposes an initial act of self-deception to work; a self-deception that in other words is not opposed to rational government but its foundation. The Pentagon papers were a secret analysis of the Vietnam War, commissioned by US Secretary of Defense Robert McNamara in 1967. The analysis, when published in the New York Times in 1971, revealed how the US government had been engaged in systematic lies to justify the US engagement in the war in Vietnam, lying not only to the media and to the public, but also to Congress. The American government had essentially lied to itself, fabricating a picture of the threat of communism in Southeast Asia that ended up becoming a political reality. The Nixon government, when it came into power and decided to escalate the war, therefore sought not to hide secrets that few knew about. Rather, it attempted to reconstruct facts that by that time had become common knowledge. Deceiving by reconstructing reality, Arendt claims, entails the need for a new understanding of elite manipulation. The classical notion of rational politics conceives of a political elite that is able to "deceive others without deceiving themselves" (Arendt 1993: 253). Contemporary politics, on the other hand, is a forum for the telling of lies that the elite (along with many other people) already believes to be true: "it is as though the normal process of self-deceiving were reversed; it was not as though deception ended with self-deception. The deceivers started with self-deception" (Arendt 1972: 35). Modern political lies, Arendt contends, are therefore different from "traditional political lies" in that they constitute a "rearrangement of the whole factual texture—the making of another reality, as it were, into which they will fit without seam, crack, or fissure, exactly as the facts fitted into their original context" (1993: 253). Arendt's analysis suggests the need to rethink the notion of deception and manipulation in political analysis. Conventional analysis of political manipulation often assumes that power elites are themselves beyond deception, rational actors who manipulate but are not themselves duped. But if successful deception depends increasingly in modern politics on self-deception, the distinction between rational elites and a duped populace begins to crumble.

The new form of political (self-)deception in an age of liberal democracy identified by Arendt is effective because it has become complicit with the new politics of sincerity and affectivity. In contemporary
politics voters look for politicians who, above all, are sincere, who "talk
straight," and who effectively convey that they "deeply feel" (Markovits 2006; 2008; Neuman, et al. 2007). Believing in the sincerity of politicians is often more important than trusting them to be right or wrong.
As long as the national leaders of the US-led coalition that invaded Iraq
in March 2003 sincerely believed Saddam Hussein to hide weapons of
mass destruction, the subsequent invalidity of this belief could somehow be politically excused, for instance. If sincerity has become a new
form of political capital, it is essential that politician believe "sincerely"
in what they say: to deceive they need first to deceive themselves—at
least on the North Atlantic Rim.

In Indonesia, I suggest, political authenticity and complicity lead a
different life. Indonesian citizens are not "the sentimental citizens" of
the polities of Europe and the United States (Marcus 2002). Therefore
the problem of power is also different. If the dilemma of power on the
North Atlantic Rim how one can trust those in power who claim themselves to be authentic, but who one suspects are not authentic, then the
dilemma of power in Indonesia is that one accepts, as given, a political
power whose authoritative legitimacy is as undeniable as it is fundamentally inauthentic. If anything, the Indonesian case pushes Arendt's revision of conventional political analysis to its logical conclusion. Power is
maintained in Indonesia, not because a masterly elite manages to dupe
an unsuspecting elite, but because a self-deceiving elite and a cynical
and dissimulating citizenry are complicit in a project where trust can be
based on the expectation of inauthenticity.

Let me give an example of how acceptance and inauthenticity co-
exists in Indonesia. Indonesians are far more optimistic than the citizens of any Western country about the efforts of their government to
curb corruption. A full 74 percent of Indonesians in the 2009 Global
Corruption Barometer, published by Transparency International, report
that they believe the present corruption-curbing efforts of their government to be effective. The corresponding number for the European
Union as whole is 24 percent, and for the United States the number is
27 percent (Transparency International 2009: 33). At the same time, in
Indonesia more citizens see their parliament as the most corrupt sector
as compared to any other country. In the same survey, 47 percent of
Indonesian respondents agree that the parliament and the legislature is
the most corrupt sector—the highest suspicion level for parliamentary
corruption among all the countries included in the 2009 Global Cor-

ruption Barometer report (Transparency International 2009: 30). The suspiciousness of Indonesians when it comes to the corruptibility of their parliament is not unfounded: 51 of the country's 560 members of parliament were under investigation for corruption in 2008 (Efendi and Faridz 2008). The paradox, in other words, is this: on a global scale, Indonesians (more than the citizens of any other country) trust the effectiveness of their own parliament to curb corruption; a parliament that Indonesians (more than the citizens in any other country in the world) simultaneously regard as corrupt.

As Benedict Anderson noted many years ago about power in Indonesia, it is beyond good and evil (Anderson 1990a). Unlike power in the West, power in Indonesia does not have to prove itself morally righteous to be accepted, or to be authentic. Instead, authenticity in Indonesia springs from power itself. But it does so in an inherently inauthentic manner. Power in Indonesia is widely accepted as a fact, rather than being measured against a moral ideal; and yet the facticity of power is "contingent," inextricably linked with inauthenticity. "Who do you vote for," I asked my adopted sister in Indonesia, a mother of two teenage boys, in the lead-up to the regional election in 2004. "Whoever wins," she immediately replied. One partakes, in other words, in the rituals of politics, but one does not do so within an epistemology of "good" and "bad" power, where trust and authenticity adhere to "good" power. Rather, one dissimulates, because dissimulation is inherent in power itself. One trusts implicitly what one knows is implicitly inauthentic.

As Liisberg argues in his chapter, trust may always entail a kind of willful deception of oneself, a good-faith trickery that involves believing in someone else while ignoring that this is really "only" a belief. Could one fairly say that Indonesian beliefs in power likewise involve a similar sort of trickery: trusting power while ignoring that it is inauthentic? Or is it in fact the notion of the authenticity of power, its epistemology, that is differently configured? I think the answer to this question is, to some degree, dependent on one's disciplinary interests. The question of whether authenticity, power, trust, and subjectivity are universal or contextual phenomena is one that runs through many of the chapters in this volume. The epistemological inclination of most philosophers is likely to choose the former, while that of anthropologists, myself included, is to choose the latter because fieldwork has appeared to reveal alternative possibilities. As an anthropologist, I am interested in the kinds of political illusions that make certain kinds of selves, and certain kinds of (dis)trust, possible. The speech acts and that which Liisberg, in his reflections and using a concept from John Searle, calls "status functions" that surround theme parks in Indonesia are one ethnographic example from a political epistemology that paradoxically links trust to inauthenticity. Forged but authentic documents represent another example.

Example 2: Forgeries

Fakes are everywhere in Indonesia, and anything can be faked: brand products, driver's licenses, exam papers, customs stamps, money, medicine, public tenders. Part of a global industry of counterfeits, many of these fakes are, and can only be, produced by state agents who employ the authentic paper, the real printers, and the actual stamps and seals of the state authorities themselves. They require "an insider" (*orang dalam*). In 2000, for instance, the governor of Bank Indonesia, who was later charged and convicted for his part in the 90-million-dollar Bank Bali corruption scandal, was accused of involvement in a forgery racket where employees at the national bank were forging money (BBC News 2000; Bubandt 2009; Strassler 2000). When the national bank is directly implicated in the production of forged currency, the dividing line between the authentic and the fake disintegrates, as does the authority of the state that underwrites the trustworthiness of one of the main expert systems in the modern world: money.

It is the pervasive nature of this kind of fake authenticity, or authentic forgery, that has produced the neologism *aspal* (Lindsey 2000; Siegel 1998). *Aspal* is an example of the kind of wordplay (*plesetan*) in which Indonesians love to engage. The concept of *aspal* mixes the word for "original" (*asli*) with the word for "fake" (*palsu*) to make a composite word that means not only "tarmac" or "bitumen," but also refers to the inherent falsity of authenticity. *Aspal* may in this second and metaphorical sense perhaps be transliterated as "authentic-fake." An *aspal* product or license is simultaneously authentic and fake. However, the term *aspal* is employed not only to denote the opacity of fakes; it was and is used—during the New Order and after—about the state itself. An apt illustration of the "authentic-fake" workings of state power is presented by the reception of fake letters. In late October 1999, thousands of copies of such a letter were dispersed into the streets of the two largest towns of North Maluku, at the time a province of some 800,000 inhabitants in the easternmost part of Indonesia.

The letter seemed to have been written by the Christian Church of Maluku. In outrageously blunt terms, it instructed Christian churches in North Maluku to organize the persecution and ethnic cleansing of one particular ethnic group of Muslims. Within a few days it sparked a riot, initiated by panic-stricken Muslims eager to stage a pre-emptive strike against the Christians. The riot killed almost a dozen people, and forcing the evacuation of Christian minorities from the two administrative capitals of Ternate and Tidore. The appearance of the fake letter was one of the main events triggering the endemic violence that broke out in the region over the following eighteen months. This violence was directly influenced by the images of religious conspiracy that the letter had helped establish (Bubandt 2008). When fighting subsided by the end of 2001, it was estimated that at least 2,000 people had lost their lives, another 1,000 had been seriously injured, and some 260,000— more than a quarter of the population in North Maluku at the time— had become internally displaced (ICG 2002: 18).

Yet the letter that had brought all this about was a fake. It was, most likely, written by Muslim bureaucrats who wanted to use the letter to portray the Christian Church as a rotten apple, a hidden political demon. The letter sought to achieve this by effectively mimicking several text features characteristic of its alleged Christian author, using Christian turns of phrase and Christian millenarian language about the Second Coming of Christ (Bubandt 2004; Bubandt 2008).

What interests me about this letter—and many other fake letters that provoked violence in Indonesia in the late 1990s—is that it worked so effectively, even though all people I spoke to, whether they were Christian or Muslim, strongly suspected that the letter was a forgery (Bubandt 2009). There is, in other words, what Umberto Eco has called a "force of falsity" at work here (Eco 1999). The notion of a force of falsity describes the historical effects that deceptions, lies, and political untruths may have. With customary mischievous wit, Eco implies that such falsity effects may be as powerful as the "truth effects" that Foucauldian analyses of power usually trace. If truths are historical forces with historical effects that can be uncovered, so, too, are falsities. To illustrate the force of falsity, Eco tells the story of a letter, allegedly penned by a certain Priest John or Prester John. The letter, which began circulating in Europe in the second half of the twelfth century, told of a Christian kingdom without vice in the Far East. Although the letter was almost certainly a deliberate fabrication, it was to have a lasting impact on European political imagination. Because of its narrative appeal to religious and political rulers alike, the letter was to have a long series of unexpected political consequences. Thus, the idea of a Christian kingdom in the East changed not only the history of the Roman Church, but also the Age of Discovery, and it was to act, so Eco argues, as an opportune argument for European colonization of the Orient (Eco 1999: 12). Through historical serendipity, as it were, a false "geographical fantasy gradually generated a political project" (Eco 1999: 12). In a Western context, so it would seem, the efficacy of the force of falsehood is dependent on the falsehood remaining undetected. Indonesian politics, however, rarely if ever offers a vantage point from which veracity is visible. Indeed, I propose that the force of falsity that the fake letter in North Maluku evinced did not depend on the deception remaining undetected. Rather, it is a deception that was strongly suspected, but which was still authoritative enough to have a social effect. I would argue that the reason why fakes like this one are effective, even when they are known to be fake, is related to the authentic-fake nature of power in Indonesia.

The fake letter in North Maluku thus mimicked not only an imagined Christian author; it was also in mimicry of a conventional state letter. It contained all the trappings of an official letter, including official-looking headings, a structure that divided it into numbered sections, and prolific use of the same bureaucratic phrases and official signs, such as the backward slash, that also characterize official letters. State codes were, in other words, used to make the forgery authentic, with "state legibility" being borrowed to underwrite the authority of the letter (see Das 2004 for an analysis of state (il)legibility). But by the same token, these same state codes also put the letter's authenticity into question, opening it to an "aspal" reading that regarded it as a likely fake. The letter was, in this sense, a striking mixture of forgery and authenticity claims. It was the very use of state codes that contributed to its reception as a fake—an instance of an *aspal* or "authentic-fake" state. At once authoritative and widely suspected of being fake, letters such as the fake letter in North Maluku were circulating evidence of the seemingly counterfeit nature of state authority itself. The efficacy of this particular fake letter (and the many others like it, see Bubandt 2004) reverses the logic of the *aspal* state: while the state, for instance in its theme parks, claims to be the producer of the authenticity of the park's artifacts in ways that for many, Indonesians are inherently inauthentic, the fake letter, by mimicking a state whose authenticity is always-already fake, raises the likelihood of their inauthenticity—even as they are roundly accepted as authoritative (see Bubandt and Willerslev, 2015).

My suggestion that the efficacy of falsehood in Indonesia is independent of its detectability since state facts by definition are both authentic and inauthentic implies that what Liisberg in his chapter calls "tolerance of ambiguity" is a political necessity in Indonesia. This runs counter to received wisdom about Indonesians who are often described as being adverse to ambiguity and uncertainty. For instance, Geert Hofstede, who has "uncertainty avoidance" as one of the five dimensions in his interesting numerical and statistical analysis of cultural difference, suggests that Indonesians have a relatively high dislike of uncertainty. My case suggests the opposite: Ambiguity is an epistemological condition of possibility for the existence of "state facts" in Indonesia. Indonesians in that sense appear to have a remarkably high tolerance for uncertainty and ambiguity. Like Liisberg, I am wary of numerical models such as that of Hofstede that seek to gauge this "tolerance." Power is a pragmatic paradox fraught with epistemological dilemmas (in both the so-called East and the so-called West), rather than a value dimension that can be measured numerically, as Hofstede contends (see also McSweeney 2002). The people in Indonesia that I know definitely have a fairly high avoidance of uncertainty when it comes to social conventions, the need to avoid public failure, or the propensity to smooth over conflict. But they are masters at maneuvering the political landscape of uncertainty and ambiguity that Indonesian history and state authorities have imposed on them. Uncertainty avoidance is therefore highly varied in different Indonesian contexts. Political history in Indonesia has cultivated high degrees of uncertainty and ambiguity, to which Indonesians have found their own ways of accommodation.

State power in Indonesia is the object of acceptance and trust (by virtue of the "just-so-ness" of power), but its facticity (or its objective existence) is inherently inauthentic. One may trust the givenness of power (and mimic its authoritative signs), but the claim to authenticity of power and its authoritative signs are entirely untrustworthy. Every claim to the originally new (as in the Jakarta theme park), or to authoritative authenticity (as in state letters), is haunted by the specter of the authentic-fake—falsity and authenticity being not opposites, but mutually constitutive in and of power (see Siegel 1998 for a detailed analysis of this paradox).

In this sense, power in Indonesia is less than "certain" and more than "probable," to speak with Sartre (see Liisberg's chapter). Rather, power is "metastable": it presents "an autonomous and durable form" (Sartre 1956: 90), whose very durability and authenticity is paradoxically precarious, made possible by its constant disintegration, its inherent inauthenticity. In this sense, Liisberg is right, I think, when he proposes "the absurdity that in Indonesia nothing is more authentic than (self)-deception."

Conclusion

So what is the broader relevance of this analysis for the theme of trusting the new? I contend that Indonesian politics works as a "counter-ethnography" because it suggests that both fidelity and novelty are cultural facts; that they are semiotic, emotional phenomena produced within a certain political epistemology in which truth and falsity are configured in particular and often paradoxical ways. Power in Indonesia is beyond good and evil, its authenticity (for instance in theme parks) is haunted by inauthenticity, while its inauthentic copies (fake letters, counterfeit bank notes, licenses, or brand products) are credible in spite of their assumed falsity. Power is also beyond the dichotomy of past and future, and the political epistemology of "the new" is therefore not entwined in the same constellation of trust, authenticity, and suspicion as it is in Euro-American modernity. In the Indonesian political version of modernity, "the new" is politically claimed to be authentic by virtue of power, but power itself is inherently inauthentic. That is the essence of the idea of *aspal*, the "authentic-fake"—and that is the aporia of power, trust, and the new in Indonesia.

I suggest, in other words, that neither "trust" nor "the new" are stable phenomena with universal properties. My ethnographic counter-example may serve to remind us that our notions of trust and novelty are linked to a particular political sensibility, subjective ontology, and epistemology of authenticity and truth that is distinctive of a certain political and philosophical tradition in the West. If there are multiple modernities out there, there are also other political and cultural epistemologies of the new and of trust. Put a bit differently, trust and novelty are open to comparative study because they are bent into certain shapes within particular political epistemologies.

These epistemologies are in the modern world fed, firstly, as I have argued, by particular ways of organizing notions of power and authenticity as well as by particular political histories of state-society relations. Secondly, it is important to underline that no such epistemology exists in isolation. The Indonesian approach to power, which, for the sake of expediency, I have outrageously portrayed as uniform, is not *sui generis*. The "Indonesian" epistemology of power, as I have caricatured it here, is also fostered by a particular position within the global political economy. John and Jean Comaroff have proposed that neo-liberal geo-politics have made counterfeit products an increasingly important form of Third World production (Comaroff and Comaroff 2006: 10). In the industrialist and imperialist world of yesteryear, Third World countries supplied the raw materials, while the First World created added value from these products and sold them back to the Third World. In the current post-industrialist, out-sourced liberal economy, the former Third World produces our brand names, and yet the added value still ends up in the First World. According to the Comaroffs, the production of fake products that masquerade as authentic brands is, under these circumstances, an attempt by Third World elites to magically control global forms of economic hegemony; a failing endeavor to appropriate the magic and the profit of the neoliberal mode of production.

The global production of the authentically new is, in other words, unevenly distributed. Authentic products emerge out of the Global North, while the Global South is largely left to copy and dabble in forgeries. The same division of labor could be said to characterize the domain of global politics: "Real" democratic futures are very much seen to be fashioned predominantly in the Global North, while poorer "imitations" of democracy appear to emerge in the Global South. Trusting the New, in this global landscape, has very different conditions of possibility in the Global South and the Global North.

Trust as the Life Magic of Self-Deception

A Philosophical-Psychological Investigation into Tolerance of Ambiguity

Sune Liisberg

Our human social world is, to a large extent, a world of probabilities and possible interpretations, and so it consists of all kinds of ambiguity with which we must cope. This is the underlying existential assumption of the present chapter, in which I propose the general claim that trusting behavior is intimately related to a human category that psychologists, since the 1940s, have labeled "ambiguity tolerance." I thereby take up a suggestion that psychologist Robert W. Norton (1975: 618) put forth as one of several desiderata for further investigations into ambiguity tolerance, namely the question: "How is trusting behavior related to tolerance of ambiguity?"

Tolerance of ambiguity is an important theme for a variety of branches in psychology (Furnham and Ribchester 1995: 179, 196), and although my reflections upon the question of how trusting behavior relates to ambiguity are primarily of a philosophical nature, I do continually take into account empirical psychological research in the field.

The overall aim of the first two sections is to indicate that trusting behavior can be interpreted as a way in which human beings cope with ambiguous situations. On one hand, ambiguity in human relations seems to be a challenge to trusting behavior. On the other hand, trusting behavior must be a manifestation of some degree of tolerance of ambiguity; if I need to "disambiguate" the other person's gestures and verbal ex-

---

Notes for this section begin on page 174.

pressions piecemeal in order to trust him or her, then the whole point of exhibiting trusting behavior seems to be contradicted. First, I survey various psychological research done on the concept of ambiguity (in) tolerance. Second, I argue, from a phenomenological point of view, that the phenomenon of ambiguity is conditioned by the finitude of our intuition and, in interpersonal relations, by freedom as well.

A second claim I make in the following section is that tolerance of ambiguity presupposes a benign form of self-deception. The last two sections therefore examine the relations between intersubjectivity, self-deception, and tolerance of ambiguity; I argue that trust as an interpersonal attitude and behavior is a form of self-deception in good faith. In other words, I argue that trust builds on positive illusions about the other as a strategy for coping with ambiguity. Finally, these considerations constitute the backdrop for my reflections on Nils Bubandt's anthropological fieldwork in Indonesia, which I have also incorporated into the last two sections.

Psychological Approaches to Ambiguity Tolerance

In psychological research, the notion of ambiguity tolerance was first treated comprehensively by Else Frenkel-Brunswik in the late 1940s (Norton 1975: 607; Furnham and Ribchester 1995: 179–80). In fact, it was Frenkel-Brunswik who suggested the label "tolerance vs. intolerance of ambiguity," which seemed to her to be "one of the basic variables in both the emotional and the cognitive orientation of a person toward life" (Frenkel-Brunswik 1949: 113; cf. 1948). Accordingly, psychologists have since assumed that there is an intimate link between a person's degree of ambiguity tolerance and how that person deals with life in general. As Norton states, "How a person psychologically copes with ambiguous information affects the perception, interpretation, and weighting of cognitions. Because a person's degree of ambiguity tolerance interacts in any situation in which there is too little, too much, or seemingly contradictory information, this trait touches many behavioral phenomena" (Norton 1975: 607). However, the use of the term "ambiguity" in psychological research has, itself, been quite ambiguous. Norton (1975: 608) enumerates eight categories that have been utilized to define this term over the years. Ambiguity has been considered as: (1) multiple meanings; (2) vagueness, incompleteness, fragmentedness; (3) a probability; (4) a lack of structure; (5) a lack of information; (6) uncertainty; (7) inconsistencies; and (8) a lack of clarity.

As I will attempt to argue in this and the following sections, it is the category of "probability" that seems to relate most closely to trusting behavior. Yet this does not eliminate the relevance of addressing aspects of some of the other categories, especially "uncertainty," for the purposes of the discussion below.

Frenkel-Brunswik (1948) highlights that a person who is intolerant of ambiguity is disinclined to "think in terms of *probability*," and favors "black-and-white stereotypes." In addition, she notes that "ambiguity of cognitive responses must be seen as a reflection of the uncertainties existing in the environment itself, thus opening up the field of 'probability' as a new area of psychological research" (Frenkel-Brunswik 1949: 121).[1] So we may propose that willingness to think in terms of probability, in Frenkel-Brunswik's view, is a main feature of being tolerant of ambiguity.

While Frenkel-Brunswik (1948; 1949) was especially interested in establishing the relationship between intolerance of ambiguity and ethnic prejudice in children, Stanley Budner, another renowned researcher in the field, for his part undertook an "analysis of intolerance of ambiguity as an interesting variable in its own right" (Budner 1962: 29). Budner begins by investigating the term "ambiguous situations." Ambiguous situations are "characterized by novelty, complexity, or insolubility" (Budner 1962: 30), and intolerance of ambiguity is the "tendency to perceive (i.e. interpret) ambiguous situations as sources of threat" (Budner 1962: 49).

With his notion of ambiguous situations, Budner seems to emphasize certain kinds of uncertainties in the environment, which Frenkel-Brunswik connects with willingness/unwillingness to think in terms of probability. But Budner's investigation also establishes that intolerance of ambiguity is not itself a "localizable" phenomenon; it does not exist "in itself" but is a broader term that is displayed through certain predilections of a person. If a person favors censorship, for instance, it is not because intolerance of ambiguity has caused him to favor it, "rather, favoring censorship (in most situations) is part of being intolerant of ambiguity" (Budner 1962: 49). Hence, Budner does not understand ambiguity intolerance in essentialist terms; rather, as he states, intolerance of ambiguity is a term that we apply to certain *forms* of behavior, for instance censorship—"in most situations" (as he himself adds in parentheses).

This indicates that we should merely assume that there are *degrees* of tolerance/intolerance, meaning that a person can neither be *absolutely* intolerant nor *absolutely* tolerant toward ambiguity. Even so, a person can naturally display *more or less* tolerance, and in my view a clear example of how a low tolerance for ambiguity can manifest itself is in the form of distrusting behavior, revealed by attempts to take control over the environment. A high tolerance for ambiguity, on the other hand, would—all things being equal—be displayed as a higher degree of trusting, and perhaps even foolhardy, behavior. So, what I claim is that the degree of ambiguity tolerance we can ascribe to a person is likely also to be manifested in trusting or, respectively, distrusting behavior being exhibited by that person.[2]

Ambiguity tolerance must also be manifested in the way in which a person behaves with regard to the future, insofar as the phenomenon "future" in principle implies the possibility of occurrences of things that are new or complex, or problems I might not be able to solve—in brief, "future" implies ambiguity as regards probabilities as well as uncertainties. The latter assumption finds support in Geert Hofstede's (2001) analysis of what he labels "uncertainty avoidance" in terms of strategies of coping: "Uncertainty about the future is a basic fact of human life with which we try to cope through the domains of technology, law, and religion. In organizations these take the form of technology, rules, and ritual" (Hofstede 2001: 145). Not unlike Budner's definition of ambiguity intolerance consisting in a tendency to interpret ambiguous situations as sources of threat, Hofstede, at the level of a given society's "cultural programming" of its members, defines uncertainty avoidance as regarding an uncomfortable feeling that occurs in unstructured situations, since these "are novel, unknown, surprising, different from usual" (Hofstede 2001: xix–xx).

Hofstede's term "uncertainty avoidance," relates more explicitly, though, to the phenomenon of anxiety than to the phenomenon of trust. Trusting or, respectively, distrusting behavior rather seems to concern (the avoidance of) risk-taking. Taking risks involves a willingness to think in terms of probability, which, according to Hofstede, is not the same as a willingness to live with uncertainty:

> Uncertainty is to risk as anxiety is to fear. Fear and risk are both focused on something specific: an object in the case of fear, an event in the case of risk. Risk is often expressed in a percentage of probability that a particular event may happen. Anxiety and uncertainty are both diffuse feelings. Anxiety has no object, and uncertainty has no probability attached to it. It is a situation in which anything can happen and one has no idea what. As soon as uncertainty is expressed as risk, it ceases to be a source of anxiety. It may be a source of fear but it may also be accepted as routine, such as the risk involved in driving a car or practicing a dangerous sport (Hofstede 2001: 148).

And so, as far as trust is concerned, we can choose the phenomenon of risk-taking to exemplify that even though we know that, in principle, there is always a *possibility* of something unexpected and perhaps even terrible occurring, we may say to ourselves that it will *probably* not come to pass. In this sense, a willingness to think in terms of probability can actually, in our daily lives, promote trusting behavior, which at times may be hard to differentiate from the kind of routine that Hofstede mentions in the previous quotation.

A Philosophical Approach to Ambiguity Tolerance

However important the psychological research efforts treated in the preceding section are for the present discussion of trust seen in relation to the tolerance vs. intolerance of ambiguity, they do suffer from the circumstance that they measure ambiguity tolerance by using different scales that do not relate clearly to one another (see Kenny and Ginsberg 1958: 300; Furnham and Ribchester 1995: 189–90). A philosophical approach might help to provide a more generalized view.

Let me return once again to the notion of "probability." It seems clear that whenever we experience "certainty," here—as we shall see—as opposed to "probability," the need for trust vanishes with respect to that certainty. For instance, a quick Cartesian reflection reveals to me that it is certain that I exist. There is no need for trust in that case, although Descartes's cogito argument opens up an enormous field of other problems that I will refrain from discussing here.

Within the context of materialistic theories of mind, Richard Rorty has argued that others have no criteria, whatsoever, by which to correct me as being mistaken with regard to the first-person reports that I give of my own sensations and thoughts. This "incorrigibility" of whether and how something appears to me, and appears *as such*, is thus the "mark of the mental"—that is, the very definition of the privacy of mental states—whereas "we do have criteria for setting aside all reports about everything else" (Rorty 1970: 413).

This means, as I understand Rorty, that the subjective experiential realm is characterized by a certainty of evidence as to whether and how something appears to me in my first-person perspective, whereas as soon as I generate claims about the nature of the object in question, I am—as Sartre states in a similar line of reasoning—"passing from the certain to the probable" (Sartre 2010a: 5). Correspondingly, Sartre remarks that "what is called an *object* is said to be probable" (Sartre 1995: 252).

The reason for this is that objects of perception (objects of the imagination need special elaboration; see Sartre 2010a) always give themselves away by profiles or aspects. Due to our embodiment we cannot have a "view from nowhere"; we must make do with the finitude of our intuition, which defines the horizon for our temporary perceptions (Sartre 1995: 306). So it is that my experience of an object is never adequate with respect to the *nature* of that object; and therefore, in "perception, knowledge is formed slowly," for "the object of perception constantly overflows consciousness" (Sartre 2010a: 10).

The following anthropological description, made by Bernhard Waldenfels, seems to emphasize this point as a source of ambiguity: "Human beings normally tolerate some ambiguity because they assume that reality is not there to honor rules, but that rules merely render help and safeguard [*wahrnehmen*] certain order functions.[3] But reality itself always allows for many more possibilities, so that the human is distinguishable from the brutish by the ability that humans have to live with ambiguous situations—doing something, even though I know that what I interpret or understand in this way does not exhaust all possibilities, and that it is not finalized wisdom" (Waldenfels 2000: 198–99; my translation). We may conclude from this passage that, regarding ambiguity tolerance, the specific human is not only implied in the finitude of our intuition, but is also implied in the *temporal* awareness that human beings have *of* this finitude as a human condition.[4] Thus, tolerating some ambiguity at the same time means being able to deliberate the awareness that we have of our finitude—it is, so to speak, taking a "cool" approach to things as a way to cope with this awareness.

So one general condition for ambiguity as a human factor seems to be the finitude of our intuition, to which we attach the sphere of the "probable" in terms of the world's richness, possible meanings, interpretations, and so on. This is important with regard to trusting behavior as an interpersonal phenomenon, insofar as one central aspect of the relation between concrete human beings is that it is perceptively mediated (see Sartre 2010b).

It seems to me that another general human condition linked to ambiguity is freedom, especially freedom seen against the backdrop of that which Merleau-Ponty defines as the specifically human consisting in "the capacity of going beyond created structures in order to create others" (Merleau-Ponty 1963: 175). Although Merleau-Ponty does not address the notion of freedom in the context of that quotation, I think that he presupposes it implicitly: going beyond created structures in order to create others seems to presuppose freedom, insofar as such a re-structuring, arguably, presupposes *questioning* the meaning of the created structures already at hand.

Human freedom, according to Sartre, is "the necessary condition for the question" (1995: 33). This implies, among other things, that human beings themselves—as the jealous lover or spouse knows only too well—partake in generating ambiguity, for instance in the form of novelties or complexities that, as we know from Budner (see above), characterize ambiguous situations and which may occur through certain actions or be revealed by certain questions or in conversations. Furthermore, the mere initiation of the creation of other structures presupposes an awareness of alternatives and possibilities for creating a new situation beyond an actual, existing situation: "What then is freedom? To be born is both to be born of the world and to be born into the world. The world is already constituted, but also never completely constituted, in the first case we are acted upon, in the second case we are open to an infinite number of possibilities. But this analysis is still abstract, for we exist in both ways at once. There is, therefore, never determinism and never absolute choice, I am never a thing and never bare consciousness" (Merleau-Ponty 1989: 453).

Freedom thus potentially generates ambiguities between human beings, for if I am never a thing and never bare consciousness, then it seems that I—and by extrapolation every human being—must resist absolute disambiguation, not only in my relation to others, but even and also in relation to myself, since some of my self-experiences occur in situations that I cannot plan. Ambiguities are everywhere in our everyday lives, though mostly on the fringes of consciousness, without being taken up for consideration (see Dreyfus 1992: 109). But *if* they are considered, an intolerance of ambiguity would, most likely, be manifested in tendencies to distrust and to attempt to take control over what originates in freedom. This could be said to be the human condition under which we behave trustfully or distrustfully toward one another: Potentially we are trustful when ambiguities stay on the fringes of consciousness; potentially distrustful when they are considered.

Intersubjectivity and Conflict

Merleau-Ponty contends that we should apply the term "probability" to understand more adequately the condition of personal freedom. Going against Sartre, he argues that it may well be possible that a given person will suddenly change—but is it also probable? This is a question that we must take into account when theorizing about the freedom of a concrete person; that is, we "must recognize a sort of sedimentation of our life" (Merleau-Ponty 1989: 441; see 442).

Merleau-Ponty is effectively formulating a basis for regarding trusting behavior as being relatively unproblematic, since—as we have seen—

we tend to trust the probable, here in the sense that the other has a specific *habitualness,* rather than the merely possible or uncertain. Of course we can also distrust another person because of his or her specific habitualness, all of which entails that the tension between trust and distrust relates to a tension between positively or, respectively, negatively evaluated probability.

Sartre, for his part, seriously challenges trusting behavior, in that he stresses the category of the possible with regard to freedom and includes a strong element of uncertainty in interhuman relations (see Sartre 1995: 262).[5] First, because the other, being the limit of my freedom, can, in principle, always surprise me; second, because the other "holds a secret—the secret of what I am" (Sartre 1995: 364). To Sartre, therefore, the essence of intersubjective relations is conflict (Sartre 1995: 429), and this essential conflict originates in an experience of *certainty* concerning the *existence* of others, who, consequently, cannot be reduced to figments of the imagination.

The crucial point for Sartre is that deep within ourselves we are certain of the other in "his capacity of being 'of interest' to our being" (Sartre 1993: 369; my translation). The other is not a part of my being in any ontological—or mystical—sense. The other is someone I meet and who judges me from the *outside* of the lived experience that I am of my own existence, which I do not judge as such. It is only through the gaze of the other that I am being subjected to standards and propriety, and it is thus due to the simultaneous existence of viewpoints other than mine that I learn to see myself as someone who can be described—or judged—in terms of "what," i.e. in terms of *qualities* such as tall, small, good, mean, helpful, courageous, trustworthy, etc.

In this sense, I need "the mediation of the Other in order to be what I am" (Sartre 1995: 289). When I am ashamed, for instance, it is because I recognize or admit "that I *am* as the Other sees me" (Sartre 1995: 222). Shame "therefore realizes an intimate relation of myself to myself" (Sartre 1995: 221), except for the fact that the "objective truth" or the "value judgment" about what I am evades me—it is in the hands of someone else (see Sartre 1995: 267, 363). But my basic freedom can never, as long as I live, be captured and encapsulated in a final judgment about what I am. So one only has to reverse the situation, making my viewpoint the point of departure for judgments about the other, in order to imagine the inherent circularity of conflict that is ultimately involved in Sartre's theory of intersubjectivity, and which, I contend, also entails a crucial point of relevance with regard to the theme of trust as a concrete interpersonal attitude and behavior. For we could well ask: If the other as a *subject* is certain to me, why do we need trust? The answer is that what is certain is simply the *existence* of concrete subjects other than me (see Sartre 1995: 282, 301). But the secret of what I am to the other remains ambiguous, that is, probable or uncertain; I am simply "in danger" before the other. These interhuman conditions might, indeed, provoke overt conflict. But they might as well motivate self-deceptive strategies understood as efforts to somehow "flee the being which I am" (Sartre 1995: 261; cf. Sartre 1992: 428).

Based on Sartre's analysis of the phenomenon of "bad faith" (*mauvaise foi*), which is, in effect, self-deception, I will now elaborate on the argument that self-deception relates closely to the conflictual conditions of interhuman relations. In such relations, I will further argue, self-deception must be considered as a way of coping with ambiguity. In the final section I propose, by way of conclusion, that there is also a form of self-deception that should be considered as *good faith*, which represents an attitude of trust and as such stimulates trusting behavior.

Self-Deception as Bad Faith

Self-deception, bad faith, is a possibility, because the human being "can take negative attitudes with respect to himself" (Sartre 1995: 47). This implies that we must distinguish clearly between a lie and self-deception. When I lie, I deceive the other about something that I know to be true. The lie does not concern my own conviction. What the lie generally does is that it affirms to us that consciousness "exists by nature as *hidden from the Other*" (Sartre 1995: 48–49). Consequently, Sartre contends, in line with Husserl, that the consciousness of the other appears to me as an absence—and vice versa; that is, the consciousness of the other gives itself to my intuition "as a perpetual question—still better, as a perpetual freedom"; the *meaning* of his or her "look is not a fact in the world, and this is what makes me feel uncomfortable" (Sartre 1995: 61–62).

As mentioned, the other holds the secret of what I am, and this being which I am remains ambiguous, since it "preserves a certain indetermination, a certain unpredictability" caused, not only by my lack of knowledge about the other's mind, but also by the other's freedom which "is revealed to me across the uneasy indetermination of the being which I am for him." (Sartre 1995: 262). In other words, the meaning of the other's look is, in essence, ambiguous for—as I have sought to substantiate above—ambiguity in interhuman relations originates in freedom. I might thus, in perpetual paranoia, ask myself: Am I being deceived here? And this question is always—and not just as an instance of paranoia—a manifestation of intolerance of ambiguity, that is, of a distrusting attitude.[6] So it would be fair to say that the questioning freedom that characterizes the appearance of the other opens and challenges the field of trusting or, respectively, distrusting behavior.

Whereas the lie affirms that the consciousness of the other exists as hidden to me, which might, indeed, provoke distrustful attitudes and behaviors, self-deception, on the other hand, affirms the *meta-stable* structure of consciousness itself, since the deceiver and the deceived are one and the same person. I deceive myself when I hide the truth *from myself*, when I suppress facts about myself in order to believe that something else is the case. How can this come about?

According to Sartre, one deceives oneself as one goes to sleep. Consequently, deceiving oneself is like engaging in a dream (see Sartre 1995: 68). Yet self-deception is a conscious project of censorship, and as such it is a strategy of coping by which a human being tolerates a degree of confusion between ideal and real circumstances by *believing* in this confusion: "The true problem of bad faith stems evidently from the fact that bad faith is *faith*. It can not be either a cynical lie or certainty—if certainty is the intuitive possession of the object. But if we take belief as meaning the adherence of being to its object when the object is not given or is given indistinctly, then bad faith is belief; and the essential problem of bad faith is a problem of belief" (Sartre 1995: 67). Let us note here, firstly, that the kind of belief we encounter in self-deception as bad faith is a belief that defies ambiguity insofar as the object in question is not given, or is given indistinctly. To believe that I can transform the *function* of being a waiter into an "absolute" *fact* about what I am—to take Sartre's example—is to defy the ambiguous process of human existence, which is "condemned to be free" (Sartre 1995: 129). In addition, Sartre remarks that the "strange proliferation [*scissiparité*] that we call *existence*" simply excludes the possibility that *beliefs* could ever be certitudes (Sartre 1988: 544; my translation). If I, for instance, tell my friend Pierre that I trust him as a friend—that I really believe in his friendship—then according to Sartre, "I immediately give rise to the counterposition in myself, 'I am not sure.' Here sincerity turns into bad faith because it is going to neglect the quiet voice that says: 'I really only believe it'" (Sartre 1992: 475). To Sartre, therefore, "authenticity would be to maintain the tension by positing that to believe is to believe that one believes and that it is only belief, it is also not to believe" (Sartre 1992: 476). This is the most demanding challenge to authentic existence, because it requires upholding a *permanent awareness* of the tension, in its capacity *as tension*, between sincerity and the perpetual risk of self-deception in every human project.

According to Nils Bubandt, in Indonesia falsity and authenticity are not considered as opposites but as features that are mutually constitutive of power. In this light, the strength of political power in Indonesia seems to be due to a certain tolerance that the people of Indonesia have of the conjuring tricks by which the state declares certain social phenomena to be authentic: "We might call it a museum now because someday everything in it will be antique," as the Indonesian First Lady (as maintained by Bubandt) says of the brand new artifacts in the museum of the Taman Mini Theme Park. But how can the Indonesian government effectuate the *belief* that authenticity can be a matter of declaration?

In one of his latest books on social ontology, philosopher John Searle proposes the general thesis that all institutional facts, meaning facts that depend on human agreement, are created by speech acts of a certain kind, which Searle calls "Declarations." Declarations "change the world by declaring that a state of affairs exists and thus bringing that state of affairs into existence" (Searle 2010: 12). Now is this not exactly what happens with regard to authenticity in Indonesia as Bubandt describes it? If this is so, we may ask how declarations relate to authenticity. While thinking about Bubandt's chapter, I came across this statement in Sartre's *Notebooks for an Ethics*: "If you seek authenticity for authenticity's sake, you are no longer authentic" (1992: 4). Seeking authenticity in order to be authentic is, by definition, inauthentic, which is to say: self-deceptive. This seems to be consistent with the results of Bubandt's fieldwork in Indonesia and his claim, based on a quote from Hannah Arendt, that modern political lies originate in the politicians' self-deception insofar, that is, as the politician's lie implies a pretension of, and a belief in, his or her own genuineness. For the quotation from Sartre entails, in effect, that I cannot declare without contradiction: "Right now I am being authentic." This goes for everything else as well, given that as soon as I declare something to be authentic, because I want it to be authentic, I have nothing but my metastable *belief* to cling to. It is a mere postulate that can, nevertheless, be quite effective. What seems especially interesting here with regard to Bubandt's chapter is that the immanent structure of Sartre's ontology of "ambiguous" subjectivity—which Bubandt, for his purposes, proposes to move from the existential realm to a political realm—can give rise to a surprisingly effective state power. The effect is surprising because it is revealed by Bubandt as paradoxical, and in this respect I am tempted to immediately propose the absurdity that in Indonesia there is nothing more authentic than self-deception.

Authenticity is a coming to terms with the circumstance that, because of the strange proliferation of the human existence, I never am what I am in any fixed or unquestionable sense, since we have to deal with "human reality as a being which is what it is not and which is not what it is" (Sartre 1995: 58). Existentially, this is to say that in a human life there is a tension between transcendence and facticity in the sense that I *have* to be what I am not, meaning a transcending projection of myself toward my future meaning, and *have* not to be what I am, meaning the facticity of my past actions (see Sartre 1995: 59–60, 118, 125–29).

Here we can reiterate, along with Merleau-Ponty: I am never a thing and never bare consciousness.[7] We can do so because, whereas the example with the waiter addresses a self-deceptive behavior in a person who believes—or perhaps, rather, make-believes—that he is simply a factical, mechanical "thing," there is another self-deceptive strategy that consists in believing that one can be bare consciousness, i.e. pure transcendence or "all intellect." Sartre's example of this is a woman who goes on an obviously romantic date and nevertheless clings to the belief that the man who has invited her out is "only" interested in an intellectual conversation about life—while she ignores *the fact* about herself that she has actually gone on *a date* (see Sartre 1995: 55–56).

In both of the examples given above, the goal is "to put oneself out of reach" (Sartre 1995: 65); it is an escape, as Sartre also states. Furthermore, it is important to emphasize that "ambiguity [is] necessary for bad faith" (Sartre 1995: 57), because the way to put yourself out of reach, in the case of bad faith, is to somehow confuse the order of things with the order of freedom, dodging the unpleasant responsibilities implied in human existence. At the same time, both of the above attempts to escape are, in effect, escapes from ambiguity—or better, escapes from ambiguous situations perceived as sources of threat in some sense. Insofar as I am "in danger" before the other, and that this is the main motivation underlying self-deceptive strategies, Sartre's analysis may thus be said to demonstrate that self-deception is essentially *realized* as an attempt to cope with ambiguous *social* situations.

Conclusion: Trust as the Life Magic of Self-Deception

According to Frenkel-Brunswik (1939), so-called "auto-illusions," which are illusions about the self, occur as a person's strategy for coping with his or her shortcomings in certain social contexts. She remarks, with an expression from Henrik Ibsen, that self-deception can be comforting as a kind of merciful "life-lie." But in the end this is still a negative notion of self-deception, since life-lies are comforting *at the price* of endangering one's possibility to adjust to the environment (see Frenkel-Brunswik 1939: 414).

In her book, *Positive Illusions,* the psychologist Shelley E. Taylor for her part emphasizes a purely positive notion of auto-illusions, for instance in what she calls "creative self-deception," which, according to her views, characterizes the healthy mind to quite a significant extent: "That is, rather than being firmly in touch with reality, the normal human mind distorts incoming information in a positive direction. In particular, people think of themselves, their future, and their ability to have an impact on what goes on around them in a more positive manner than reality can sustain. ... I argue that the normal human mind is oriented toward mental health and that at every turn it construes events in a manner that promotes benign fictions about the self, the world, and the future" (Taylor 1989: xi).

My point is that *trust* belongs to the category of such benign fictions, which Taylor also calls "positive illusions." But whereas Taylor emphasizes positive illusions about oneself, I am interested in positive illusions about the other. Trusting behavior arguably also presupposes benign fictions about the self, the world, and the future—or, as Friedrich Nietzsche has put it in a different context: in order to act you must be embraced with a veil of illusion (see Nietzsche 1999: 57). Let me just add to this that trusting behavior further implies having positive illusions, i.e. benign fictions or ideas about the other. Such a positive illusion comes to the fore in the following passage in Sartre: "I believe that my friend Pierre feels friendship for me. I believe it *in good faith.* I believe it but I do not have for it any self-evident intuition, for the nature of the object does not lend itself to intuition. I *believe* it; that is, I allow myself to give in to all impulses to trust it; I decide to believe in it, and to maintain myself in this decision; I conduct myself, finally, as if I were certain of it—and all this in the synthetic unity of one and the same attitude" (Sartre 1995: 68–69). This is an example of how Sartre conceives of good faith—apparently as opposed to bad faith. But what characterizes the attitude that Sartre is addressing here? My answer remains the same: self-deception. Good faith is actually realized *as faith* or *belief* within the same unitary and *metastable* structure of our conscious existence—along with the dimension of being for others—as bad faith is (see Sartre 1995: 57, 70). That is, neither bad nor good faith has any stable base outside of being *faith*; that is, belief. So we need a wider term that covers both good faith and bad faith, since—according to Sartre—the real opposite of bad faith is not good faith but *authenticity* (Sartre 1995: 70). And that wider term, I contend, is "self-deception."

One might say that if I am in good faith I do not deceive myself; it can only be the other who may deceive me without my knowledge. But in order to be in good faith I must tolerate some ambiguity. Maybe Pierre is my friend—I *really believe* that he is, and I *trust* him as a friend. But I also *know* that it is something I believe, that is to say, the only certain thing—in Rorty's sense of "incorrigible"—is that I believe Pierre to be my friend. As a matter of fact, the *nature* of Pierre's friendship remains a probability (see Sartre 1992: 476). It is not an open possibility or an uncertainty, because I have many indications that he is my friend. But Pierre's friendship is, nevertheless, a probability. He may eventually surprise me so negatively that the range allowing for ambiguities due to my positive illusion about him is transgressed. And just as surely: I may disappoint him as well.

This is not to say that my trust in Pierre's friendship is essentially inconsistent, because—as mentioned—I have many indications of it from all the years we have been acquainted. But it is to say that my belief presupposes a certain positive illusion—or fiction, or idea—about this concrete other, and the belief that I have on the basis of this illusion is, in effect, a manifestation of ambiguity tolerance, meaning a willingness to think in terms of probability.

But why is Pierre's friendship not *merely* a probability to me? Why is it also, arguably, an illusion? The answer is that it is both. The interpretive move from probability to illusion is significant, though. Regarded as a mere probability, I would not be able to state more than a "maybe" with respect to the question whether Pierre is my friend. On the other hand, if I say and mean: "certainly, he is a good friend of mine," then I—as a result of my willingness to think in terms of probability—transgress the dimension of mere probability. I am assuming more than reality—also probable reality—can sustain: I *actually* do believe he is my friend, that is, I trust him, which is to say, I believe our relationship has a *future*.

So the point I am trying to make is that I need a kind of benign illusion in order to act on a probability *as if* it were certain. In this sense, trust can be said to be a self-deceptive strategy, in good faith, for coping with the ambiguities linked, mainly, to the category of "probability." Very briefly put, one could also say that trusting someone means not minding ambiguity in your relationship with that person. At least this is my suggestion for an answer to Norton's question about how trusting behavior relates to tolerance of ambiguity, which I posed at the beginning of this chapter.

By way of conclusion, I will define the positive illusion about the other as the condition of possibility for trusting behavior which consists in ignoring the mere fact that perception by necessity mediates, and that individual freedom sets limits to, concrete interhuman relations with regard to the question of whether or not I can trust other people. If trust were not linked to a benign fiction, but to a certainty, it would be hard to explain, for instance, the kind of magical phenomenon (which I perceive as a variant of the so-called Pygmalion effect[8]) consisting in this: If you trust someone, you may actually evoke trustworthy behavior in that person, and vice versa. If this is so, then the realization of trust as a coping strategy in the face of ambiguity can also be understood as a form of "life magic,"[9] insofar as the positive illusion about the other has a certain *social* meaning, function, and effect in human life; all of which defies the fact that the probable intentions of the other cannot be anticipated in terms of certainty.

Social Facts of Magic: A Final Reflection

There is another social aspect of magic in modernity that I would finally like to consider in relation to Bubandt's chapter: political ontology, which is concerned with what can be said to exist *only because of political* mediation; that is, certain human agreements. However, we all know that, at least within proper democratic societies, agreements and disagreements live side by side. It therefore cannot be particular agreements that constitute a democratic society ontologically; it must rather be something of the sort that John Searle calls "status functions," which are collectively recognized institutional facts that enable individuals to realize certain functions, such as being the First Lady of Indonesia, a university professor, or a waiter in a café (cf. Searle 2010: 7). Furthermore, Searle remarks that democratic status functions are "based [among other things] on a Background presupposition of tolerance of disagreement" (Searle 2010: 172), which can actually be said to be a model for ambiguity tolerance at the societal level. On this background, the question must be how the democratic status functions at governmental level are recognized collectively in Indonesia.

Firstly, it seems clear to me that these status functions have something like a pact with ambiguity, for instance as regards the so-called authentic-fakes (*aspals*) that Bubandt addresses as a common phenomenon in Indonesia. *Aspal* is even used to denote the state itself, because it partakes in producing forgeries, as is the case in Bubandt's example of the letter, which I consider below.

Secondly, the population perceives the status functions of the state as being "inherently inauthentic," in Bubandt's words. Nevertheless, the state has what Searle calls "deontic powers," which means rights as well as obligations (Searle 2010: 8–9, 146). In the particular case of Indonesia, for example, the government has the *right*—or, perhaps more correctly put, *believes* it has the right (and apparently no one objects)— to declare certain phenomena to be authentic, although these phenomena, as a matter of fact, *are* inauthentic or at least have no history. This is an emphatically contingent right, but it apparently works. On the other hand, being a democratic institution, the Indonesian government, for instance, has the *obligation* to occasionally call an election. However, this is supposedly inauthentic as well, given the pervasive attitude that, as Bubandt quotes his adopted sister, in Indonesia you "vote for whoever wins."

Against this backdrop, I think that Bubandt's description and analysis of Indonesian modernity demonstrate a phenomenon that I would term "magical social facts." Firstly, magic can be defined as the belief that it is possible to act *at a distance* (see Sartre 1992: 333). In my view, this makes magic a part of the family of Searle's "Declarations." I find further support for this suggestion in Marcel Mauss's thesis that magic is not primarily associative, as James Frazer (1993) classically defined it in a Humean line of reasoning, but rather—in a Kantian line of reasoning—that magic is a *judgment* that creates and constitutes a state of affairs *ex nihilo* in "the moment of the conjuring trick" (Mauss 2009: 152). Secondly, Mauss suggests that magic implies something like a Searlian "status function," since magic "is always a matter of the respective values recognized by society. These values do not depend, in fact, on the intrinsic qualities of a thing or a person, but on the status or rank attributed to them by all-powerful public opinion, by its prejudices. They are social facts not experimental facts. And this is excellently demonstrated by the magical power of words and the fact that very often the magical power of an object derives from its name" (Mauss 2009: 148).

Bubandt proposes, with a notion from Umberto Eco, that there is a certain "force of falsity" at play in Indonesia (and elsewhere, as well). When bureaucrats working for the government succeed in producing forgeries, such as the false letter that started a riot between Muslims and Christians, even though it was strongly suspected that the letter was a forgery, it may have been due to a certain experience of the object having a "magical power" deriving from its *name*—in this case the *aspal* name, since the letter was perceived by the population as an authentic-fake. The point is that the letter apparently had the same effect as if it were authentic. Consequently, the deception implied was somehow tolerated, in the same way that you might self-deceptively, though in a benign form, allow yourself to become affectively puzzled by a magician's conjuring tricks, although you know that you have no reason to believe in them.

As anthropologist Peter Pels has remarked with regard to the presence of magic *in* modernity: In magic, generally speaking, there is a "dialectics of publicity and secrecy, and revelation and concealment," which also in modernity is a way "in which external authority conjures up magical beliefs and subject positions" (Pels 2003: 31). This implies, in my view, that ambiguity is necessary for magic, and also that, arguably, the *aspal* phenomenon is an instance of magical dialectics.

Furthermore, Giora Keinan (1994) has argued that there is an intimate relationship between real-life magical thinking, stress, and a low tolerance for ambiguity. And so I suppose that if a person—or perhaps even a whole community—is massively challenged to be tolerant of ambiguities, meaning it is driven into a state of stress under pressure from ambiguous tricks worked by an external authority, the result could be a persistent doubt about one's own rational judgment, which in turn may pave the way for associative magical thinking. I really cannot say whether this is actually what is happening in Indonesia. I have observed, however, that according to Bubandt, the tolerance of ambiguity is a "political necessity in Indonesia." Moreover, I think that the political ontology of the Indonesian society, as described and analyzed by Bubandt, must constitute a serious challenge to trusting behavior with regard to the country's attempts to succeed with its "experiment with democracy," as Bubandt calls it. For it must indeed be harder than usual for a people to maintain a positive illusion about its politicians in a situation where people are forced to consider anything coming from the political sphere as a potential threat—that is, as a powerful instance of ambiguity and inauthenticity.

Notes

1. Frenkel-Brunswik is referring here to a report on a rat experiment, "Probability as a Determiner of Rat Behavior," carried out by Egon Brunswik. The latter characterizes his report as "an attempt to study the learning response of organisms to ambiguous means to a certain end, within the field of overt action" (Brunswik 1939: 175). It is beyond the objective of this chapter, however, to engage in a comparative psychological discourse.

2. Seanor and Meaton (2008) have also, but in quite a different discourse than mine, suggested that there is an intimate relation between ambiguity and trusting/distrusting behavior.

3. An extensive note by Waldenfels has been left out here.

4. Ambiguity tolerance not only distinguishes man from brute, as Waldenfels argues, but also distinguishes man from machine. For tolerance of ambiguity, according to Hubert Dreyfus, is one of the things that "computers can't do," since ambiguity tolerance is one of four types of human "information processing ... which have resisted formalization in terms of heuristic rules" (Dreyfus 1992: 206).

5. One could argue, however, that in effect Sartre and Merleau-Ponty do not differ that much. From the point of view of Sartre's theory of the original choice that a person spontaneously makes of himself, but which only an existential psychoanalysis may help him to uncover, Sartre, in consequence, is very close to Merleau-Ponty's point about freedom and probability (cf. Sartre 1995: 557ff.).

6. As I argued above, we are never absolutely tolerant of ambiguity, nor are we ever absolutely intolerant of it.

7. Some might wish to object to this stance that in Sartre, consciousness is always bare consciousness and can be limited only by itself. That is true (see Sartre 1995: xxxi). But *man* is not bare or pure consciousness; man is a concrete being-in-the-world "in which consciousness, like the phenomenon, constitutes only moments" (Sartre 1995: 3).

8. "The Pygmalion effect" refers to Robert Rosenthal and Lenore Jacobsen's (1968) experiments with "interpersonal self-fulfilling prophecies" (1968: vii) in educational situations. Roughly, their experiments show that the mere positive expectation from the teacher to his/her pupils has a similarly positive effect on the pupils' performance, compared to equally intelligent pupils who are not subjected to positive expectations.

9. See Hass (2008) for an elaboration of the notion of "life magic" as it relates to, and differs from, "staged magic."

REFERENCES

Acciaioli, Greg. 1985. "Culture As Art: From Practice to Spectacle in Indonesia." *Canberra Anthropology* 8, no. 1–2: 148–72.

Anderson, Benedict. 1990a. "The Idea of Power in Javanese Culture." In *Language and Power: Exploring Political Culture in Indonesia,* edited by B. Anderson. Ithaca, NY: Cornell University Press.

———. 1990b. *Language and Power: Exploring Political Cultures in Indonesia.* Ithaca, NY: Cornell University Press.

———. 1992. *Imagined Communities: Reflections on the Origin and Spread of Nationalism.* London: Verso.

Arendt, Hannah. 1972. *Crises of the Republic.* New York: Harcourt Brace Jovanovich.

———. 1993. *Between Past and Present: Eight Exercises in Political Thought.* New York: Penguin Books.

Argyrou, Vassos. 2000. "Reflexive Modernization and Other Mythical Realities." *Anthropological Theory* 3, no. 1: 27–41.

BBC News. 2000. Indonesia Bank Chief in Forgery Row. 8 December 2000. Available at http://news.bbc.co.uk/2/hi/business/1060962.stm. Accessed 17 March 2008.

Beck, Ulrich, Anthony Giddens, and Scott Lash, eds. 1994. *Reflexive Modernization: Politics, Tradition, and Aesthetics in the Modern Social Order.* Cambridge: Polity Press.

Berman, Marshall. 1982. *All That Is Solid Melts Into Air: The Experience of Modernity.* London: Verso.

Brunswik, Egon. 1939. "Probability as a Determiner of Rat Behavior." *Journal of Experimental Psychology* 25, no. 2: 175–97.

Bubandt, Nils. 2004. "Violence and Millenarian Modernity in Eastern Indonesia." In *Cargo, Cult, and Culture Critique,* edited by H. Jebens. Honolulu: University of Hawai'i Press.

———. 2008. "Rumors, Pamphlets, and the Politics of Paranoia in Indonesia." *Journal of Asian Studies* 67, no. 3: 789–817.

———. 2009. "From the Enemy's Point of View: Violence, Empathy, and the Ethnography of Fakes." *Cultural Anthropology* 24, no. 3: 553–88.

———. 2014a. *The Empty Seashell: Witchcraft and Doubt on an Indonesian Island.* Ithaca, NY: Cornell University Press.

———. 2014b. *Democracy, Corruption and the Politics of Spirits in Contemporary Indonesia.* London: Routledge.

Bubandt, Nils, and Rane Willerslev. 2015. "The Dark Side of Empathy: Mimesis, Deception, and the Magic of Alterity." *Comparative Studies in Society and History* 57, no. 1.

Budner, Stanley. 1962. "Intolerance of Ambiguity as a Personality Variable." *Journal of Personality* 30, no. 1: 29–50.

Comaroff, John, and Jean Comaroff. 2006. "Law and Disorder in the Postcolony: An Introduction." In *Law and Disorder in the Postcolony,* edited by J. Comaroff and J. Comaroff. Chicago, IL: University of Chicago Press.

Cribb, Robert. 2001. "How Many Deaths? Problems in the Statistics of Massacre in Indonesia (1965–1966) and East Timor (1975–1980)." In *Violence in Indonesia,* edited by Ingrid Wessel and G. Wimhöfer. Hamburg: Abera.

Das, Veena. 2004. "The Signature of the State: The Paradox of Illegibility." In *Anthropology in the Margins of the State,* edited by V. Das and D. Poole. Oxford: James Curry.

Dean, Mitchell. 1999. *Governmentality: Power and Rule in Modern Society.* London: Sage.

Derrida, Jacques. 2005. *The Politics of Friendship.* London: Verso.

Dreyfus, Hubert L. 1992. *What Computers Still Can't Do: A Critique of Artificial Reason.* Cambridge, MA: MIT Press.

Eco, Umberto. 1999. *Serendipities: Language and Lunacy.* London: Phoenix.

Efendi, Cecep, and Djan Faridz. 2008. "Democracy with Falling Representation." *The Jakarta Post,* 6 October 2008.

Eisenstadt, Shmuel, ed. 2002. *Multiple Modernities.* New Brunswick, NJ: Transaction Publishers.

Errington, Shelly. 1998. *The Death of Authentic Primitive Art and Other Tales of Progress.* Berkeley: University of California Press.

Foucault, Michel. 1980. *Power/Knowledge: Selected Interviews and Other Writings, 1972–1977.* Brighton, UK: Harvester.

———. 1991. "Governmentality." In *The Foucault Effect: Studies in Governmentality,* edited by Graham Burchell, Michel Foucault, Colin Gordon, and Peter Miller. London: Harvester and Wheatsheaf.

Frazer, James. 1993. *The Golden Bough: A Study of Magic and Religion.* Hertfordshire, UK: Wordsworth Editions.

Frenkel-Brunswik, Else. 1939. "Mechanisms of Self-Deception." *The Journal of Social Psychology* 10, no. 3: 409–20.

———. 1948. "Tolerance toward ambiguity as a personality variable." *The American Psychologist* 3, no. 7: 268.

———. 1949. "Intolerance of Ambiguity as an Emotional and Perceptual Personality Variable." *Journal of Personality* 18, no. 1: 108–43.

Fukuyama, Francis. 1995. *Trust: The Social Virtues and the Creation of Prosperity.* New York: Free Press.

Furnham, Adrian, and Tracy Ribchester. 1995. "Tolerance of Ambiguity: A Review of the Concept, Its Measurements and Applications." *Current Psychology* 14, no. 3: 179–99.

Gaonkar, Dilip Parameshwar, ed. 2001. *Alternative Modernities.* Durham, NC: Duke University Press.

Giddens, Anthony. 1990. *The Consequences of Modernity.* Cambridge: Polity Press.

———. 1991. *Modernity and Self-Identity: Self and Society in the Late Modern Age.* Cambridge: Polity Press.

Habermas, Jürgen. 1987. *The Philosophical Discourse of Modernity.* Cambridge, MA: The MIT Press.

Hardin, Russell. 2006. *Trust.* Cambridge: Polity Press.

Hass, Lawrence. 2008. "Life Magic and Staged Magic: A Hidden Intertwining." In *Performing Magic on the Western Stage: From the Eighteenth Century to the Present,* edited by Francesca Coppa, Lawrence Hass, and James Peck, 13–31. New York: Palgrave Macmillan.

Heelas, Paul. 2008. *Spiritualities of Life: New Age Romanticism and Consumptive Capitalism.* Malden, MA: Blackwell Publishing.

Hetherington, Marc. 2007. *Why Trust Matters: Declining Political Trust and the Demise of American Liberalism.* Princeton, NJ: Princeton University Press.

Hofstede, Geert. 2001. *Culture's Consequences: Comparing Values, Behaviors, Institutions, and Organizations Across Nations,* 2nd ed. Thousand Oaks, CA: Sage.

ICG. 2002. *Indonesia: The Search for Peace in Maluku.* Jakarta/Brussel: International Crisis Group. Available at http://www.crisisgroup.org.

Keinan, Giora. 1994. "Effects of Stress and Tolerance of Ambiguity on Magical Thinking." *Journal of Personality and Social Psychology* 67, no. 1: 48–55.

Kenny, Douglas T., and Rose Ginsberg. 1958. "The Specificity of Intolerance of Ambiguity Measures." *The Journal of Abnormal and Social Psychology* 56, no. 3: 300–304.

Knauft, Bruce, ed. 2002. *Critically Modern: Alternatives, Alterities, Anthropologies.* Bloomington: Indiana University Press.

Kumar, Krishnan. 1995. *From Post-Industrial to Post-Modern Society. New Theories of the Contemporary World.* Oxford: Blackwell.

Lindsey, Tim. 2000. "Black Letter, Black Market, and Bad Faith: Corruption and the Failure of Law Reform." In *Indonesia in Transition: Social Aspects of Reformasi and Crisis,* edited by Chris Manning and Peter van Dierman, 278–92. Singapore: Institute of Southeast Asian Studies.

Marcus, George. 2002. *The Sentimental Citizen: Emotion in Democratic Politics.* University Park: Pennsylvania State University Press.

Markovits, Elisabeth. 2006. "The Trouble with Being Earnest: Deliberative Democracy and the Sincerity Norm." *The Journal of Political Philosophy* 14, no. 3: 249–69.

———. 2008. *The Politics of Sincerity: Plato, Frank Speech, and Democratic Judgment.* University Park: Pennsylvania State University Press.

Mauss, Marcel. 2009. *A General Theory of Magic.* Translated by Robert Brain. London: Routledge.

McSweeney, Brendan. 2002. "Hofstede's Model of National Cultural Differences and their Consequences: A Triumph of Faith—A Failure of Analysis." *Human Relations* 55, no. 1: 89–118.

Merleau-Ponty, Maurice. 1963. *The Structure of Behavior.* Translated by Alden Fisher. Boston: Beacon Press.

———. 1989. *Phenomenology of Perception.* Translated by Colin Smith. London: Routledge.

Neuman, W. Russell, George Marcus, Ann Crigler, and Michael Mackuen, eds. 2007. *The Affect Effect: Dynamics of Emotion in Political Thinking and Behavior.* Chicago, IL: University of Chicago Press.

Nietzsche, Friedrich. 1999. *Die Geburt der Tragödie.* In *Kritische Studienausgabe*, vol. 1, edited by Giorgio Colli and Mazzino Montinari. Munich: DTV/de Gruyter.

Norton, Robert W. 1975. "Measurement of Ambiguity Tolerance." *Journal of Personality Assessment* 39, no. 6: 607–19.

Nye, Joseph, ed. 1997. *Why People Don't Trust Government.* Cambridge, MA: Harvard University Press.

Pels, Peter. 2003. "Introduction: Magic and Modernity." In *Magic and Modernity: Interfaces of Revelation and Concealment,* edited by Birgit Meyer and Peter Pels. Stanford, CA: Stanford University Press.

Pemberton, John. 1994. "Recollections from 'Beautiful Indonesia' (Somewhere Beyond the Postmodern)." *Public Culture* 6, no. 2: 241–62.

Putnam, Robert. 2000. *Bowling Alone: The Collapse and Revival of American Community.* New York: Simon & Schuster.

Rorty, Richard. 1970. "Incorrigibility as the Mark of the Mental." *The Journal of Philosophy* 67, no. 12: 399–424.

Rose, Nikolas. 1998. *Inventing Ourselves: Psychology, Power, and Personhood.* Cambridge: Cambridge University Press.

———. 1999. *Governing the Soul: The Shaping of the Private Self.* London: Free Association Books.

Rosenthal, Robert, and Lenore Jacobson. 1968. *Pygmalion in the Classroom: Teacher Expectation and Pupils' Intellectual Development.* New York: Holt, Rinehart and Winston.

Said, Edward. 1995. *Orientalism: Western Conceptions of the Orient.* London: Penguin Books.

Sartre, Jean-Paul. 1956. *Being and Nothingness: A Phenomenological Essay on Ontology.* Translated by Hazel E. Barnes. New York: Washington Square Press.

———. 1988. *L'Idiot de la famille: Gustave Flaubert de 1821 à 1857,* vol. 3. Paris: Gallimard.

———. 1992. *Notebooks for an Ethics.* Translated by David Pellauer. Chicago, IL: University of Chicago Press.

———. 1993. "Conscience de soi et connaissance de soi." In *Selbstbewusstseinstheorien von Fichte bis Sartre,* edited by Manfred Frank. Frankfurt: Suhrkamp.

———. 1995. *Being and Nothingness: An Essay on Phenomenological Ontology.* Translated by Hazel E. Barnes. London: Routledge.

———. 2010a. *The Imaginary: A Phenomenological Psychology of the Imagination.* Translated by Jonathan Webber. London: Routledge.

———. 2010b. *Sketch for a Theory of the Emotions.* Translated by Philip Mairet. London: Routledge.

Sayer, Derek. 1991. *Capitalism and Modernity: An Excursus on Marx and Weber.* London: Routledge.

Scott, James. 1998. *Seeing Like a State: How Certain Schemes to Improve the Human Condition Have Failed.* New Haven, CT: Yale University Press.

Seanor, Pam, and Julia Meaton. 2008. "Learning from Failure, Ambiguity and Trust in Social Enterprise." *Social Enterprise Journal* 4, no. 1: 24–40.

Searle, John. 2010. *Making the Social World: The Structure of Human Civilization.* Oxford: Oxford University Press.

Siegel, James. 1998. *A New Criminal Type in Jakarta: Counter-Revolution Today.* Durham, NC: Duke University Press.

Strassler, Karen. 2000. "Currency and Fingerprints: Authentic Reproductions and Political Communication in Indonesia's 'Reform Era'." *Indonesia* 70, October: 71–82.

Taylor, Charles. 1991. *The Ethics of Authenticity.* Cambridge, MA: Harvard University Press.

Taylor, Shelley E. 1989. *Positive Illusions: Creative Self-Deception and the Healthy Mind.* New York: Basic Books.

Tilly, Charles. 2005. *Trust and Rule.* Cambridge: Cambridge University Press.

Transparency International. 2009. *Global Corruption Barometer 2009.* Berlin: Transparency International.

Trilling, Lionel. 1972. *Sincerity and Authenticity.* Cambridge, MA: Harvard University Press.

Uslaner, Eric. 2002. *The Moral Foundation of Trust.* Cambridge: Cambridge University Press.

Waldenfels, Bernhard. 2000. *Das leibliche Selbst: Vorlesungen zur Phänomenologie der Leiblichkeit.* Frankfurt: Suhrkamp.

Yurchak, Alexei. 2006. *Everything Was Forever, Until It Was No More: The Last Soviet Generation.* Princeton, NJ: Princeton University Press.

GIFT-GIVING AND POWER BETWEEN TRUST AND HOPE

JOINT STATEMENT

Sverre Raffnsøe and Hirokazu Miyazaki

The chapters in this dialogue insist on elucidating trust and hope as they are enacted in their delicate relationship to each other and to other human and social phenomena of similar vital importance, such as knowledge and experience, power, gift-giving, freedom, agency, and, ultimately, grace and sleep. Trust and hope are thus to be understood as modes of existence that are distinct and significant, and play a part within a larger social fabric. As attitudes that are turned toward, and modes of being that are affected by, an uncharted future still to be nego-tiated, hope and trust concomitantly transcend the given social context and in so doing open the way for the yet-to-be in general.

Drawing on insights from philosophy—especially Bloch, but also Benjamin and Rorty—Miyazaki's anthropological work has led us to consider hope as an implicit "common operative in all knowledge for-mation" in order to confront the "most fundamental problem" concern-ing our knowledge of "what knowledge is for" (Miyazaki 2004: 9). It may well be that "all men by nature desire to know," as declared in the opening sentence of Aristotle's *Metaphysics*, a founding declaration of Western first philosophy (Aristotle 1989: 980a). On closer inspection, however, this raises the question of why we take such an intense inter-est in knowledge and come together in a profound will to know. If we begin to address this question seriously, hope appears as a yet-to-be-apprehended motivating factor for seeking knowledge. We do not merely strive to know because we want to master and be in control in a certain given situation (Adorno and Horkheimer 1992). The quest for knowl-edge should also be understood within the context of an open, tempo-rally oriented existence that cannot help cherishing dreams of "a better life … that might be possible (*das möglich wäre*)" (Bloch 1985, vol. 1: 1). To remain a true conscience of tomorrow, however, hope, as the expectancy of possibilities yet to come, must also be based on knowledge. If not, hope risks becoming mere reverie, as Raffnsøe argues in his chapter. Similarly, Miyazaki contends that by giving attention to and comprehending hope as a prevalent leading principle, philosophy and anthropology can become knowledgeable of hope, drawing attention to and gaining knowledge of the hope inherent in knowledge, as well as drawing attention to and gaining knowledge of knowledge as an inherent condition of hope.

Equally, as Raffnsøe furthermore argues, trust seems to occupy an intermediate and central position between knowledge and hope. On the one hand, trust maintains a close but somewhat ambiguous relationship to knowledge. The conscious decision to adopt a trusting attitude to some extent rests on the fact that knowledge of past and present experiences give us reason to trust. On the other hand, the decision to rely upon someone or something transcends established knowledge by taking a risk in a future that is not entirely foreseeable. Both authors consequently agree that even though trust is based on knowledge and past experience, it is also motivated by hope. The resolution to take a risk and leap into the future is almost impossible to adopt if the experienced conditions are not concurrently perceived as conditions that allow the initiation of something that is still in its infancy. As an anticipatory being affected actively by something that transcends the conditions given, hope seems to pave the way and be a prerequisite for showing trust.

Consequently, the relationship between trust, hope, and knowledge seems so intimate that these three are not only linked externally, but are, rather, intrinsically interdependent.

By giving attention to and comprehending trust, hope, and knowledge as interdependent and relating to a wider context, anthropology and philosophy avoid being professions of faith. Instead of confessing allegiance or adhering to certain given values or entities in order to develop their peculiar nature in isolation from other entities, philosophy and anthropology are able to articulate the specificity of trust, hope, and knowledge as pervasive aspects of human existence, irreducible to each other in as much as they relate to one another within a given social context; a context that they transcend, since they are also turned toward anticipating and negotiating the future.

This common approach to trust, hope, and knowledge is developed in its various bearings throughout this dialogue, which opens with Raffnsøe's longer chapter "Empowering Trust in the New: Trust and Power as Capacities." Miyazaki's contribution "Hope in the Gift—Hope in Sleep" takes the form of a shorter commentary, accentuating and transposing certain points developed in Raffnsøe's chapter.

Both chapters stress that the conception of trust as being motivated by hope as well as based on knowledge and experience, as suggested by Raffnsøe, can be further elucidated by relating it to the simultaneously free and obligatory character of giving, receiving, and reciprocating that Marcel Mauss has famously articulated in *The Gift*. When we hand over part of our possessions, or part of ourselves, by entrusting ourselves to others, we simultaneously place these others under an obligation to take care of and reciprocate this gift in a proper way. In this fashion we are able to affect others in ways that effect (that is, bring about) a change in their dispositions to act. As a consequence, showing trust also emerges as a particularly refined form of exercising power, and indeed as a form that is able to make the best of human freedom.

However, while agreeing that showing trust follows the logic of gift-giving, the chapters highlight different aspects of gift-giving and trust. When comprehending trust and gift-giving as ways to exercise power, Raffnsøe's chapter stresses an important active element in both. Even though we expose ourselves, as we deliver ourselves over to others by showing trust or giving gifts, it is insufficient to perceive these lines of action as acts of unconditional surrender. Showing trust and giving gifts should also be considered as attempts to deal effectively with issues of powerlessness and as ways to assert human agency. Giving gifts and showing trust are also lines of action undertaken to build up hope that something might happen, and thus they are ways to position oneself as powerful and active.

Miyazaki's chapter, on the contrary, stresses the moment of abeyance of agency in the ritual of gift-giving and in trust, since the completion of one side's action is delegated to the other side, whether it is to the gift-receiving side or ultimately to God. In this manner the moment of uncertainty, unknowability, and helplessness is deferred and hence obviated again and again. In this context, hope emerges as a capacity to rest assured and embrace human uncertainty and powerlessness, as one entrusts oneself into another's keeping. Precisely by postponing human agency and leaving scope for not necessarily well-earned acts of mercy, one may be able to receive, to find peace and rest, in ways that enable one to recuperate and recommit oneself to acts of trust.

When stressing the deference of agency that is manifest in gift-giving as a precondition for trust and human agency in general, Miyazaki gives prominence to points developed throughout Raffnsøe's chapter but especially accentuated in its last section part. Here Raffnsøe underscores that the inception of humanity also entails the experience and the recognition of a dependency on extrinsic factors that cannot be dominated, not only within the body politic at large but also within the human body. According to Raffnsøe, the postponement of human will and agency that is evident in trust and gift-giving thereby draws attention to a somewhat ambiguous affective humane interdependency in which unfamiliar forces make themselves felt in uncanny and productive ways. By contrast, Miyazaki makes a case for the necessity of transgressing performative, interactional, and relational modes of being through acts of self-surrender in order to keep hope alive.

In this way, the exchange in the dialogue that unfolds takes the form of a mutually challenging gift-giving. The division of labor in the exchange nicely mirrors the differences in opinion and approach.

The reader remains free to speculate on the extent to which the differences displayed at various levels in the exchange could be seen as occasioned by, and as expressions of, the differences in outlook and modes of existence that come together and blend in the dialogue. These differences might be occasioned by, and be expressions of, tensions between a religious and a secularized outlook, or antagonisms between a Western metaphysics of the will seeking to know its own limitations and an Eastern commemoration of the limits of the self and the will. It might also be the case that a philosophical request to "know thyself" by asserting yourself and your free speech in order to situate yourself within a larger context meet and exchange with an anthropological commemoration of the necessity to surrender to the other in order to become aware of yourself and your own contribution. As a consequence, there is still ample room for further illuminating exchanges between anthropology and philosophy.

EMPOWERING TRUST IN THE NEW

Trust and Power as Capacities

Sverre Raffnsøe

During the past century, management has become an all-embracing concept and a phenomenon with a profound and pervasive impact on the communities and the lives of individuals in the Western hemisphere. As soon as we have to confront and solve problems in organizations and society, to improve our performance or to reorganize, we look for better and more efficient ways not only to wield physical resources but also, and especially, to direct and conduct human efforts and behavior (Wren 2005: 3).

Management as a ubiquitous activity implies an ongoing exertion of power. Pouvoir is *a* sine qua non of management. We have to "be able" (lat. *potere)* to do or to effect something. More specifically, we must have the ability or capacity to affect people in order to make them behave in ways they would not otherwise behave (Dahl 1957; Morriss [1987] 2002: 13).

Management also seems to presuppose something irreducible to power, however. Lately, it has become commonplace to draw attention to the fact that management heavily relies upon trust. Concurrently, sociological and economic theory, and especially managerial practice and theory, emphasize the importance of trust in management (Misztal 1996; Gambetta 1988). Trust is routinely marketed as an all-important value and a managerial resource, a not-to-be-taken-for-granted resolve (Misztal 1996: 16) to show "confidence in or reliance on some quality or attributes of a person or thing, or the truth of a statement" (Oxford English Dictionary: entry for "trust"). Arguably, it helps to "facilitate cooperation," "lowers transaction costs," "promotes smooth and efficient market exchanges," and "improves" the ability of companies "to adapt and develop" (Wicks, Berman, and Jones 1999: 99).

Indeed, trust is often considered a counter-concept to managerial power in the traditional sense: a concept that encapsulates all the positive effects of minimizing direct uses of power (Fukuyama 1995), while at the same time ensuring mutual obligations. Trust is associated with liberating and empowering employees and creating open spaces for innovation and expression. As we experience difficulty in exerting power within management and turn to trust, we seem to stumble upon an unexpectedly simple and efficient answer.

In contradistinction to this "segregation" between trust and power, a basic assumption of this chapter is that the two are closely interrelated and must be approached accordingly by management. This point is of consequence not only to the management of particular firms or organizations, but to the management in and of society in general. Consequently, the chapter purposes to re-examine and rethink trust and power in order to arrive at a more refined understanding of both notions, permitting us to cope with not only their mutual irreducibility but also with their inseparability and interdependency. This objective is quite challenging, as there are serious impediments preventing its realization.

The first section of my chapter examines the present context within which we place trust in trust. At first glance, trust appears to be a universal positive value, in both moral and economical terms, but upon closer inspection it proves to have the status of a problematic, and all too scarce, resource. On the one hand, trust is in great demand and widely hailed, since it has become an increasingly important prerequisite for modern organizational life and for modern society. On the other hand, trust appears to be fragile, scarce, and fraught with problems since we tend to understand and manage it in ways that prove detrimental to it. A principal cause for the misconception and mismanagement of trust and power is the conception of trust and power as external to and incompatible with each other. The second section examines an omnipresent, received notion of power as command, coercion, control, and calculation that forces us to imagine trust and power as separate realms and prevents a proper understanding and handling of trust.

The third section develops an alternative notion of power, permitting us to understand and relate to trust and power as complementary and interdependent dimensions. Here power appears as a capacity to affect the dispositions of others. When exercising power with this end in view, we begin to focus on another very real aspect of the world: the virtual. Further developing the wide-ranging implications of this displacement, the fourth section shows how this more refined conception of power enables us to consider and relate to trusting as an active and deliberate exercise of power. In the wake of this more refined understanding of both power and trust, it is possible to conceive of trust as an anticipatory affect. In contrast to mere confidence, then, trust is essentially to be understood as a resolve to bear an actively experienced risk by confiding in the new and unknown. Closely associated with knowledge and hope, trust is thus essentially turned toward the new and is to be conceived of as a way of negotiating the future. Not only does trust anticipate and relate to the plane of the virtual. Trust may also be a way to actively influence the dispositions and the conduct of other people. Since trust affects people's dispositions to act, and also the way they express themselves, showing trust can be conceived of and practiced as an exercise of power and as a way to direct people in a more refined manner.

The Present Challenge: Why We Place Trust in Trust

At present, the universal value of trust in management is asserted almost everywhere. Observers preach the virtue of trust by stating that "in business, politics, marriage—indeed in any significant relationship— trust is the essential precondition upon which all real success depends" (Solomon and Flores 2001: back cover). By presenting trust as a universal value per se and placing our trust in trust, we seem to be progressing toward a better world in general—a world of trustworthiness, credibility, authenticity, and efficiency.

Still, the picture of simple progress with regard to the recognition of trust appears misleading the moment we ask why we have come to feel the need for trust so pressingly in recent years. Researchers often assert that managers and management literature have hitherto overlooked and underestimated "the elusive notion of trust" (Gambetta 1988: 9; Barney and Hansen 1994; Calton and Lad 1995). Similarly, other scholars draw attention to the fact that in economics, too, trust has long been regarded as a "background environment," a kind of basic tacit assumption necessary in economic transactions and interactions (Dasgupta 1988: 49).

In addition to stressing the inherent virtues and advantages of trust, researchers seeking to explain the present popularity of trust often draw our attention to the erosion of the traditional basis of society and the appearance of a mobile and global society. According to Hart, trust becomes "central to social life when neither traditional certainties nor modern probabilities hold" (Hart 1988: 191). Even when stressing that confidence, or familiarity (*Vertrautheit*) remains a condition sine qua non both for trust and distrust (Luhmann 1973: 19), Luhmann makes a similar point: The erosion of the past handed down as a given and unproblematized *Lebenswelt* (Luhmann 1973: 22) and the birth of an increasingly complex social world (Luhmann 1973: 16) call for trust as a way to cope with these very challenges. Since these transitions are general and have taken place over a long time, however, they provide only part of the reason for the relatively sudden rise in popularity of the notion of trust, particularly within management.

An additional reason behind the discovery of the importance of trust in management is, no doubt, more recent trends toward self-management within organizational culture and managerial theory and practice (Raffnsøe 2010, 2011; Lopdrup-Hjorth 2011; Bramming et al. 2011). A demand for more and better management is created by the propagation of self-management, which has a long-rooted genesis but has only spread relatively recently. At the same time, however, it creates a critical situation for management. Management now has to face a new challenge: that of managing people or units that manage themselves (Raffnsøe 2010; Leth and Raffnsøe 2011).

In settings where managers have to manage freedom, the command and control approach so dear to traditional management appears to be neither legitimate nor productive. These basic principles of business management evolved, along with the creation of the large corporations and the managerial revolution during the nineteenth century, as the "visible hand" of the manager (Chandler 1977, 1990) increasingly replaced the "invisible hand" of the market" (Smith 1976: 184; 1991: 400) as a way "to advance the interest of the society," even "without intending it, without knowing it" (Smith 1976: 185). The principles were at last formulated succinctly, as management finally aspired to the status of a scientific discipline with Taylor's *Principles of Scientific Management* at the beginning of the twentieth century (Taylor 1967).

If the issue is how to manage units or individuals that are supposed to behave and develop in unforeseeable ways, however, then command and coercion, calculation and control seem a lot less productive and appear to be less viable ways to gain approval and create commitment. In this case, trust may seem an obvious alternative to the established approach in order to attenuate or replace the all-too-visible hand of the manager. As the "confident anticipation" (Webster's Third New International Dictionary: entry for "trust") that the other will live up to our expectations, mutual trust seems to establish a binding reciprocal relationship that allows for freedom and ensures dynamic cooperation and coordination (Solomon and Flores 2001; Fukuyama 1995). Building (on) trust, management avoids the manager's visible, all too heavy-handed and restraining touch, while conforming with Adam Smith's invisible hand to create "the possibility of cooperation without coercion" (Friedman 1999).

Thus, trust appears as part of the response to the current crisis in management that has been created by the erosion of familiarity, the increase in complexity, and the propagation of self-management and freedom in modern work life. The seeking of refuge in trust, and the attempt to conjure up trust, emerges not so much as a matter of managerial benevolence but rather as a matter of necessity in the absence of a better alternative.

We have come to realize the importance of trust because it has become *problematic*. It has become a field of first-rate importance that raises pressing and highly important questions to which we have no final answers or solutions. Trust is in demand, and is lacking, and we feel the necessity to create and maintain trust without knowing exactly how to go about doing so.

The Challenge of Philosophical Investigation: Power and Trust as Transcendental, Interdependent Conditions of Management

The edifying depiction of progress with regard to trust in management is also tarnished by the way in which we practice trust in management. According to Solomon and Flores, "business executives these days talk a great deal about trust, but mainly to bemoan its absence" (2001: 22). This is also due to the fact that managers tend to manage their organizations in ways that make the employees ill-disposed toward placing trust in the management. Managers conceive of power and trust as two separate realms, and therefore feel they face a choice between mutually exclusive alternatives.

In practice, this conception of the relationship between power and trust makes management inclined to commute incessantly back and forth between these realms. Employees sense this shuttling back and forth and come to see management as incoherent and untrustworthy. What is more, this division undermines trust, no matter how strongly the management may glorify it. Trust appears as an alternative domain into which the manager can escape when the domain of power fails.

Shuttle management is detrimental, however, since in practice management can no more do without power than it can do without trust. Both aspects of management must be present on a daily basis if a company is to prosper, or an organization function. Therefore management needs to replace the "either–or" perception of power and trust with a perception of "both–and." Management is in no way possible without power and the exercise thereof, but in the absence of trust, the manager's initiatives will be constantly resisted. However, if the manager does not exercise power and set the agenda, it will be equally impossible to win trust as a manager.

Since power and trust are both indispensable aspects of management, the manager must be able to perceive them as complementary and interdependent, rather than as mutually exclusive and incompatible. Management must be able to take trust into account whenever it focuses on exercising power, and vice versa.

Upon closer inspection, the reciprocal relationship between power and trust implies that not only are they inseparable in the sense that they are continuously linked externally; they are also intrinsically and internally linked. This means that trust always contains an aspect of power. When the leader places trust in his employees or establishes trust-relations between himself and his employees, he is also already exercising power. Trust is also a (kind of) power, albeit one that differs from the conventional. Reversely, it means that power already involves trust. When the manager exercises power and creates new constellations of power, new relations of trust are simultaneously established. Exercising power actively can also be seen as a way of creating trust.

It follows, then, that not only are trust and power two necessary aspects of, and preconditions for, management; they also form necessary prerequisites for one another. They constitute transcendental conditions for the possibility of management that are mutually interdependent and internally linked. Rephrasing a famous statement made by Kant in his *Critique of Pure Reason* (Kant 1976a: 98), one could formulate the point like this: Within management, the exercise of power without trust is empty. Conversely, within management the appeal and the recourse to trust without power are blind.

As a consequence, power and trust are not mere practical problems that the manager can solve. On the contrary, they are basic transcendental conditions of management that the manager and the managed must take care to reestablish on a daily basis, as managing is neither feasible nor practicable in their absence. They are ever-present, closely related circumstances that demand constant attention.

Yet to give proper attention to trust and power as closely interrelated conditions for managers in the theory and practice of management, it is necessary to think through power and trust in a new way to make it clear that they do not exclude one another, and to show how they are interconnected and mutually depend on one another.

For philosophy, it is an obvious task thus to discuss, problematize, and distance oneself from widely held conceptions that permeate a given practice in order to expound the conditions that make that very same practice possible at a more basic level, and also in order to be able to re-address important issues in well-established practice. The effort to formulate basic implicit, and often neglected, conditions of the possibility of vital importance for practice found its emblematic expression in Kant's transcendental philosophy (Kant 1976a, 1976b, 1976d). Still, this endeavor can be regarded as an overriding concern motivating the entire Western philosophical tradition, most markedly in the long-standing ontological tradition from Plato and the pre-Socratics to our own time, which has attempted to formulate the basic nature of being that is fraught with consequences for how humans can live and interact.

This kind of transcendental and ontological examination distinguishes itself from an empirical study in any traditional sense of the word, whether it be of a sociological, historical, or even anthropological nature. The examination is not primarily concerned with giving an accurate and exhaustive description of what actually happens. The point is to examine the conditions for the world's appearance and attaining being. Note, however, that this is done so as to attain a distance from the already given limitations, which is not the same as simply disregarding them, since they are in effect for good reasons.

In some respects, examining and stating the conditions for the world's attaining being is less comprehensive than describing reality. The aim is "merely" to examine a level that we relate to, and which prescribes how we may live and interact. In this sense, philosophical inquiry is ultimately concerned with "ought" rather than "is." On the other hand, the prescriptive guidelines determine how we may come to influence the world and leave our traces upon it. In this respect, then, the level of ambition is higher in this kind of investigation. The level of normativity determines what we are basically able to conceive and implement, and thereby what can become real and attain existence in a wider sense. As such, the level of normativity takes precedence over the factual; it is more important than the real and more essential than the being.

Philosophy considered as a tendency to problematize and "look behind" the basis for common-sense assumptions is an extension of everyday life, since this involves a tendency to problematize itself and common sense (*doxa*). It is an integral aspect of "everyday" life that it is, in itself, a process of constant learning; that one is constantly inclined to view the given at a more basic level. Philosophy is therefore not merely done out of desire, ability, or a surplus of intellectual energy, but also out of need, distress, and necessity. In this sense, philosophy is unavoidable.

As has been indicated, the inquiry into humankind's place in the world, taking as its outset the self's non-obvious relations to the self and to the world, has played a decisive role since Socrates, and possibly even since the pre-Socratic philosophers. Philosophy has been coupled ever since to the aim of giving an account of the self and the other, and of oneself in relation to others. In this sense, philosophy has maintained an intimate relationship to responsibility and accountability (Butler 2005). I simply cannot appear as a self until I am able to account for my self and my relationship with others, and thereby come into existence as a responsible being. Being called upon to account for my self and my relationship with others may raise a number of unanswered ethical questions.

The Inherited Notion of Power and its Relation to Trust

If we are to perceive the correlation between power and trust and to take it into due account, we must reconsider the received notions of power in as much as they force us to end up with the "either–or" of management and invite us to practice shuttle management. We have to rethink these limited commonsensical notions to pave the way for a more subtle understanding of, and approach to, power and trust.

The Received Concept of Power:
Command, Coercion, Control, and Calculation

With regard to power, we are obliged to reconsider "the four Cs," which dominate the way we conceptualize power: command, coercion, and control, all closely linked to calculation. In the first place, we have to confront the received notions of power as *command (1)* and *coercion (2)*. When we exercise power by commanding others, we tell them to do or to abstain from doing something specific. We express a certain wish, desire, or demand in such a way that we feel entitled to expect that they will comply with it.

If necessary, we may even back up our wish by threatening with certain unpleasant or even harmful sanctions (Hart 1979: 19). In cases like this, we achieve power by way of coercing other people. To command and to coerce may be very efficient ways to force other people to do things they would not otherwise have done. It permits the agent to obtain and to hold power over other people in an enduring, stable, and precise manner.

Exercising power in this manner even gives the agent the gratification of being or feeling in *control (3)*. We direct the behavior of other people in such a way that *they* know exactly what to do, and in such a way that *we* know exactly what they will do and also know what to do if they do *not* do it.[1] If we exercise power in a way that makes us able to control other people, we are able to dominate them to such an extent that ultimately we appear to be the true cause of what they do.[2] We are able to have our way, and make our will prevail, to the extent that we appear to be the true and sovereign holders of power, so that the others are, at best, our auxiliary arms or tools.

Exercising power in this manner is closely associated with *calculation (4)*. By commanding, coercing, and controlling other people, we make sure that they do not act in unpredictable but predetermined ways. We see to it that we are able to foresee what is going to happen and are thus able to calculate the range of potential consequences.

The Prevailing Notion of Rule

Rather than being one option among many, power exercised and conceptualized as command, coercion, control, and calculation is to be regarded as the primary and norm-setting mode of power—at least, but not exclusively, in Western societies. Asserting itself against the existing network of feudal structures of dependence and rivalry (Luhmann 1989: 67), the Roman Catholic Church originally adopted this approach in order to establish itself as an overarching "counter-power" against the network of existing feudal structures of dependence (Raffnsøe 2001: 123). Subsequently, this approach was assumed and further developed by the more centralized form of monarchical power that appeared in the late Middle Ages (Raffnsøe 2003: 11–12).[3] In the theory and practice of the Holy See and of absolute monarchy, power is essentially exercised in the form of command, coercion, and control.

The modern Western European territorial states, and later nation-states, continue to rest on the same notion of power. They remain centered on a supreme sovereign authority, forming the capital of the territory, whether this authority be an absolute monarch or the parliament of a representative democracy (Raffnsøe 2003). The established power structure creates a state of internal peace and agreement[4] as it expresses its will in the form of general standing mandatory orders. These orders are imperative statements to be obeyed by anyone concerned, simply because they are issued by someone in the position to do so. Moreover, they are orders that will be backed by sanctions if they are not complied with (Hart 1979: 18–25). Such commands establish a clear-cut, binary division of the world, since every kind of activity is classified either as a transgression of the imperatives or as a permitted activity that takes place within the limits prescribed. According to this long-standing juridical conception and institutionalization of power, power is essentially that which marks the boundaries within which we should remain, and hence it limits and represses us (Foucault 2003: 15). At the end of the day, to the extent that we follow this restrictive conception, power amounts to an ability to either put to death, or to let live (Foucault 1976: 178).

The conception of power as an expression of will mainly limiting other people prevails in a number of agenda-setting political thinkers and philosophers in the Western tradition, ranging from Bodin, Locke (1963), and Hume (Morriss [1987] 2002: 15) over Rousseau (1964: 379–80), Bentham (1977, 1983), and Austin (J. Austin 1968; Raffnsøe 1996: 131) and right up to Freud (Foucault 2003: 15). It reaches an ideal typical expression in Hobbes, according to whom society is not to be presupposed, but is established through acts described as initiating commands issued by a central sovereign authority creating common-wealth ex nihilo, again and again, almost like "God in the creation" (Hobbes 1979: 82, 163–64). This conception is also very much present in Kant (1976b: 30; 1976e: 156) and Hegel (1972: 231, 249, 257–320).

Within this tradition the exercise of power is very closely associated with the notion of *rule*. Not only is the person or the authority that displays power and force expected to make the determining decisions; they are also supposed to be in charge by attending to the whole and creating and overseeing the unity of the entity that they govern. In addition to the literature and the practice previously mentioned, this notion of rule is presupposed and developed in an extensive literature that aims to instruct and counsel princes to enable them to assume the position of ruler. Inaugurated by Plato's seventh letter to Dionysius of Syracuse and Xenophon's *Cyropaedia*, an ongoing tradition of *mirrors for princes* finds a classical expression in St. Thomas's *On Princely Government to the King of Cyprus* (Aquinas 1974).

According to this tradition, the ruler must govern by assuming the position of the *helmsman* (Aquinas 1974: 3). By virtue of his natural and acquired capabilities and merits, he should be able to rise above his fellow beings and exercise dominance. Assuming his natural position above the crew, the helmsman should be able to dominate them and ensure a steady course, as he takes command, indicates the common destination, and finds the means to reach this goal.

Rule, Power, and Trust

So, through a long and convoluted historical process, the notion of the ruler has become the point of reference for agents aspiring to power, as concurrently the concepts of command, coercion, and control have come to dominate the way we understand and exercise power.

Insofar as the manager understands his exercise of power along these lines, he tends to claim for himself the position of a ruler, maintaining his position by taking recourse to command, coercion, and control. As stated at the beginning of this chapter, that has in fact been a common approach to, and for, management as it developed within corporations from the beginning of the nineteenth century (Wren 2005: 77–152).

There have been number of valid reasons for adopting this now-classic notion of power. Exercising power in this fashion has ensured stability and predictability for the governing as well as the governed. Hobbes went so far as to claim that this vertical power formed the will and reason of human society and was essential to common wealth (Hobbes 1979: 81).

That said, the model has numerous drawbacks as well. Along with this mainly restrictive conception of power, a certain restricted conception of power has gained almost hegemonic status. It is quite a simple and crude model of power, as it tends to reduce power exercised over and through other human beings to a brutish sort of power at the far end of the spectrum. Power becomes similar to the force exerted by human beings over things that "gives the capacity to modify, use, consume or destroy them" (Foucault 1982: 217). Consequently, exercising power along the lines set out by this notion of power makes it very difficult to cope with challenges posed by the advent of self-management and freedom, in the endeavor to make positive use of this unforeseeable dynamic in various ways.

Moreover, as long as we act within this classical but very limited conception of power (let us call it Power I), it is impossible to perceive trust as a way to exercise power. When we effect something, or make something happen by showing trust, we do not force other people to make it happen or command them to carry it out. Nor do we necessarily check whether it happens. Insofar as we choose to rely on trust, we take risks and accordingly we risk being disappointed (Luhmann 1976). We are simply no longer able to remain in command and in control in the traditional way. Machiavelli's *The Prince* bears witness to the insurmountable difficulties of inspiring trust that princes face as they try "to avoid … being under the control of other people" and maintain control of their own people and territory (1977: 65).

Not only is it impossible to perceive trust as power if power forms an unquestioned starting premise. There is simply no room and no place for trust at all, be it in theory or in practice. As long as we adhere to this limited and limiting conception of power, we implicitly remain within a social contract based not on trust, but on distrust. When trying to organize a coherent society, we begin with the assumption that others will always end up deceiving us, at least if we are unable to establish unanimously binding commands and back them up by force. As we strive to organize society, and to create community and cooperation, our starting point is the worst-case scenario, so to speak, and we begin to organize society accordingly. Exercising power in the manner perpetuated in the Western tradition, we turn our back on the experience of risk that is inherent in trust and end up suppressing human freedom in order to eradicate the possibility that we may be deceived in the future.

As already indicated, Hobbes's *Leviathan* may serve as an outstanding example of the attempt to construct a confidence-inspiring social contract based on distrust, command, control, and recourse to force. Concurrently, however, he demonstrated the fragility of the construct. According to Hobbes, distrust remained ever present, for instance as a ubiquitous "disposition" to "WARRE," affecting all fellow citizens at each and every moment (Hobbes 1979: 185–87).

Yet in his own pointed way, Hobbes simultaneously happens to demonstrate a general, basic, tragic irony inherent in this approach to power and trust. We strive to soothe our anxiety that we may be betrayed, and society fall apart, by creating and upholding a reliable and trustworthy social order that transcends this very menace, as it is based on protective measures against it. But by these very measures, we manage to conjure up precisely those spirits that we are trying to confine, to the effect that they re-emerge as ever-present forces.

Unwittingly, then, we adopt an approach that resembles the ruler's line of action in *King Lear* (Shakespeare 1977). Trying to protect himself and make sure that he is cared for, King Lear ends up rejecting Cordelia, his daughter who is "closest at heart" and loves him most dearly (also according to the etymology of her name). Distancing himself from that which should have been closest to his heart, and from the one who could have supported him, the king finally finds himself utterly abandoned.

An Alternative Notion of Power

As a consequence of the received notion of power, we are forced to perceive and treat trust as a phenomenon situated outside the realm and the range of power. We can no longer consider ourselves to be rulers in the traditional sense of the word if we want to be able to conceive of trust as a kind of power. In order to make room for understanding trust as power, we must conceive of power in a different, more subtle, and more encompassing way (Power II).

Power as a Capacity

According to this more subtle conception, exercising power is not reducible to ruling. If we say that someone has power, we do not necessarily assert that he has power over and controls someone else. What we claim is that he has the power to do something or make something happen. Consequently, power must essentially be conceived of as a certain capacity or ability.

A person does not have power, however, simply by virtue of the fact that he is able to have an impact of some kind, or exert some influence. Power is more than the ability to affect someone or something. For if it were no more than that, then a noisy passerby who provoked his assailant would have been in power. Power is a performative act (J. L. Austin 1980) in a more directive way than that, since the ability to do something must be understood as the ability to bring about or accomplish something more specific than just a change of some sort. Having power is also, and even essentially so, the ability to effect. It is the ability to bring about or obtain some more or less specific outcome that does not necessarily pre-exist.

In other words, according to this more subtle and general conception of power (Power II), it should be understood as the capacity to affect someone or something, not just in any way, but in ways that effect or bring about certain outcomes, or at least make them more likely.[5]

Dispositional Power

With this more subtle understanding of power, we enter a new plane of existence (Deleuze 1996). We no longer relate directly or primarily to the level of factual states in the world, be they past, present, or even future states of affairs. When discussing capacities, we leave the plane of factual information and begin debating dispositions—that is, tendencies or liabilities for something to happen or propensities for doing something.

Yet it is not exceptional to enter this plane. Ryle draws our attention to the fact that "a number of the words that we commonly use to describe and explain people's behavior signify dispositions and not episodes." According to Ryle, to say that a person knows something, for example, is not to say that he is in a particular state, but that he is able to perform certain things if need be. Moreover, Ryle argues that we use such terms for characterizing a wide range of objects, from atoms and matter to animals and men, as we are "constantly wanting to talk about what can be relied on to happen as well as to talk about what is actually happening" (Ryle 1966: 112). If we say, for instance, that a rubber band is "elastic," we point at a certain disposition or propensity. We indicate that the band is prone to bend and stretch if affected, and that it is likely to resume its original shape afterwards. Likewise, if we characterize a man as "choleric," we state that he is easily susceptible to anger, but not necessarily that he will be angry each and every time he is provoked, or that he will be angry right now.

In the extreme case, the choleric person may in fact never burst into a fit of anger, given that he is never sufficiently provoked, just as the rubber band may remain elastic during its entire existence without actually being forced to bend or stretch. Still, the dispositions may exist even if they are never triggered or put into action and therefore remain unobservable. Dispositions per se belong to the realm of the "unobservable," even though it is normal to expect them to manifest themselves in what occurs and thus to be perceptible in that way.

Power conceived as a capacity (Power II) also belongs to this same plane of existence, even though the concept refers specifically to the capacity to effect certain social dispositions. When we assert that someone has power, we claim that he or she has the capacity to affect others to the effect that that they become prone to doing certain things or behaving in certain ways.

The Plane of the Virtual

When addressing questions of power and dispositions, we leave the realm of the factual (Ryle 1966: 112). Instead of confining ourselves to paying attention to actual objects and the actual, we begin to focus on another very real aspect of the world: the virtual (Deleuze 1991: 42–43, 81; 1996). The virtual does not present itself in the form of a certain "whatness" (Heidegger 1976, 1980b) or exist in an intimate pure present (Derrida 1967, 1972). Instead "the virtual" refers to that which makes itself felt as something that acts in and through the present considered as a *Vorhandenheit,* as something at hand (Heidegger 1979, 43c).

As a consequence, the virtual is not to be conceived of as the possible, but as that which effects and is felt through its effects. "It is more apparitional than empirical" (Massumi 2002: 135). The virtual is developed through, and works in, the present as a substance, or as a being and a force (*virtus*) that is operative within it (Leibniz 1969: 26–27). The virtual is a "coming into being, registering as becoming" (Massumi 2002: 135).

This force constitutes the genetic condition of real experience (Deleuze 1991) as it continually modifies the given and forces it to reshape. Giving impetus to the present, the virtual not only sets it in motion, but causes it to unfold itself to the effect that it transcends itself, further developing in certain determinate directions. As an "outside coming in" (Massumi 2002: 135), the virtual makes itself felt when certain trends are coming into force. It acts as a normative influence, to the effect that it predisposes social reality to further develop in certain directions.

When discussing power issues, we focus on the virtual and the dispositional in the sense described as we try to investigate and unfold the level of prescription as the crucial aspect of social reality. We articulate a level upon which we establish guidelines for how it is that we, in interaction with the surrounding world, can emerge and leave our mark. This prescriptive level is a most genuine and important aspect of reality; with regard to power and trust it should be given precedence over the actual insofar as the actual is understood as that which is the case.

The prescriptive level is important, because it has a determining effect not only on what exists, but also on what we imagine possible, and also, therefore, on what is—on being in the broadest sense. Not only does the prescriptive in this sense gain precedence over the actual; it is seen as more important than the existing. The prescriptive has already played a guiding or piloting role as soon as the real can be known as an object of knowledge, as soon as one can imagine the possible as something that might happen, as soon as one can point out the potentially realizable as something one can hope for, or act in order to bring about (Raffnsøe 2002, vol. 3: 373).

According to the conceptualization of power as a capacity, we are capable of exercising power to the extent that we have the competence and the ability to affect others in ways that influence their dispositions, meaning their tendency and ability to unfold themselves as they behave and act in specific ways. In practice, then, power is exercised and is felt as an activity that affects a restructuring of other people's fields of actions. Power conceived of at the level of Power II is to be understood and analyzed as "a mode of actions upon actions" (Foucault 1982: 220). We exercise power to the extent that, through our activity and actions, we are capable of structuring other people's fields of possible actions.

Consequently, power is also to be conceived of as a capacity to "conduct conduct (*conduire des conduites*)" (Foucault 1984: 315).[6] Power is the capability to direct the way people relate to themselves and behave, and it is the capacity to do so in and by the way we relate to and direct ourselves. By conducting our own and other people's conduct, we are able to produce certain effects, to make a certain range of not fully pre-defined outcomes more likely than others.

Power as the Management of Freedom

According to this view, then, the exercise of power is closely associated with the exercise/use of freedom. Since the exercise of power does not fully determine the outcome, power presupposes freedom conceived of as the absence of external impediments (liberty) (as for instance in Kant 1976c: 755) and as the possibility and ability to make choices according to our inner will ("essential," "inner," or moral freedom) (Kant 1976b: 299; 1976d: 78; and elsewhere). In as much as the exercise of power is a mode of action and (re)action upon the actions of others in which we try to overcome and govern the actions of others, yet another demanding conception of freedom presents itself as an active imma-nent condition of possibility for the exercise of power. It is freedom as conceived of in the request formulated by Kant and the Enlightenment for mankind's "emergence" from the easy state of "self-incurred imma-turity" to which people tend, when, due to laziness or cowardice, they submit themselves to "alien guidance" (Kant 1976e: 53).

In this request, freedom confronts us in the form of a demanding challenge or obligation to renounce the easy dependence on external circumstance, and to seize power courageously and resolutely through an independent mode of reflection and action that permits us to over-come the initially given conditions and the impediments and demands they impose upon us. Freedom is understood as an ongoing challenge and obligation to *become* free, an obligation that we have to face and live up to as, by emancipating ourselves, we try to attain maturity (Kant 1976e; Raffnsøe 2010) and assume responsibility for ourselves (Butler 2005).

This relative freedom serves as an internal but irreducible condition of possibility for the exercise of power. At the very heart of the power lie the "intransitivity (*intransivité*)" and irreducibility of freedom and "the insubmissiveness and unmanageability (*rétivité*)" of the will (Foucault 1984: 315).[7] The participants' reciprocal endeavor to overcome existing or potential unfreedom (or in its most extreme form, servitude) and attain maturity constantly challenges the existing power relations and provokes them to reaffirm themselves by unfolding themselves anew.

Superficially, then, power and freedom are contrary terms that may seem incompatible with one another. However, they are certainly not contradictions that exclude each other. Scrutinized more closely, the ir-reducible contrariness between power and freedom creates an ongoing tension and antagonism between them, an ongoing struggle to gain the upper hand in which they provoke each other mutually, thereby forcing each other to transgress the immediately given form. In contradistinction to the doctrine that more power entails less freedom and more freedom presupposes freedom from power, according to this analysis power and freedom may enhance one another, implying more freedom and power. The more freedom is asserted, the more power is forced to exert and expand itself, thereby gaining range and momentum. The more power is exercised as the capacity to influence the dispositions of others, the more it challenges freedom to reaffirm itself as a capacity to emerge as a mature human being by overcoming the challenges posed by alien guidance.

This conception of power tallies with Foucault's statement that power "is exercised only over free subjects, and only insofar as they are free" (1982: 221). It is possible to account for the traditional notion and practice of power within this conception of power, but as a very crude form of power. Exercised and practiced as Power I, power is characterized by the fact that those in power take freedom into consideration, but primarily as a challenge to be minimized by restricting human freedom. As they reduce human beings to passivity, people exercising power in this manner may try to avoid resistance. When doing so, however, they first and foremost act directly upon human beings as objects that can be handled, modified, and used as such. They do not seriously and positively take into account the way people act and exert themselves. At the end of the day, this objectifying and mainly negative display of power in many respects comes close to the simple use of force, or even to violence. Reducing free subjects to subjugated objects, Power I amounts to the exercise of power in a crude and unproductive form.

An Alternative Conception of Trust

Trust versus Confidence

Within the more refined notion of power developed here as Power II, trust can be perceived as a kind of power. Defined as something over and above mere confidence, showing trust may be enacted and perceived as a conscious and reflected way to exercise power.

Simply having confidence in someone or something is a relatively unreflective form of conduct, in that it is the (usually pre-unconscious) adoption of an attitude to continue as before, to depend on a setting that has hitherto been experienced as unproblematic. By contrast, trust involves the adoption of a more active stance, which is especially called for within a modern context where many former familiarities are said to be eroded and self-management is prevalent. Trust is the active resolve to rely and gamble on the reliability of other people or circumstances, despite experienced uncertainty and unpredictability.

So unlike confidentiality, trust is a way of relating to and dealing with unfamiliarity and freedom, as it involves an active resolve to take risks, despite the awareness that one's expectations may be disappointed. Showing trust is essentially a venture, transcending not only what is the case, but also to some extent transcending past experiences (Luhmann 1973: 27). While confidence is oriented toward and determined by the past, trust is essentially oriented toward the future not only in the sense of future expectations (Luhmann 1973: 20), but also in the sense of something essentially unpredictable that may be foreclosed in the future (Løgstrup 1997: 8–28). When we trust someone or something, we actively adopt the attitude to choose risk in anticipation of some future gain that we might not be prepared to predict (Solomon and Flores 2001).

Trust, Fear, and Hope as Anticipatory Affective Attitudes

With the active resolve to show trust, consequently we enter the plane of the dispositional and the virtual. We begin to give prominence to what can be relied on and what may reasonably be expected to happen, over what is actually the case. And we do so with an acute awareness of the risk involved, since an irreducible outside is entering the scene, most likely to shatter or surpass our expectations in various respects.

Hence, conceived of at this level, trust is essentially to be understood as actively trusting the new and unknown. The resolution to actively take a risk and leap into the future is motivated by the conviction that the future will meet and perhaps even surpass the given expectations.

As a firm though emotional conviction turned toward the future, trust is closely related to "anticipatory affects (*Erwartungsaffekte*)" (Bloch 1985, vol. 1: 82–83) such as hope and fear, but in reverse ways. The dread that the future will bring us *nothing* (good) counters and restrains our ability to show trust in the present. In contrast, the longing for *something* (else) to come makes us more inclined to trust.

When we are afraid, what frightens us is less an already given definite past or present threat. What predominantly causes dread is, instead, the anticipation that something negative is going to happen, something terrible that we often cannot entirely predict, but which we cannot avert and must passively undergo. Being affected in this way by the expectation of an anticipated negative future seems to counteract the ability to trust. When predominant, an "anticipation of hurt or injury" (Ahmed

2004: 65) in a given situation makes it almost impossible to adopt a trusting attitude in and to the present.

By contrast, hope—an anticipatory being affected actively by, and yearning for, something that transcends the conditions given in predictable or unpredictable ways—not only counterbalances the tendency to be overwhelmed passively by fear, but concomitantly paves the way for trust. When hoping and trusting, we do not resign ourselves to our fate, as in the case of despair, sloth, and helplessness. Instead of being overwhelmed by the state of things as we find them and projecting that experience onto the future, we make the best of things as we relate to them as conditions for initiating something else that is still in its infancy. When hoping, we cannot help cherishing and being affected by dreams of "a better life ... that might be possible (*das möglich wäre*)" (Bloch 1985, vol. 1: 1). When adopting a trusting attitude, we are detecting whether experience supports anticipations to such an extent that we could, and maybe even should, take the risk of relying upon the experienced conditions, despite an experienced uncertainty. In both cases, however, the anticipation of further fulfillment moves us, as it forces us to reaffirm the given conditions, and ourselves, by reforming them.

Trust as an Informed and Engaging Gift-Giving

When hoping and trusting, we anticipate and focus on an ontology of the yet-to-be as it is mediated through the given here-and-now. In this respect, trust and hope differ from confidence, despair, and power in the limited sense, in that the former resemble dispositional power in drawing attention to the plane of the virtual.

Unlike confidence, but like power, the display of trust may be understood as a capacity or an ability to do something. When showing trust, we concurrently affect the dispositions of others. Entrusting ourselves to others, we hand over part of ourselves to others and thus let others gain power over us. As a consequence, we risk being let down, disappointed, or even betrayed. Precisely because we entrust ourselves to others and take risks, however, we concomitantly begin to affect others to (the) effect that what we fear becomes less likely to happen. In some odd sense, showing trust and thereby delivering oneself over to others has a challenging side to it; a challenge that we must measure up to in the world that we begin constructing together in this way. By exposing part of ourselves or our possessions to others, we act and thereby actively issue the ethical demand that these others should prove themselves worthy of our trust, and should live up to it, whether they actually end up doing this or not (Løgstrup 1997: 8–28).

In this respect, showing trust follows the logic of gift-giving as it has been articulated in anthropological studies, especially by Mauss (1995) and Levi-Strauss (1949). When giving gifts to others, we start creating a total social reality that interferes with and, at least partly, sets aside individual interests. We begin to establish a social bond, in the form of a "moral contract," obliging the participants to enter a reciprocal exchange in which they should, in the long run, preferably give more than they have received, as they return part of their possessions and themselves (Mauss 1995: 148, 271). If gift-giving is habitually associated with freedom, luxury, and generosity, it should equally be understood as a juridically and ethically very demanding social activity.

Similarly, when we hand over part of our possessions or of ourselves by entrusting ourselves to others, we place them under the obligation to take care of and reciprocate this peculiar kind of gift in a proper way. By placing their future activity under the auspices of this obligation, we are able to affect others in ways that effect a change in their dispositions to act. We are able to influence the way people relate to themselves and behave, in and by the way we relate to ourselves as we exhibit trust. Consequently, the resolve to show trust is also a way to exercise power. In particular, it is an exercise of power that is able to take human independence actively into account to make the best of self-management.

Still, whether we are prepared to take the risk of adopting a trusting attitude also depends to some extent on whether past and present experiences give us reason to trust. A trusting attitude must be based on relevant supportive knowledge if trust is to be more than just a starry-eyed confidence, or an obstinate resolve to maintain a certain moral stance by cherishing trust as a universal fixed ethical value (Luhmann 1973). Even when explicitly voiced as trust in the new, trust maintains a close relationship to knowledge (Luhmann 1973; Misztal 1996).[8]

Management by Trust

So on the basis of the account given, the decision to show trust may be conceived of as actively endorsed risk-taking, adopted in anticipation of an additional gain that is not otherwise to be obtained. Up to a point, trust is motivated by relevantly corroborating knowledge and experience. Beyond that, the resolve to adopt a trusting attitude is motivated by hope as an inveterate being affected by a coming into being that transcends the conditions given. In addition, such a stance is supported by the expectation that by handing over a part of ourselves or of our possessions to others in this way, we begin establishing a binding social contract; a mutual ethico-juridical obligation to attend to this gift-giving in a proper way, also by preferably rendering more than we have received. Since this mutual obligation affects the dispositions to act and works as a virtual force that is operative and felt through its effects, showing trust can most decidedly be conceived of as a way to exercise power. Undoubtedly, actively trusting people has the capacity to affect them and make them behave in ways they would not otherwise behave (Dahl 1957).

Once trust is perceived in this way, showing trust can not only be understood as a way to effect something by exercising power, but also approached as a strong vessel for management in its effort to direct and conduct human endeavors and behavior. Management and the exercise of power in a refined and more efficient sense, as Power II, are impossible without trust. In this case, management openly moves beyond the ability to command, coerce, and control as it incorporates gift-giving as an essential and indispensable element. Only if managers are capable of exercising power in this more refined sense will they be able to maintain employee confidence in management, and create confidence-inspiring relationships in today's organizations. At this level, management, power, and trust appear to be obviously interdependent, rather than incompatible. And even as *pouvoir* in the sense elaborated on earlier appears as a sine qua non for management, so trust appears as an unavoidable condition of possibility for management conceived of as a sophisticated way to exercise power.

Acknowledging that gift-giving is a highly obliging activity affecting people's dispositions to act, managers may openly ply the trade of management as an activity of bestowing as well. For instance, managers may offer rewards, give recognition, resources, and feedback to others, even as they may entrust them with the responsibility of handling and managing certain tasks.

In exchange, when showing trust in this manner, managers should acknowledge that they thereby begin to establish binding relationships to and between the people entrusted with these gifts; relationships which affect their disposition to act. This exercise of power in turn furnishes the manager with good reason to believe that in a sufficient number of instances the receivers will take care of the "goods" in an appropriate way and reciprocate by rendering more than what was originally entrusted to them.

Thus, managers should not only be aware that they are taking risks, and consequently be prepared for disappointment now and again. When showing trust, managers should also recognize that they are exercising power and conducting human conduct in ways so demanding that they are very difficult to fully live up to. Consequently, they should be prepared to appreciate the effort to do so even when it fails, and to maintain that the risk was worth taking even when they are disappointed.

Notes

Parts of this contribution appeared first in *Journal of Political Power* 6, no. 2: 241–60, and are reproduced with the permission of the journal.

1. In fifteenth-century Europe, control was habitually associated with the activity of checking accounts and verifying that they were right by comparison with an existing duplicate register that they were supposed to conform to (Onions 1966: 211).
2. Dahl makes this point: "for the assertion 'C has power over R', one can substitute the assertion, 'C's behavior causes R's behavior'" (Dahl 2002: 16).
3. *Dictatus Papae*, issued by Gregory VII in 1075, and *The Assizes of Ariano*, promulgated by *Roger II* of Sicily in 1140, represent early examples of this development (Raffnsøe 2003). In his capacity as king of Sicily, the German Emperor Frederick II later published the more comprehensive *Liber Augustalis* in 1231 (Frederick II 1971).
4. In its earliest, most original form, the term "status" meant "a state of peace," (Luhmann 1989: 83). Only later did the term come to refer to the actor establishing and guaranteeing a peaceful state, if necessary by recourse to force.
5. At one end of the spectrum, "someone" or "somebody" could be any(-)body in movement or activity. At the other end of the spectrum, the being affected, by someone or by myself, could eventually be me. To simplify matters, however, during the rest of this chapter I shall confine myself to focusing on discussing the capacity to affect others.
6. The earlier English "translation" of Foucault's French text somewhat misleadingly reads: "guiding the possibility of conduct" (Foucault 1982: 221).
7. The earlier English "translation" of the French text reads: "the intransigence of freedom" and "the recalcitrance of the will" (Foucault 1982: 221–22).
8. This is equally true of hope. To remain a true conscience of tomorrow, hope, as the expectancy of possibilities yet to come, must also be based on knowledge. If not, hope risks becoming mere reverie, be it as "a disposition of the soul to persuade itself that what it covets will happen (L'espérance est une disposition de l'âme à se persuader que ce qu'elle desire adviendra)" (Descartes 1996: 203; own trans., SR) or as "eine Jenseits-Hoffnung," an "evil of evils" capable of making those who suffer hold out, but also likely to make them put up with the conditions given (Nietzsche 1979: 1183).
   At the same time, it is quite misleading to understand knowledge-seeking as an activity exclusively concerned with the past and the present. Investigations in philosophy and anthropology have led us to consider hope as an implicit "common operative in all knowledge formation" in order to confront the "most fundamental problem" concerning knowledge, which is "what knowledge is for" (Miyazaki 2004: 9).

HOPE IN THE GIFT— HOPE IN SLEEP

Hirokazu Miyazaki

In his chapter, "Empowering Trust in the New: Trust and Power as Capacities," Sverre Raffnsøe investigates the currently pervasive and yet underexamined "trust in trust" as an unproblematic "universal value" in the context of management and management studies. Raffnsøe seeks to define trust in terms of its delicate relationship with power. In his view, trust becomes an effective tool of management when it is recognized as "an active and deliberate exercise of power." What makes Raffnsøe's formulation of trust particularly compelling is his insistence that trust is "motivated by hope" as well as by "knowledge and experience." In other words, there is always an element of uncertainty, unknowability, and indeterminacy in trust, and trust is partially defined by its openness to the future unknown. Raffnsøe offers the gift as an image of trust as a hopeful performance of power. In line with the thoughts that Marcel Mauss famously articulates in *The Gift*, Raffnsøe's attention focuses on the simultaneously free and obligatory character of giving, receiving, and reciprocating: "When we hand over part of our possessions or of ourselves by entrusting ourselves to others, we place them under the obligation to take care of and reciprocate this peculiar kind of gift in a proper way. By placing their future activity under the auspices of this obligation, we are able to affect others in ways that effect a change in their dispositions to act. We are able to influence the way people relate to themselves and behave, in and by the way we relate to ourselves as we exhibit trust" (Raffnsøe in this volume). In this context, trust emerges as a particular "exercise of power" that leaves room for "human freedom." In this sense Raffnsøe's goal is to turn management and management studies into a more humane endeavor capa-

ble of embracing human fallibility and sparking unexpected creativity
and resilience.

No doubt this is an intellectually broad and ambitious interjection
into the field of management studies. My response is limited in scope.
It focuses on Raffnsøe's deployment of the anthropological category of
the gift as a model of trust. I revisit my own earlier ethnographic examination of indigenous Fijian gift-giving, specifically drawing attention to
a particular kind of trust entailed in the Fijian gift and the distinctively
interactional fashion in which the gift obviates the problem of uncertainty, unknowability, and indeterminacy. I then juxtapose the gift-based
model of trust and the labor and work invested in such trust, with an
image of sleep that Catholic theologian Hans Urs von Balthasar invokes
as the ultimate form of trust in his theology of Christian hope. Finally,
I consider the implications of these contrasting models of trust for an
understanding of Japan's crisis following the earthquake, tsunami, and
nuclear disasters of 11 March 2011. To the extent that Japan's crisis is
a crisis of management, here I implicitly revisit Raffnsøe's conceptual
reformulation of the relationship among knowledge, trust, and power
in management. My discussion focuses on the dissonance between the
Japanese government's campaign to promote *kizuna* (bonds), a gift-
like form of relationality characterized by a sense of obligation and indebtedness, between victims of the disasters and the rest of the nation,
on the one hand, and a more quiet, diffused, and yet persistent sense
of distrust among Japanese citizens in their government's management
of (or its capacity to manage) the crisis, on the other hand. I suggest
that Balthasar's notion of sleep as a model of trust surfaces as a compelling response to a situation overloaded with the labor of both trust
and distrust.

Obviating Trust

In my book *The Method of Hope: Anthropology, Philosophy, and Fijian
Knowledge*, I examine a ritual moment in indigenous Fijian mortuary
gift-giving in which gift-givers wait for gift-receivers' response after presenting their gifts (Miyazaki 2004). Holding whale's teeth (*tabua*), the
most significant exchange objects in indigenous Fijian gift-giving, the
spokesman for the gift-givers kneels on the floor and waits for someone
from the gift-receiving side to take the valuables away from him. If
Raffnsøe sees knowledge (experience) and hope in trust, it is precisely
trust in that sense that is at stake at this moment. The trust that gift-givers
place in gift-receivers is anchored simultaneously in knowledge and hope.

In indigenous Fijian gift-giving—which is a part of all kinds of gatherings, from mortuary rites to weddings and conferences—gifts are rarely rejected outright. It is expected that gift-receivers will receive and accept gifts in a respectful and dignified fashion. It is obligatory for indigenous Fijian gift-receivers to receive gifts, to borrow Mauss's original formulation. The moment of waiting is therefore partially about whether gift-receivers conform to this expectation.

That is not the whole story, however. There is a real sense of uncertainty and unpredictability in indigenous Fijian gift-giving. That is because the efficacy of ritual gift-giving is not known until after the fact. Even if gifts are accepted, gifts can be rendered inadequate by later rumors and gossip. Speeches may be deemed poorly executed. Reciprocal gifts may be regarded as insufficient. Illness and death among ritual participants following a gift-giving event may confirm such views. In this context, the efficacy of ritual gift-giving is ultimately unknowable. Hence, the trust that gift-givers place in gift-receivers is also based on hope, that is, hope for the efficacy of the gift.

There is also a second moment of waiting in indigenous Fijian gift-giving. After gifts are accepted, the spokesman for the gift-receivers typically declares that love (*veilomani*) is "the only valuable." Eternal life is invoked as what love alone could ultimately deliver (almost all indigenous Fijians are Christians). All this implies that the act of gift-giving is not ultimately important. The speech delivered by the spokesman for the gift-receivers typically ends with a prayer for God's blessing on all those present.

I have theorized these ritual moments as moments of abeyance of agency. At the first moment, the spokesman for the gift-givers places gift-givers' agency in abeyance temporarily by subjecting gift-givers to the mercy of the gift-receivers. At the second moment, the spokesman for the gift-receivers in turn subjects both sides to God's ultimate mercy. In both cases the completion of one side's action is delegated to the other side, whether it is the gift-receiving side or God.

This play of agency effectively obviates the problem of uncertainty, unknowability, and indeterminacy in indigenous Fijian mortuary gift-giving in two ways. First, the gift-receivers' acceptance of gifts generates hope for God's mercy (the gift of eternal life). This confirms the indigenous Fijian conviction that the proper manner of attendance through submission should elicit the proper type of response and mercy. This confirmation serves as a reason for ultimate hope.

Second, the invocation of hope for God's response (God's mercy) obviates the unknowability of the efficacy of the gift-giving itself. The ultimate unknowability of God's intentions ("Only God knows," as in-

digenous Fijians routinely remark) overrides any human effort to interpret and scrutinize the efficacy of human action (in the form of gossip,
rumors, and so on). In other words, in indigenous Fijian gift-giving, the
problem of uncertainty, unknowability, and indeterminacy is ritually
deferred and thus obviated again and again.[1]

Such continual deferral and obviation in turn repeatedly generates
a moment of "not yet" (Bloch 1986, vol. 1). In this context, hope—the
"not yet"—emerges as a capacity to embrace the profound uncertainty,
unknowability, and indeterminacy of life (and afterlife); to reorient
oneself repeatedly from disappointment and fear; and to commit oneself once again to an act of trust (or the abeyance of agency, in my
vocabulary).

The gift-based model of trust is distinctively performative, interactional, and relational, and the intricate strategic manipulation of agency
(gift-givers versus gift-receivers; or humans versus God) allows hope to
be made anew as a motivator of trust (cf. Raffnsøe in this volume). If
there is something lacking in the gift-based model of trust, however, it
is precisely what its performative, interactional, and relational emphasis occludes. Is it enough for us to keep working on social interaction in
order to keep hope alive?

Putting the Labor of Trust to Rest

Hans Urs von Balthasar, an influential twentieth-century Catholic theologian, posits a slightly different take on trust in his theology of hope.
Balthasar is known for his distinctive, and arguably heretical, position
on hell (see Balthasar 1988: 163). In his view, Christians ought not to
pretend to know God's intentions regarding who is to be saved. Balthasar sees it as the duty of Christians to "have hope for all men" (1988:
163) whether they are Christians or not. For him, the unknowability
of God's intentions is critical to Christian hope and needs to be taken
seriously. For Balthasar, hope, a well-established theological counter-
point to knowledge (certain knowledge, to be more precise), serves as
a method for embracing, and even enriching, such ultimate unknowability and mystery.

It is important to note that the model of the gift serves as an important framework for Balthasar's theology (see, for example, his discussion of the principle of reciprocity in the Trinity). But in his extensive
discussion of the nature of Christian hope, Balthasar introduces an image that seems to exceed the framework of the gift. This is an image of
sleep as an "ultimate" form of "self-surrender" (Balthasar 1998: 187–

88). Salvation may be a gift, but in this context it is not regarded as the direct yield of the reciprocal relationship between humans and God. It emerges as a by-product of ultimate surrender, that is, sleep.

Balthasar's theology of hope is largely inspired by Charles Péguy's poem, "The Portal of the Mystery of Hope" (Péguy 1996). For Péguy, as Balthasar explains, hope is like children:[2] "What inspires him [Péguy] is not so much some goal to be reached in the future as the inexhaustible delight of children who, with their energy and tireless legs, happily repeat the same journey over and over again ... The poet attributes something of the child's vitality to theological hope, on God's part or on man's; for neither of them, ultimately, loses his way, despite fear, grief, anxiety and mortal danger" (Balthasar 1998: 187). Sleep, and night "that is created for sleeping" (Balthasar 1998: 188), emerges as an image of the ultimate form of trust. This trust in turn generates hope. Balthasar points to the following part of Péguy's poem in which God speaks of those who refuse to sleep:

> I'am talking about those who work and who don't sleep.
> I pity them. I'm talking about those ... who don't have the courage, don't have the confidence, don't sleep ...
> They have the courage to work. They don't have the courage to do nothing.
> They possess the virtue of work. They don't possess the virtue of doing nothing.
> Of relaxing. Of resting. Of sleeping ...
> They look after their affairs well during the day.
> But they don't want to give them to me to look after during the night.
> As if I weren't capable of looking after them for one night.
> He who doesn't sleep is unfaithful to Hope (Péguy 1996: 125–26).

What is most striking about Péguy's poem is where it ends. At the end of the poem, Péguy recounts the night in which God witnessed his Son's burial. Balthasar summarizes the ending as follows:

> God recalls [the centrality of sleep to hope] one particular night which came down like a linen cloth to cover the body of his dead Son. It shrouded his sleep in ultimate self-surrender to the Father, and his last hope in him who had apparently disappeared forever. The poet does not insist, does not theologize. He simply takes the best God has designed for his children, namely the renewal of hope in sleep, and combines it with the darkest reality of trinitarian forsakenness (the Father having witnessed the execution of his Son) and the night that has seen the burial of this horror (Balthasar 1998: 188).

Here even God lets sleep and night take over.

I do not intend to elaborate on the broader theological significance of Balthasar's reflections on hope here. The simpler point that I would like to make in response to Raffnsøe's reworking of the concept of trust is this: The model of sleep may offer an alternative, non-interactional, and non-relational model for comprehending the way trust and hope are made anew as capacities.

There is a certain dose of mystery in Balthasar's theology, but perhaps there is a point at which the distinctively secular problem of self-management, and the associated problem of how to manage employees who are expected to manage themselves, gains some traction with this brief theological exploration. Trust is energized not only by hope for reciprocity and more general human sociality, but also by the hopefulness of a rested body and mind. It is fairly self-evident from our daily experience that only a rested body and mind is capable of embracing failure and disappointment and placing trust once again in others.[3] If, as many ethnographic studies have shown, the gift is work (and continual work, to be more precise), sleep is an apt supplement to the gift. In some context, however, sleep may surface as more than a mere supplement to work. I now turn to the crisis of trust in post-Fukushima Japan.

Creating a Space for Resting in the Midst of a Crisis

It was in the midst of Japan's crisis following the earthquake, tsunami, and nuclear disasters when I was reminded of Balthasar's formulation of sleep as a model of hope. In the early afternoon of 11 March 2011, Eastern Japan was hit by a magnitude 9.0 earthquake and shortly later by a massive tsunami. Largely due to the tsunami, more than 15,000 people lost their lives and more than 2,600 people are still missing today. The natural disasters were followed by a nuclear disaster at Fukushima Dai-ichi nuclear power plant. The meltdowns and explosions at the nuclear power plant caused radioactive substance to spread all over a wide area of Eastern Japan. Thousands of residents of the areas surrounding the nuclear power plant were evacuated or voluntarily relocated to other parts of the country.

Immediately following the triple disasters, the Japanese government launched a campaign of *kizuna* (bonds), a call for the nation to unite and support victims of the disasters in Eastern Japan together. The campaign exploited a gift-like sense of obligation and indebtedness to those affected by the tsunami and the nuclear disaster. The idea of *kizuna* served as the predominant framework for the Japanese government's varied efforts to manage the profound uncertainty of the situation logistically, financially, and politically. At the outset, the gravity and seriousness of the nuclear crisis was unclear largely due to the conscious effort to downplay the crisis on the part of Tokyo Electric Power Company (TEPCO), the operator of the nuclear power plant, the nuclear regulatory authority, and the media. The government's emphasis on *kizuna* was a conscious effort to manage this managerial uncertainty.

The crisis was also partially financial. Already heavily indebted, the government needed to secure funding for massive reconstruction work. TEPCO, the largest issuer of corporate bonds in the country, to which mega banks and insurance firms had deep financial exposure, now faced numerous compensation claims and expensive reactor decommission work and immediately surfaced as a threat to the entire economic system. The introduction of new individual and corporate taxes for the reconstruction of tsunami-affected regions, and the injection of massive private and public funds into a mechanism the government set up to keep TEPCO afloat, were all argued for and executed in the name of the victims of the nuclear disaster.

The government also called for various forms of more tangible commitment from the nation. The government made every effort to assure the public of the safety of agricultural products from Fukushima and its vicinity and urged consumers to purchase and eat those products to show their support for Fukushima. The government also implemented a policy to widely distribute potentially radioactive debris from tsunami-affected regions to the rest of the country. In the summer of 2011, the government urged the public to save energy so that the nation might survive the shortage of electronic power due to the shutdown of most of the country's nuclear power plants for safety inspection.

The campaign of *kizuna* took for granted a certain sense of reciprocal trust, not dissimilar to the kind of gift-like trust articulated by Raffnsøe—the government's trust in citizens to unite and strive to overcome the crisis together and citizens' reciprocal trust in the government. However, the campaign failed to garner trust in the campaign itself. Instead, it engendered a deep sense of distrust in the government. The government's efforts to manage the crisis were resisted, albeit quietly, by citizens in many different ways. The government was not able to persuade many citizens to purchase and consume vegetables from Fukushima. The government also encountered strong resistance from various municipal governments and residents to the transportation of potentially radioactive debris to their regions for processing.

Yet, the *kizuna* campaign demanded a great deal of labor and work on the part of citizens beyond volunteering work in tsunami-affected regions, financial contributions to recovery and reconstruction efforts, and various individual efforts to save energy. Their quiet resistance to the campaign itself was labor-intensive. Everyday life in East Japan changed due to the contamination of water and food with radioactive substance. Citizens began daily and routinely to check the amount of radioactive substance in water, air, and food. They also began desperately and yet quietly to search for safer food and water.

What made such work even more burdensome and stressful was the way the *kizuna* campaign made it difficult for citizens to voice their concerns. Citizens' quiet avoidance of food from Fukushima, and their reluctance to accept potentially radioactive debris, were often described in the media as evidence of the lack or loss of *kizuna* in the country. The language of trust embedded in the campaign silenced voices of dissent. Amidst the profoundly uncertain situation, one thing was clear: The nation was exhausted by all the work demanded by both *kizuna* and the quiet resistance to it.

In the midst of this exhaustion, I recalled Balthasar's notion of sleep as a model of hope mentioned above. The idea struck me as simultaneously problematic and compelling in this particular context. On the one hand, it seemed highly problematic precisely because it undermined my own and other citizens' urge to act in the midst of the national crisis. True, the campaign of *kizuna* sounded intuitively objectionable to many partly because it reminded them of the wartime total mobilization campaign, and partly because it disregarded the gravity and magnitude of the ongoing nuclear disaster. And yet, along with many other citizens, I felt obligated to act and search for other ways to contribute to the situation. The call for "self-surrender" seemed to undermine all the work being performed in the name of either trust or distrust.

On the other hand, the idea of sleep seemed compelling precisely because I was deeply exhausted not only by my own daily struggle to avoid exposure to radioactive substance but also by all the work, both positively and negatively, demanded by the campaign of *kizuna*. Balthasar's theology made me realize that it was absolutely necessary for anyone to find time to rest, even briefly, during a crisis. Neither the government's campaign of *kizuna* nor many citizens' quiet campaign of distrust seemed to have left room for such resting.

The need for sleep was briefly invoked in the context of the government's effort to manage the crisis. In the initial few days following the disasters, Yukio Edano, then cabinet spokesperson, became the primary government source of information about the unfolding nuclear disaster. Edano's seemingly sincere effort, day and night, to provide as much information as possible about the crisis and the government's management of the crisis for the public was generally well-received by citizens. Edano's around-the-clock effort prompted a widely retweeted tweet, "Edano, sleep" ("Edano, nero"). But the tweet only indexed the widely shared appreciation of Edano's unceasing communicative efforts in the context of distrust in the government rather than an appreciation of his and the equally exhausted nation's need for sleep.

Japan's crisis is perhaps an extreme case of the problem of trust (and the lack thereof) in management. Indeed, the problem of management always entails the question of how to manage (and balance) work time and rest time. However, the shift from the gift metaphor to the sleep metaphor I suggest here ultimately points to the virtue of a willingness to stop managing altogether (and "do nothing"), at least for a moment. Trust entailed in sleeping is antithetical to the kind of trust entailed in management (and the gift).

Concluding Remarks

The gift is arguably the single most important and longest lasting contribution of anthropology to philosophy. And yet, in anthropology, the debate about Mauss's text, *The Gift,* is still ongoing (see, for instance, Miyazaki 2010). The gift serves as a constant point of disagreement among anthropologists, and the subject remains generative of new theoretical insights for the discipline (Strathern 2006). This disciplinary condition at times makes it difficult for anthropologists to have a meaningful academic dialogue with those outside their discipline who deploy the gift as an analytical framework.

In this response, I have sought to follow my own disciplinary instinct judiciously and have focused on the philosopher Raffnsøe's deployment of the category of the gift in his philosophical discussion of trust and power. My goal has been not so much to critique his use of the gift as to perform my own trust in the gift. As I have argued elsewhere, anthropologists' continual trust in the gift lies in the extensibility of the category (Miyazaki 2005, 2010). Anthropologists have sought to extend anthropological theories of the gift to a broad range of contemporary topics from organ transplants to financial transactions. By extending the gift, anthropologists have also expanded the contours of the category of the gift. Anthropologists have sought to keep the gift an open category in the spirit of its underlying openness. By juxtaposing the gift to the idea of sleep, I have sought to achieve the same effect by putting this disciplinary trust to rest.

Notes

1. For a similar analysis of the ritual staging of radical uncertainty, unknowability, and indeterminacy, see Webb Keane's account of Eastern Indonesian gift-giving rituals (Keane 1997).
2. Péguy writes,

   "Children don't even think about being tired.
   They run like little puppies. They make the trip twenty times.
   And, consequently, twenty times more than they needed to.
   What does it matter to them. They know well that at night
   (But they don't even think about it)
   They will fall asleep
   n their bed or even at the table
   And that sleep is the end of everything.
   This is their secret, this is the secret to being indefatigable.
   Indefatigable as children.
   Indefatigable like the child Hope.
   And always to start over again in the morning" (Péguy 1996: 123).
3. In his presentation to the "Hope in Law and the Economy" conference held in New York City in April 2010, Ghassan Hage made a similar observation about the hopefulness of a rested body.

REFERENCES

Adorno, Theodor W., and Max Horkheimer. 1992. *Dialektik der Aufklärung.* Frankfurt: Suhrkamp.

Ahmed, Sara. 2004. *The Cultural Politics of Emotions.* Edinburgh: Edinburgh University Press.

Aquinas, Thomas. 1974. "On Princely Government to the King of Cyprus [De regimine principum ad regem cypri]." In *Aquinas: Selected Political Writings,* edited by Alessandro P. D'Entreves. Oxford: Oxford University Press.

Aristotle. 1989. *Metaphysics.* Cambridge, MA: Harvard University Press.

Austin, John. 1968. *The Province of Jurisprudence Determined and the Uses of the Study of Jurisprudence.* London: Weidenfeld and Nicolson.

Austin, John L. 1980. *How to Do Things with Words.* Oxford: Oxford University Press.

von Balthasar, Hans Urs. 1988. *Dare We Hope "That All Men Be Saved"? With a Short Discourse on Hell.* Translated by David Kipp and Lothar Krauth. San Francisco: Ignatius Press.

———. 1998. *Theo-Drama: Theological Dramatic Theory.* Vol. 3, *The Last Act.* Translated by Graham Harrison. San Francisco: Ignatius Press.

Barney, Jay B., and Mark B. Hansen. 1994. "Trustworthiness as a Source of Competitive Advantage." *Strategic Management Journal* 15: 175–90.

Bentham, Jeremy. 1977. *A Comment on the Commentaries and a Fragment on Government.* London: Athlone Press.

———. 1983. "Constitutional Code." In *The Collected Works of Jeremy Bentham,* vol. 1, edited by R. Rosen and J. H. Burns. Oxford: Clarendon Press

Bloch, Ernst 1985. *Das Prinzip Hoffnung,* vol. 1–3. Frankfurt: Suhrkamp Verlag.

———. 1986. *The Principle of Hope,* vol. 1–3. Translated by Neville Plaice, Stephen Plaice, and Paul Knight. Cambridge, MA: MIT Press.

Bramming, Pia, et al. 2011. "Roundtable: Management of Self-management." *Ephemera* 11, no. 2: 212–24. Available at http://www.ephemeraweb.org.

Butler, Judith. 2005. *Giving an Account of Oneself.* New York: Fordham University Press.

Calton, Jerry M., and Lawrence J. Lad. 1995. "Social Contracting as a Trust-Building Process of Network Governance." *Business Ethics Quarterly* 15, no. 2: 271–95.

Cavell, Stanley. 2003. *Disowning Knowledge in Six Plays of Shakespeare.* Cambridge: Cambridge University Press.

Chandler, Alfred D. Jr. 1977. *The Visible Hand: The Managerial Revolution in American Business.* Cambridge, MA: Harvard University Press.

———. 1990. *Scale and Scope: The Dynamics of Industrial Capitalism.* Cambridge, MA: The Belknap Press.

Covey, Stephen M. R. 2006. *The Speed of Trust.* New York: Free Press.

Dahl, Robert A. 1957. "The Concept of Power." *Behavioral Science* 2, no. 3: 201–15.

———. 2002. "Power." In *Power: A Reader,* edited by Mark Haugaard. Manchester: Manchester University Press.

Danto, Arthur C. 1973. *Analytical Philosophy of Action.* Cambridge: Cambridge University Press.

Dasgupta, Partha. 1988. "Trust as Commodity." In *Trust: Making and Breaking Cooperative Relations,* edited by Diego Gambetta. New York: Basil Blackwell.

Deleuze, Gilles. 1991. *Bergsonism.* New York: Zone.

———. 1996. "L'actuel et le Virtuel." In *Dialogues,* edited by Gilles Deleuze and Claire Parnet. Paris: Flammarion.

Derrida, Jacques. 1967. *De la Grammatologie.* Paris: Les Éditions de Minuit.

———. 1972. "Ousia et Grammè." In *Marges de la philosophie.* Paris: Les Éditions de Minuit.

Descartes, René. 1996. *Les passions de l'âme.* Paris: Flammarion.

Foucault, Michel. 1976. *La Volonté de Savoir.* Paris: Editions de Gallimard.

———. 1980. "Two Lectures." In *Power Knowledge: Selected Interviews and Other Writings,* edited by Colin Gordon. New York: Pantheon Books.

———. 1982. "Afterword: The Subject and Power." In *Michel Foucault: Beyond Structuralism and Hermeneutics,* by Hubert L. Dreyfus and Paul Rabinow. Chicago: University of Chicago Press.

———. 1984. "Deux Essays sur le Sujet et le Pouvoir." In *Michel Foucault: Un Parcours Philosophique: Avec un Entretien et Deux Essays de Michel Foucault,* edited by Hubert L. Dreyfus and Paul Rabinow. Paris: Éditions Gallimard.

———. 2003. *"Society Must Be Defended": Lectures at the Collège de France 1975–1976.* Basingstoke, UK: Macmillan.

———. 2007. *Security, Territory, and Population: Lectures at the Collège de France 1977–1978.* London: Penguin Books.

Frederick II. 1971. *The Liber Augustalis; or, Constitutions of Melfi, Promulgated by the Emperor Frederick II for the Kingdom of Sicily in 1231.* Syracuse, NY: Syracuse University Press.

Friedman, Nelson. 1999. Introduction to "I, Pencil: My Family Tree as told to Leonard E. Read." Irvington-on-Hudson, NY: The Foundation for Economic Education, Inc. Available at http://www.econlib.org/library/Essays/rdPncl0.html.

Fukuyama, Francis. 1995. *Trust: The Social Virtues and the Creation of Prosperity.* London: Hamish Hamilton.

Gambetta, Diego. 1988. "Foreword." In *Trust: Making and Breaking Cooperative Relations,* edited by Diego Gambetta. New York: Basil Blackwell.

Hage, Ghassan. 2010. Presentation at the "Techniques of Hope" conference. New York, NY. April 2010.

Hart, Herbert L. A. 1979. *The Concept of Law.* Oxford: Clarendon Press.

Hart, John K. 1988. "Kinship, Contract, and Trust: The Economic Organization of Migrants in an African City Slum." In *Trust: Making, and Breaking Cooperative Relations,* edited by Diego Gambetta. New York: Basil Blackwell.

Hegel, Georg W. F. 1972. *Grundlinien der Philosophie des Rechts.* Frankfurt: Ullstein.

Heidegger, Martin. 1976. *Platons Lehre von der Wahrheit.* Bern: Francke Verlag.

———. 1979. *Sein und Zeit.* Tübingen: Niemeyer.

———. 1980a. "Der Ursprung des Kunstwerkes." In *Holzwege.* Frankfurt: Vittorio Klostermann.

———. 1980b. "Die Zeit des Weltbildes." In *Holzwege.* Frankfurt: Vittorio Klostermann.

Hobbes, Thomas. 1969. *The Elements of Law.* London: Frank Cass.

———. 1979. *Leviathan.* Middlesex, UK: Penguin Books.

Kant, Immannuel. 1976a. *Kritik der reinen Vernunft,* vol. 1. In *Werkausgabe,* vol. 3, edited by W. Weischedel. Frankfurt: Suhrkamp.

———. 1976b. *Grundlegung zur Metaphysik der Sitten.* In *Werkausgabe,* vol. 7, edited by W. Weischedel. Frankfurt: Suhrkamp.

———. 1976c. *Metaphysik der Sitten.* In *Werkausgabe,* vol. 8, edited by W. Weischedel. Frankfurt: Suhrkamp.

———. 1976d. *Kritik der Urteilskraft.* In *Werkausgabe,* vol. 10, edited by W. Weischedel. Frankfurt: Suhrkamp.

———. 1976e. "Beantwortung der Frage: Was ist Aufklärung." In *Werkausgabe,* vol. 10, edited by W. Weischedel. Frankfurt: Suhrkamp.

Keane, Webb. 1997. *Signs of Recognition: Powers and Hazards of Representation in an Indonesian Society.* Berkeley: University of California Press.

Kohn, Marek. 2008. *Trust: Self-Interest and the Common Good.* Oxford: Oxford University Press.

Leibniz, Gottfried W. 1956. *Vernunftprinzipien der Natur und der Gnade. Monadologie.* Hamburg: Felix Meiner Verlag.

Leth, Jørgen, and Sverre Raffnsøe. 2011. "Tripping up the Perfect." In *Ephemera* 11, no. 2: 189–203. Available at http://www.ephemeraweb.org.

Levi-Strauss, Claude. 1949. *Les Structures Élémentaires de la Parenté.* Paris: Presses Universitaires de France.

Lewis, Carlton T., and Charles Short. 1879. *A Latin Dictionary.* Oxford: Clarendon Press.

Locke, John. 1963. *Two Treatises of Government.* Cambridge: Cambridge University Press.

Lopdrup-Hjorth, Thomas. 2011. "Governing Work Through Self-Management". In *Ephemera* 11, no. 2: 97–104. Available at http://www.ephemeraweb.org.

Luhmann, Niklas. 1973. *Vertrauen: Ein Mechanismus der Reduktion sozialer Komplexität.* Stuttgart: Verdinand Enke Verlag.

———. 1989. "Staat und Staatsräson im Übergang von traditionaler Herrschaft zu moderner Politik." In *Gesellschaftsstruktur und Semantik,* vol. 3. Frankfurt: Suhrkamp.

Løgstrup, Knud E. 1997. *The Ethical Demand.* Translated by Theodor I. Jensen and Gary Puckering, revised by Hans Fink and Alasdair MacIntyre. Notre Dame, IN: University of Notre Dame Press.

Machiavelli, Niccolò. 1977. *The Prince.* New York: W.W. Norton.

Massumi, Brian. 2002. *Parables for the Virtual.* Durham, NC: Duke University Press.

Mauss, Marcel. 1995. *Essai sur le don: forme et raison de l'échange dans les sociétés archaïques.* In *Sociologie et Anthropologie.* Paris: Presses Universitaires de France.

———. 2010. The Gift : *The Form and Reason for Exchange in Archaic Societies.* London: Routledge Classics.

Misztal, Barbara A. 1996. *Trust in Modern Societies.* Cambridge: Polity Press.

Miyazaki, Hirokazu. 2004. *The Method of Hope: Anthropology, Philosophy, and Fijian Knowledge.* Stanford, CA: Stanford University Press.

———. 2005. "From Sugar Cane to 'Swords': Hope and the Extensibility of the Gift in Fiji." *Journal of the Royal Anthropological Institute* 11, no. 2: 277–95.

———. 2010 "Gifts and Exchange." In *The Oxford Handbook of Material Culture Studies,* edited by Dan Hicks and Mary Beaudry. Oxford: Oxford University Press.

Morriss, Peter. (1987) 2002. *Power: A Philosophical Analysis.* Manchester: Manchester University Press.

Nietzsche, Friedrich. 1979. *Der Antichrist: Fluch auf das Christentum.* In *Werke III,* Friedrich Nietzsche. Frankfurt: Ullstein.

Onions, Charles T. 1966. *Oxford Dictionary of English Etymology.* Oxford: Oxford University Press.

Oxford English Dictionary. Available at http://www.oed.com.

Péguy, Charles. 1996. *The Portal of the Mystery of Hope.* Translated by David Louis Schindler Jr. Grand Rapids, MI: William B. Eerdmans.

Putnam, Robert D. 2000. *Bowling Alone: The Collapse and Revival of American Community.* New York: Simon & Schuster Paperbacks.

Raffnsøe, Sverre. 1996. "Reorganizing Society." In *Law, Justice and the State IV,* edited by Mikael M. Karlsson and Olafur P. Jonsson. Berlin: Archiv für Rechts- und Sozialphilosophie.

———. 2001. "Order Ordealed: Norms and Social Coherence in the Age of Law." *Readings in Philosophy and Science Studies* 1: 120–46.

———. 2002. "English Summary." In *Sameksistens Uden Common Sense, Doctoral Dissertation,* vol. 3, by Sverre Raffnsøe, 372–414. Copenhagen: Akademisk Forlag.

———. 2003. "The Rise of the Network Society". Copenhagen: MPP WP 24/2003. Available at http://xn--raffnse-v1a.com/wp-content/uploads/

Sverre-Raffnsøe%B8e-The-Rise-of-the-Network-Society-An-outline-of-the-dissertation-2003.pdf.

———. 2010. "The Obligation of Self-management: The Social Bonds of Freedom." In *Villum Foundation & Velux Foundation, Annual Report 2009,* edited by K. J. Petersen and H. Tronier. Søborg: Villum Foundation & Velux Foundation.

———. 2012. "The Five Obstructions: Experiencing the Human Side of Enterprise." In *Ephemera* 11, no. 2: 176–88. Available at http://www.ephemer aweb.org.

Rousseau, Jean-Jacques. 1964. *Du Contrat Social: Ecrits politiques.* Paris: Gallimard.

Ryle, Gilbert. 1966. *The Concept of Mind.* Middlesex, UK: Penguin Books.

Shakespeare, William. 1977. "King Lear." In *The Complete Works of William Shakespeare.* London: Murray Sales & Service Co.

Smith, Adam. 1976. *The Theory of Moral Sentiments.* Oxford: Oxford University Press.

———. 1991. *The Wealth of Nations.* London: Random Century Group.

Solomon, Robert C., and Fernando Flores. 2001. *Building Trust in Business, Politics, Relationships, and Life.* Oxford: Oxford University Press.

Strathern, Marilyn. 2006. "A Community of Critics? Thoughts on New Knowledge." *Journal of the Royal Anthropological Institute* 12, no. 1: 191–209.

Taylor, Frederick W. 1967. *The Principles of Scientific Management.* New York: W.W. Norton.

Webster's Third New International Dictionary. Available at http://www.mwu .eb.com.

Wicks, Andrew, Shawn L. Berman, and Thomas M. Jones. 1999. "The Structure of Optimal Trust: Moral and Strategic Implications." *Academy of Management Review* 24, no. 1: 99–116.

Wren, Daniel A. 2005. *The History of Management Thought.* Hoboken, NJ: John Wiley & Sons.

WITH KIERKEGAARD IN AFRICA

JOINT STATEMENT

Anders Moe Rasmussen and Hans Lucht

This interdisciplinary exchange concerns the connection between self-transcendence and hope. It is an exchange of thoughts rooted in very different academic traditions but concerned with the same topic and the same problem. Anders Moe Rasmussen gives an account of a fundamental feature of being human, namely our capacity to transcend ourselves and our world, thereby interpreting hope as a special kind of self-transcendence. Hans Lucht, on the other hand, uses a concrete ethnographic study to explore how hope is experientially kept alive in the everyday give and take of human life. Even in situations involving the utmost uncertainty and danger, Lucht argues, existential reciprocity nourishes a hope that whatever is given up, or lost, to powers outside one's control, will potentially be substituted by something of commensurate worth. Distinguishing between different forms of self-transcendence, Rasmussen specifically deals with two distinctive ways in which a human being can distance himself from the world, and from himself. Humans have the capacity to step outside themselves in such a way that they radically call themselves into question as being nothing but products of an anonymous process, devoid of any meaning and significance. This is where the phenomenon of hope is born, as the counterpart to the experience of utter uncertainty and distress. Hope, however, is also a kind of self-relation, as it concerns an understanding of one's life and world as a unity and a whole. This is illustrated through an interpretation of Søren Kierkegaard's notion of faith as it is propounded in his book *Fear and Trembling,* in relation to the bible story of Abraham's sacrifice of Isaac. Lucht deals with this same story, and with Kierkegaard's interpretation of it, in an account of his ethnographic fieldwork in a small Ghanaian fishing community, where villagers struggle to come to terms with losing loved ones who undertake the high-risk venture of emigrating to Europe.

Self, Hope, and the Unconditional
Kierkegaard on Faith and Hope

Anders Moe Rasmussen

After years of pragmatic and strategic thinking within the contemporary political debate, the concept of hope has reappeared on the agenda, most prominently in the American president Barack Obama's rhetoric of hope. This is interesting news, as it holds the potential to revitalize both the political and the cultural debate, which are stuck in discourse theory and the platitudes of anti-ideology. However, the exact meaning of this new talk of hope still remains somewhat unclear. What is more, we have yet to consider whether it makes any sense at all to speak about hope in a contemporary context. Perhaps the disappearance of utopian thought over the last two to three decades, and the emergence of an "engineering model" for society, is simply a consequence of the long-drawn-out process of secularization reaching back to the modern Enlightenment. This observation could be supported by the fact that the concept of hope is intimately connected with religious thought and language; that is, with the language of an afterlife or a world beyond the one we know. I am not divulging any deep, dark secret by stating that these religious ideas have been under severe attack over the past three to four hundred years. The criticism of religion, which was such a fundamental part of the Enlightenment project, was directed not only against the idea of God as the creator and sustainer of the world, but just as much against the idea of a god being the redeemer, or the idea that a supranatural world existed.

Accordingly, the currently evolving model of both social life and individual existence as an engineering project could be seen as just an-

Notes for this section begin on page 242.

other expression of the last step in modern Enlightenment culture; the final victory of the idea of finitude. But as everyone knows, in painting the current situation we must use many shades of gray, as the so-called secularization theories that announce the end of religion seem to have failed utterly—and perhaps the new discourse of hope has to do with the much-debated return of God. Yet despite recent talk of God, we still face great difficulties when thinking and talking about hope in a contemporary context. There is still the pressing question of whether it makes sense to talk about hope without any references, implicit or explicit, to the religious idea of an ultimately better world, a world beyond. If, indeed, we are living in a secularized world, this raises a most severe and seemingly unsolvable problem, as it must equally be maintained that hope seems to be a basic feature of human existence. Despite secularization and despite the hypostasis of finitude, we seem exceedingly reluctant to abandon the notion of hope. And so the essential question is whether it is possible to speak of hope without any reference to the idea of an afterlife and a world beyond this one. What does hope mean when disconnected from this idea, and what are the consequences of giving up hope? Is it a fact that for us, the sons and daughters of modernity, nihilism is the only option, meaning nihilism in the twofold sense of either resignation or aggressive self-assertion. These two questions set out the general framework for my investigation of Søren Kierkegaard's concept of hope, asserting that the work of Kierkegaard not only offers a very precise diagnosis of the malaise of modern culture, but also prescribes some very interesting remedies to cure it. Before turning to Kierkegaard, however, it is appropriate to assess the sense in which hope can reasonably be said to be a basic feature of human existence, and this exercise calls for some general considerations concerning the nature of human beings. Only through an investigation that asks certain fundamental questions about human cognitive capacities and human agency can hope be made intelligible as a basic feature of human life.

Hope as a Basic Feature of Human Life

Fundamentally, human beings are creatures of distance, or rather distances, as human existence contains a multitude of distances. This "distance-based" quality of human life or, to put it otherwise, its decentralized nature, is also essential in understanding hope. Hope is a specific kind of distance, or a specific kind of relation toward the world and the self. Making this clear involves the initial clarification of other basic forms of distancing that characterize the human being. The following clarifies and displays three basic forms of distance, ultimately leading to an analysis of the kind of distance that characterizes hope. This undertaking is quite a complicated and complex enterprise, given that besides each form having a specific structure of its own, the various forms of distance are interconnected in an intricate network. That is why the considerations below in this chapter mainly appear as general observations that only loosely comment on the interconnectedness that exists between the different forms of distance.

In his masterpiece *Being and Time* from 1927, Martin Heidegger claimed that the fundamental feature of human existence (in German: *Dasein*) was being, as he put it, "disclosed" (*erschlossen*), and this in a twofold manner: being disclosed or open toward the world, and being disclosed or open toward oneself. According to Heidegger, human existence is not something fixed or enclosed, but rather something radically transcendent. In fact, the concept of "transcendence" plays a major role in Heidegger's early philosophy. By stating this, Heidegger thought himself to be radically breaking with the dominant strand of modern philosophical thinking stretching back to Descartes, namely the enterprise of grounding all the fundamental investigation concerning human cognition and action in the concept of subjectivity or self-consciousness. According to this tradition of philosophical thinking, human self-consciousness obtains its privileged position due to its absolute enclosedness and transparency. Without otherwise involving the philosophy of Heidegger—and actually, in certain ways the following reflections stand in direct opposition to his philosophy—we will follow Heidegger's questioning of this core idea in modern thinking, as well as his theory about being disclosed in the twofold manner mentioned above.

Let us first take a closer look at disclosing oneself to the world, which is the first basic form of distance characteristic of human existence. When talking about openness toward the world, we are addressing the classical epistemological problem concerning the nature of human experience and cognition. Accounting for this problem simultaneously implies giving an account of the human mind, since the mind plays an indispensable role in any explanation of our knowledge of the world. No cognition is separable from the knowledge that the knowing subject has of himself. In other words, knowledge of something is simply the ability to distinguish it from the elementary knowledge that one has of oneself. This intriguing relationship between mind and world can be, and has been, investigated in various ways in the history of philosophy. To avoid an excess of detail, I will confine myself to two accounts of the relationship between mind and world that merit special mention: the account given in the transcendental philosophy of Immanuel Kant, and Peter Strawson's semantic version of Kantian transcendental philosophy.

Kant's transcendental philosophy can be summed up as a demonstration of the indissoluble correlation between the unity of the self-consciousness and the unity of the world. According to Kant, we cannot interpret the unity of nature or the world without interpreting the unity of mind. In that sense we are legislators of what counts as an experience, but we can only serve as such legislators insofar as we interpret the unity of the mind in relation to the unity of the world. If we restrict theoretical reflections merely to mental activity without investigating the mind's correlative picture of the world, we are speaking of something different than mind. In proving this interconnectedness between mind and world, Kant takes, as his point of departure, the Cartesian conviction that it must be possible to know that any knowledge or experience I have is mine. This idea about the identity of the cognizing subject is absolutely fundamental to any account of knowledge of the world, and Kant never calls it into doubt. But the mere nature of the human mind does not imply that it is self-contained. When discussing the mine-ness of knowledge in terms of his famous "I think must accompany all of my thoughts" (Kant 1999: 132), Kant stresses that the "I think" implies nothing but *his* I, meaning that the self is a purely empty notion. Consequently, there is no particular thought that is part of the definition of the thinker, or rephrased: self-knowledge is never self-contained, as it always transcends itself. Not acknowledging this structure of self-consciousness in claiming that the definition of a thinker involves a particular thought is what makes up the mistake of Descartes and all other rational psychology, resulting in the insolvable problems that Kant examines in the so-called paralogism of his *Critique of Pure Reason* (1999).

We now come to Peter Strawson's semantic version of Kantian transcendental philosophy, and it is important that we distinguish between two different attempts to give a semantic account of self-consciousness. The first attempt claims that all questions concerning self-consciousness can be settled by investigating how the index-word "I" is used. The meaning of this word is to refer to, or identify, the speaker who is actually uttering the word. Consequently, the person who meaningfully utters this word stands in a relation to his or her self. The problem with this form of semantic ascent to self-consciousness is that it does not explain anything about the topic, as it presupposes rather than explains self-consciousness. The ability to use language meaningfully presupposes that the speaker himself knows what he is uttering, and likewise that he also intends to convey what he means to others.

The semantic ascent of Peter Strawson, famously put forward in *Individuals: An Essay in Descriptive Metaphysics* (1959), is of a very different nature. According to this theory, the meaning of the word "I" cannot be explained without taking other index words—such as "you" and "he"—into consideration. The use of these index words implies identifying singular entities, or rather, it implies the ability to identify, because indexicals only imply the possibility of identification. From this interconnectedness of the index words, Strawson draws the conclusion that the use of the word "I" presupposes a whole world-order, which in Strawson's terms is an order of individuals, meaning bodies and persons (persons being bodies that simultaneously can be ascribed the capability of a rational use of language). This is the semantic version of the self-transcendence or self-distance connected to human beings as knowing and cognizing individuals.

Moving on to the second form of self-transcendence, or the second form of distance characteristic of human beings, let us first look at a problem that is inherent in Strawson's semantic account of self-knowledge. The simple question of what it means for someone to be able to use the web of index words is enough to shake the whole semantic construction. The fact that the very ability to use the web of index words also implies that we are dealing with a person does not, in itself, address the question. The problem can therefore only be solved when the concept of a person can be applied to the speaker himself, and being able to do this presupposes that the speaker knows what it means to know of himself. In other words: self-consciousness can neither be derived nor explained by the use of the word "I." However, this being a fact is just another example of a general feature of self-consciousness: that it cannot be explained by anything external to itself. Self-consciousness seems to be a paradigmatic instance of something totally self-contained or self-absorbed ruling out any kind of transcendence. This is the truth of the Cartesian notion of the "ego" as *fundamentum inconcussum*. Yet once again, complexities arise: The fact that self-consciousness cannot be explained by something external to itself does not imply that it is able to explain itself. In the case of self-consciousness we encounter something that is both fundamental and irreducible, and at the same time complex and opaque. That is the enigma of self-consciousness. The complexity of self-consciousness is manifold, but all of its different complexities can be traced back to what could be called the essential structure of self-consciousness, which is the interconnectedness between what one knows in knowing oneself and what one knows *is* oneself. The "What?" and the "How?" of self-knowledge are intimately connected, but they are not connected in such a way that no distinction can be made. The fact that self-consciousness is fundamental does not imply that it can explain itself. It can neither be explained from without, nor from within.[1] Having established this, we are in a position where we must inevitably ask about the origin of self-consciousness or subjectivity—and this is the second form of distance or self-transcendence. The analysis of the complex and opaque structure of subjectivity is the philosophical counterpart of a commonly asked question: the "Whence?" of human existence. Based in ordinary life, this "Whence?" expresses a distinct form of transcendence or distance.

However, this question and this distance are also the offspring of two opposed reactions that concern human life and the human world in its totality: *nihilism* in the sense of a negation of life, and *hope* in the sense of an affirmation of life. Both nihilism and hope are interpretations of human life as a whole, or as a *totality*. I will return later to the notions of nihilism and negation, on the one hand, and hope and affirmation, on the other. But before turning to these issues, we have to ask ourselves what an interpretation of life in its totality means. Is it possible to give an account of such a perspective on life? Approaching this problem brings us closer to a third kind of distance, or a third kind of self-transcendence. While the first two forms of self-transcendence could be called theoretical, the third is of a practical nature.

Life in Its Totality

Human beings not only relate to themselves when pursuing a goal or performing an act; they also possess the ability to relate to life in its totality. This kind of self-relation is closely associated with the feature commonly attributed to human beings as that which distinguishes us from other creatures: the ability to distance ourselves from our immediate impulses and volitions, or to otherwise tame or frame our capacity to judge or evaluate our own volitions, thereby creating the potential for these volitions to change a goal of action. In this way, as famously phrased by Harry Frankfurt, freedom can be interpreted in terms of practical self-transcendence (Frankfurt 1988: 11–25). However, closely connected with this is another kind of practical self-distance, insofar as there is a way of relating to oneself that is not concerned with one's own single, particular wants and goals of action, but with life in its totality. Human beings are able not only to ask about the status of their own particular volitions, but also to ask more expansive questions such

as "How do I want to live my life?" or "How do I understand myself as
a person?" Asking this sort of second-order, practical questions implies
withdrawing oneself from the multitude of one's plans and projects to
collect oneself in reflecting on one's life as a whole. Moreover, the possibility of asking such second-order questions also opens up the problem of freedom, as it calls into question the classical Kantian notion
of freedom, referring to the capacity of human beings to deliberate between competing reasons, and thus to exercise of kind of self-causality.
When confronted with questions about what is ultimately most important in life, such deliberations are easily bypassed. However, rather than
digressing into a discussion of freedom, I will instead attempt to unfold
the phenomenology of relating to one's life in its totality.

There are two forms of relating to life in its totality, namely a passive form and an active form. The *passive form* can perhaps best be
characterized by Heidegger's concept of *Stimmung* or mood, as most
explicitly formulated in paragraph 29 of *Being and Time*. Heidegger's
concept of *Stimmung* entails two seemingly quite different aspects. On
the one hand the notion of *Stimmung*, paradigmatically through anxiety, reveals the absolute indeterminacy of human existence—which, according to Heidegger, is the fundamental structure of human existence
or *Dasein* in Heidegger's vocabulary. On the other hand, *Stimmung* entails an evaluative aspect. In both respects, *Stimmung* documents itself
in its difference from affects, insofar as moods are non-intentional affects that are not concerned with particular objects or particular states,
and in the case of evaluative moods they reveal or report the overall
state of a person. Moods such as boredom and despair entail a "totality
account" of the good things and bad things in a person's life, while at
the same time placing them in some sort of order according to their
significance for the person in question. The *active form* of relating to
life in its totality makes the passive evaluation entailed in the moods
explicit by asking the questions mentioned above: "How do I want to
live my life?" or "What is of genuine importance in life?" Asking such
questions is asking about a unity or unification of life, and the capacity
to do so is something specific to human beings. This way of relating to
life is a response to another tendency in human existence: the tendency
to engage in the manifold practices and objectives of life. This tendency
to diversify is a result of the fundamental human feature of not being
bound to the environment. Human beings are creatures that live in a
permanent state of strife between multiplicity and diffusion on the one
hand, and unification and concentration on the other. Another essential aspect of questions that concern the totality and unity of life is that
even though they are questions about a unitary "How?" of relating, the

unity is not to be found beside the manifold projects and plans, but as a unitary "How?" in the attitude toward them.

Two other features of relating to oneself as a totality must be addressed to complete the phenomenology of this third kind of self-transcendence. Although it presupposes the capacity to rise above one's immediate impulses, the practical question concerning the totality of life is not a necessary consequence of this capacity. Equally, the anthropological fact of the non-fixed character of human existence, its independence of the environment, does not produce a totality perspective on life by itself. It is connected to experiences of a certain kind; experiences in which life appears to have an incontrovertible and unavoidable clarity or evidence. This being a fact, the totality perspective is not the result of a decision; it is something that happens to us while, at the same time, we are agents interpreting our lives. Here the link between the second form of self-transcendence, the origin of subjectivity, and the third form, the totality perspective, becomes transparent—as creatures like us, without the capacity to ground ourselves, are permanently sensitive to experiences and interpretations in which life appears in a total and final perspective.

Coming back to the notion of hope, we can conceive of hope as a specific form of self-transcendence in the above-mentioned twofold sense: Hope is both an experience and an attitude. It is an experience in the sense that something happens to us that we do not produce in and of ourselves, and it is an attitude in the sense that we respond to this happening in terms of an interpretation in which life appears in total and final clarity. One more thing must be added, however. As mentioned above, hope is a reaction to what was called nihilism, meant in the specific sense of a life or worldview according to which life is nothing but an outflow indifferent to all human aspirations. Hope is striving for an image of the self that transcends the finitude of life in terms of the imperatives of self-preservation. It is the idea that the meaning of life does not equate with the pursuit of goals and their achievement. Thus, hope negates that the only significance that can be attributed to life is derived from the interests that we are simply unable to abandon. This negative aspect of hope points to a certain dialectical rationality inherent in human existence. As a final interpretation of life and world in their totality, hope entails a certain kind of knowledge. Nihilism and hope share a common root, as they are the legitimate answers to the opaqueness of subjectivity, and indeed equally legitimate answers—and so the antagonism arises. Any person who hopes knows about nihilism as the worldview that is definitely negated or ruled out, and vice versa. In other words, hope is an experience and an interpretation of life according to which life is legitimized in its aspirations, an image of the self that transcends the imperatives of self-preservation (see Henrich 1982: 131–41).

Kierkegaard on Hope and Faith

With this threefold explanation of self-transcendence in mind, we now turn to Kierkegaard's notions of hope and faith, particularly as they are developed in his book *Fear and Trembling* from 1843. In doing this we will be concentrating on the third kind of self-transcendence concerning the perspective of the totality of life. A new question regarding the third form of self-transcendence will be discussed in this context, namely whether it makes sense to talk about a totality perspective on life without introducing the idea of "transcendence" in the sense of something being "not of this world."

Before doing this, however, we will try to outline what ought to be conceived of as the overall agenda of Kierkegaard's thinking. Kierkegaard is fighting two positions: nihilism on the one hand, and religious orthodoxy on the other, and I would not hesitate to claim that this circumstance ought be taken into account in any analysis of Kierkegaardian thought. To a greater or lesser degree, this constellation of nihilism and orthodoxy is present in all of Kierkegaard's works. It is precisely this agenda that makes him a companion of classical German philosophy, from Kant to Hegel, however savagely he may fight this philosophical tradition throughout all of his writings. The force motivating all the philosophers following in Kant's footsteps is the struggle to escape the dilemma between nihilism, produced by radical Enlightenment thinkers such as Spinoza, and anti-modern religious orthodoxy.

In Kierkegaard's writings, however, nihilism means something different than Spinozean naturalism, and nihilism actually seems to have two very different meanings. On the one hand nihilism refers to a loss, or even a negation, of reality. This aspect of nihilism, which goes back to the German writer and opponent of the Enlightenment Friedrich Jacobi, plays an important role in Kierkegaard's polemics against the speculative philosophy of classical German philosophy in general, and of Hegel's philosophy in particular: Kierkegaard reflects speculative philosophy in modern culture, and vice versa, portraying modern life as unreal and lost in abstractions. On the other hand, nihilism refers to a view of life according to which human life is pointless, insignificant, and permeated by illusions about its intrinsic value. In Kierkegaard's writings, this kind of nihilism, pointing in the direction of classical interpretations of modern nihilism in Nietzsche and Heidegger, is often interwoven with the first-mentioned manifest in his concept of despair, which plays such a vital role in his work.

Nevertheless, in his book *Fear and Trembling*, which contains his interpretation of the bible story of Abraham's sacrifice of Isaac, Kierkegaard unambiguously describes a nihilistic experience of the pointlessness and insignificance of human life. In the passage called "Eulogy to Abraham" at the beginning of the book, Kierkegaard writes:

> If a human being did not have an eternal consciousness, if underlying everything there were only a wild, fermenting power that writhing in dark passions produced everything be it significant or insignificant, if a vast, never appeased emptiness hid beneath everything, what then would life be but despair? If such were the situation, if there were no sacred bond that knit humankind together, if one generation emerged after another like forest foliage, if one generation succeeded another like the singing of the birds in the forest, if a generation passed through the world as a ship though the sea, as the wind through the desert, an unthinking and unproductive performance, if an eternal oblivion, perpetually hungry, lurked in waiting for its pray and there were no power strong enough to wrench its clutches—how empty and devoid of consolation life would be! (Kierkegaard 1983: 15)

This passage is pivotal for everything that Kierkegaard writes about in the rest of the book, that is: faith and hope. Faith and hope are the response to the nihilistic nightmare portrayed in the quotation. But in talking about faith and hope Kierkegaard is not referring to the religious ideas of an afterlife or a world beyond. That is the modernity of Kierkegaard's thinking. Confronted with the possibility of the utter irrelevance of life, religious orthodoxy and religious symbols, such as the idea of a world beyond, provide no convincing answers. Religious thought has always known about the possibility of a nihilistic worldview, but up until the period of Enlightenment it had been possible to construct a bulwark of religious orthodoxy for protection. The entirely new situation for modern man, including Kierkegaard, is that these fortifications have fallen, and that is the reason why the nihilistic interpretation of life and world becomes more than a possibility, since it now appears inescapable. This is the situation that Kierkegaard is confronted with, and the background against which his reflections on hope and faith should be interpreted. Of Abraham, who he refers to as "the hero of faith," Kierkegaard writes:

> Yet Abraham had faith, and had faith for this life. In fact, if his faith had only been for a life to come he certainly would have more readily discarded everything in order to rush out of a world to which he did not belong. But Abraham's faith was not of this sort, if there is such a faith at all, for actu-

ally it is not faith but the most remote possibility of faith that faintly sees
some of its object at the most distant horizon but is separated from it by
a chasmal abyss in which doubt plays its tricks (Kierkegaard 1983: 20).[2]

Here Kierkegaard states that faith does not refer to the idea of a world
beyond. Rather, faith is completely incompatible with the idea of a world
beyond, and the rest of the book is solely concerned with explaining a
new meaning of faith and hope. This new meaning of faith is an essential part of Kierkegaard's general project of responding to the challenge
posed by a nihilistic view of life. Small wonder, then, that Kierkegaard
explains his new concept of faith and hope in anthropological terms.
To be sure, *Fear and Trembling* is a theological treatise defending faith
against reason, protesting *in casu* against Hegel's concept of faith as
something simple and unsophisticated, but it is just as much an essay
on anthropology. In his effort to show that faith is not something simple,
base, or unsophisticated, Kierkegaard describes faith in terms of move-
ments of human existence. In Kierkegaard, there is no contradiction
between theology and anthropology. Kierkegaard became the father of
modern protestant theology in claiming that one cannot talk about God
without talking about man.

In Kierkegaard's work the concept of faith refers to a variety of
things. Faith refers to Christian faith in Jesus Christ; to an epistemological concept; and to an anthropological category. In other words, faith is
explained in categories of human actions and relations. As mentioned
earlier, an important objective of his book is to portray faith and hope
as something distinct from a sentiment or an emotion. As he says:
"Precisely because resignation is antecedent, faith is no esthetic emotion but something far higher; it is not the spontaneous inclination of
the heart but the paradox of existence." (Kierkegaard 1983: 47). To describe faith in this way is to inscribe into it a notion of distance or
transcendence, which is explicitly stated in Kierkegaard's description
of faith as a "double movement." Faith is a double movement in the
sense that it is both a transcendence of the finite and a return to the
finite. Kierkegaard calls the transcending movement "resignation" and
the descending movement "movement by way of the absurd."

This brings us to the point where we can apply the taxonomy of
self-transcendence established above to Kierkegaard's work in general,
and to *Fear and Trembling* in particular. Knowing of Kierkegaard's general neglect of epistemological questions, it comes as no surprise that
the first kind of self-transcendence, the openness of the subject toward
the world, is almost entirely lacking in Kierkegaard's work. The two
other forms of self-transcendence are present, however. Kierkegaard
works with a notion of subjectivity both as a theoretical problem, con-

cerning the structure and the origin of the self, and as a practical problem, concerning existential kinds of self-relations. To a large extent, the two so-called psychological works by Kierkegaard—*The Concept of Anxiety* and *The Sickness Unto Death*—can be read as investigations into the structure and origin of the self, most explicitly witnessed in the famous opening section of *Sickness Unto Death*, where the author reveals the opacity of the self, its incapacity to ground or to explain itself, and how this inevitably raises the question of its origin. The passage reads: "The human self is such a derived, established relation, a relation that relates itself to itself and in relating itself to itself relates itself to another" (Kierkegaard 1980: 13). Posing this question about the origin of the self also implies opening up the possibility of a nihilistic interpretation of life, as developed in his investigation of the different forms of despair, which follows right after his structural analysis of the self. So Kierkegaard has both a historical or sociological theory of nihilism, and an anthropological theory. Nihilism is more than a product of modern culture; it is just that in modern culture forming a possible view on life and world inherent in human existence becomes urgent.

Moving on to the third form of self-transcendence—our ability to relate to our life in its totality—this could be said to be the essential problem in Kierkegaard's thinking and a cornerstone of his existential theory of the self. In his eminent theory of the "stages of life," which distinguishes between the aesthetical, the ethical, and the religious stage of a human life, all of the steps are, of course, significant. In a certain sense, however, the transition from the aesthetical to what Kierkegaard calls "the ethical" is the essential step that makes the religious stage a variation on the ethical; certainly a most decisive variation, but still a variation. Considering Kierkegaard's distinctive demarcation between the ethical and the religious stages, most explicitly set out in *Fear and Trembling*, this claim seems utterly inadequate. When looking more closely at what constitutes the ethical stage, namely what he calls the "choice of the self," the claim appears much more plausible. Now, what does this often-cited phrase "choice of the self" actually mean? It is, in fact, extremely difficult to identify the exact meaning of the phrase, but if we interpret it in terms of the third form of self-transcendence, the perspective on life as a totality, we can capture its essence. In looking at the way in which Kierkegaard describes the difference between the aesthetical and the ethical, it is worth noting that the aesthetical is more than pure immediacy leaving all reflection and distance behind. This implies that the ethical is more than the ability to rise above one's own immediate desires. The capacity to transcend is not something that applies uniquely to the ethical. It is just as much a part of what makes up the aesthetical. What is distinctive of the ethical is a specific kind of self-distance, that of relating to one's own life as whole, or as a totality. This kind of self-relation lies at the heart of the "choice of the self," as this notion is intimately linked with the ideas of "continuity," "collection," and "coherence" of life that dominate Kierkegaard's description of the ethical stage in the second book of *Either/Or* (Kierkegaard 1992). The decisive step in Kierkegaard's theory of "stages of life" is the step where one relates to one's life in its totality, and the religious stage, faith and hope, is nothing but a variation on, and a qualification of, this type of self-relation.

Faith and hope, in Kierkegaard's sense of these words, are to be understood in terms of self-relation. And nowhere else in the works of Kierkegaard does this become as clearly evident as in *Fear and Trembling*, where he describes what he calls the "double movement of faith." Describing faith in terms of the "double movement," which is the movement of rising above finitude and one's own particular goals and returning to them, means describing faith in anthropological terms, or rather in terms of self-relation; and the kind of self-relation entailed in faith is that of relating to life in its totality.

Conclusion

Three aspects of self-transcendence qualify the religious stage of life. First of all, there is the relation to God. Although Kierkegaard does not derive the religious, in the sense of God being radically different from the world, by means of the "choice of the self" he nevertheless shows the futility of making something earthly the absolute standard of one's life. Kierkegaard's first major work, *Either/Or*, essentially deals with the fragility of totally devoting oneself to something particular—be it a certain cause that fills one's life with meaning, or a person (family member or friend) who matters ultimately to one—because all of these standards of orientation and meaning can vanish. The nature of one's relation to God entailed in faith is such that it cannot simply be lost. This is ultimately exemplified in the Old Testament figure of Abraham, recounted in *Fear and Trembling*, where Abraham is called the "Father of faith" by virtue of his absolute obedience toward God.

Moreover, hope and faith cannot simply be products or results of a choice or a decision. Actually, we ought to conceive of hope much more as something to be received, as a command or a gift, or applying the theological vocabulary: as an act of divine grace. There can be no genuine concept of hope and faith without this aspect of passive acceptance. In Kierkegaard's *Fear and Trembling,* this aspect of passive acceptance is most dramatically articulated by God's calling of Abraham, commanding him to sacrifice his only son. Passivity, however, remains only one aspect of hope, as hope is also intimately linked with human action or human activity in the sense that hope is a response to a call. In Kierkegaard's primordial text, this active aspect of hope is illustrated by Abraham's action of resolutely setting out to fulfill the command that God has given him.

Thirdly, as stated above the relation to one's life as a whole is a question of "How?" It is a question about an attitude toward life in its totality, or an interpretation of the self and the world as a whole. Another hero of faith and hope in *Fear and Trembling* can illustrate this. A far less dramatic hero than Abraham, namely the so-called tax collector, who lives a life as commonplace as can be. Nevertheless, he has gone through the double movement, and however closely one inspects this man, nothing is revealed—and yet everything has changed:

> Here he is. The acquaintance is made, I am introduced to him. The instant I first lay eyes on him I set him apart at once; I jump back, clap my hands and say half aloud: "Good Lord, is this the man, is this really the one—he looks like a tax collector." But this is indeed the one. I move a little closer to him. Watch his slightest movement to see if it reveals a bit of heterogeneous optical telegraphy from the infinite, a glance, a facial expression, a gesture, a sadness, a smile that would betray the infinite in its heterogeneity with the finite. No! I examine his figure from top to toe to see if there may not be a crack through which the infinite would peek. No! He is solid all the way through ... And yet, yet the whole earthly figure he presents is a new creation by virtue of the absurd. He resigned everything infinitely, and then he grasped everything again by virtue of the absurd. He is continually making the movement of infinity, but he does it with such precision and assurance that he continually gets finitude out of it and no one ever suspects anything else (Kierkegaard 1983: 39–41).

Describing hope and faith in this way means picturing these concepts in terms of a radical change. This change is a change of attitude toward life as a whole, a change that does not deny finitude, but denies that finitude equates with the iron laws of self-preservation. This is also the essential point in Kierkegaard's almost heretic concept of God. In *The Sickness Unto Death,* he states his position as follows: "To pray is also to breathe, and the possibility is for the self what oxygen is for breathing. Nevertheless, possibility alone or necessity alone can no more be the condition for the breathing of prayer than oxygen or nitrogen alone can be for breathing. For prayer there must be a God, a self—and possibility—or a self and possibility in a pregnant self sense, because the being of God means that everything is possible, or that everything is possible means the being of God" (Kierkegaard, 1980: 40). This quotation entails, so to speak, the anthropological version of Kierkegaard's theological doctrine of the "absolute paradox"—God's incarnation in the transitory world—which speaks about God and the unconditional in terms of the categories "necessity" and "possibility" as existential ways of life. The ultimate point of human existence is the unity of facticity and possibility, meaning that the actual and transitory world, and one's actual and transitory life, are precisely the place where a radical change can happen. According to Kierkegaard, there is no world beyond the one we know, and faith and hope have nothing to do with such a world. This does not imply, however, that we are left with the nihilistic view of the world, according to which there is nothing more to life than the natural interest that the human being is simply unable to abandon.

Kierkegaard's interpretations of hope and faith in terms of a self-relation point to a position in which the idea of a radical change, so intimately connected to religious thought, is stripped of all religious orthodoxy. By securely establishing the idea of radical change and the idea that in the transitory, present experiences of something unconditional can take place, Kierkegaard offers us a conception of hope—such a fundamental feature of human existence—that amounts to more than plain engineering pragmatism. Hope does not resist nihilism and resignation in simple optimism of progress and growth rather than in experiences of the unconditional, but affirms transitory reality as the place where something radically new can happen.

Notes

1. For a detailed discussion of the complex structure of self-consciousness, see Dieter Henrich (1999: 49–73).
2. See also the important footnote in *Sickness Unto Death*, which reads: "Moreover, lest it be overlooked, from this point of view one will see that much of what in the world is dressed up under the name of resignation is a kind of despair; in despair to will to be one's abstract self, in despair to make the eternal suffice, and thereby to be able to defy or ignore suffering in the earthly and the temporal. The dialectic of resignation is essentially this: to will to be one's eternal self and then, when it comes to something specific in which the self suffers, not to will to be oneself, taking consolation in the thought that it might disappear in eternity and therefore feeling justified in not accepting it in time" (Kierkegaard 1980: 70).

KIERKEGAARD IN WEST AFRICA
Hope and Sacrifice in
a Ghanaian Fishing Village

Hans Lucht

Based on ethnographic fieldwork in a small fishing village on the Ghanaian coast of the Gulf of Guinea, this contribution explores how the erratic marine environment is drawn into a relationship of mutual obligation through symbolic exchange encounters. Through gift-giving and sacrifice, the positively unresponsive sea is experientially imbued with hope; hope that one's appeal for a response will be met, and that by giving one will receive something of commensurate worth in return for one's efforts. The sea is thus drawn into the fishermen's sphere of influence, and they are provided with a sense of having a say in deciding the direction of their lives. This being so, I explore whether this phenomenon of giving, and giving up, is a fundamental human response to the unequal balance of power between human desire and the world's notorious unwillingness to accommodate it. Or as Jacques T. Godbout has framed the dilemma, "Humans have always given of themselves, have always created obligations in order to achieve a modicum of serenity vis-à-vis all that overwhelms them" (Godbout 2000: 219). In dialogue with Anders Moe Rasmussen's work on Kierkegaard's notion of hope, I discuss whether this movement—the continuous giving, and giving oneself up to external powers beyond one's control—is a fundamental human strategy of substituting the indifferent and imperfect outside world of emptiness and unresponsiveness with a moral world where accounts are kept, where one has the attention of the powers by which one is sustained, and where "it does not rain on the just and unjust alike" (Kierkegaard 1985: 57). Though tested on an everyday

Notes for this section begin on page 254.

basis, this kind of existential reciprocity (Lucht 2011: 96–105), I argue, connects individual and collective needs to outside reality; it provides a real sense of participation in decision-making on vital matters, and gives hope in continuous existence.

A Breath of Fresh Air

In Senya Beraku, the small fishing village in Ghana's Central Region where I have conducted anthropological fieldwork since 2002, sacrifice is the central individual and collective strategy of maintaining hope that the villagers' all-important relationship with the marine environment and the powers dwelling there—which is the wellspring and mainstay of village life—can be continuously renewed, and life with its ups and downs can be drawn into a relationship of mutual obligations. Thus, every five years, the gods of the sea are presented with a bull. The animal is decapitated on the main square, its blood is mixed with secret herbs and collected in pots, and the pots are then paddled by young men in three different directions and the blood given to the gods. The gods consume the blood and in the process contract the obligation to allow the village fishermen access to the fish in the sea for another five years (sometimes longer, sometimes shorter) provided they adhere to various taboos. This is not to say that the fish now jump into the canoes by themselves, or that the fishermen are somehow free of the toil and hardships of fishing, but that there is hope, on the vast and empty sea; that their efforts—an appeal for a response as much as a technical matter—do not go unreciprocated. Of course, this inevitably has to happen from time to time, and great efforts are invested in speculation as to why one crew comes back empty-handed whereas another crew returns singing and celebrating, laughing and teasing the fishmongers, often their wives or sisters, who rush into the surf with pans on their heads to receive the triumphant crew. The women buy the catch and take it to the marketplace, while calling attention to certain expenses— schooling, medicine, and food—that need to be taken care of before their husbands hit the taverns. This brings a visible breath of fresh air that swirls through the streets, into the barbershops, around the gambling tables, the taverns, the grocery shops, the churches, the diviners, the marketplace, the chief fisherman's house, and the compounds of the fishermen's extended families.

By giving not only a sacrificial animal but also one's time, effort, and hard work—one's unmitigated practical engagement—the outside world somehow becomes morally obliged to give back, or is at least expected to avoid taking sinister courses of action. The world is transformed from being one of unresponsiveness and distance to a moral world with human-like attributes that one can believe in and trust. Obviously, this form of anthropomorphism is not exclusive to West African canoe fishermen. It is, instead, a common feature of human life-worlds, based not so much on a contemplative or strategic effort but rather constituting a "natural" attitude toward the world into which human beings are thrown, and which may encompass the cosmos, natural phenomena, the environment, technology, ideas, all people and things, and all the creatures in between (cf. Ingold 2006; Jackson 2002).

But this immediate world of reciprocal-exchange encounters appears to be perpetually haunted by the threat of unresponsiveness; that is, efforts may pass unnoticed, obligations may be forgotten, and the giving of symbolic gifts may be outright rejected. In canoe fishing, for instance, when after almost an hour of incredibly hard work the purse seine is retrieved and the net is empty—when the efforts put forward are not reciprocated with anything but seashells and crabs—everyone sinks into a moment of silence and individual speculation that stands in stark contrast to the intense singing and collaboration before the net was pulled in. "It's like work for nothing," the chief fisherman once bitterly remarked after such an incident, which seemingly caused the whole crew to brood over the pointlessness of their efforts. As Lévi-Strauss has pointed out, a relationship of indifference can never be restored once the exchange has been initiated, and the distance established by unresponsiveness—even when not accompanied by aggression—is in itself a source of suffering (Lévi-Strauss 1969: 59). But such setbacks in canoe fishing are not unusual, of course, and only create a moment of tension in the ongoing trust placed in the sea and the powers dwelling there, keeping in mind the long-standing and relatively successful (if sometimes erratic) history of exchanges with the marine environment, which has provided the village with a steady source of life and livelihood since the dawn of time, according to village myth. Indeed, if there were some way of avoiding the unpredictability of the sea and the sudden ruptures it causes in the life-worlds of the fishermen, trust would not be necessary (Luhmann 1991: 31).

Empirically, these little setbacks may be the clearest way of illustrating the centrality of existential reciprocity in the practical maintenance of the fabric of everyday life, in the sense that focusing on those little events where one's efforts are thwarted and a rupture suddenly occurs—momentarily inhibiting or freezing human action, even to the extent of calling one's very existence into question—speaks of a practical framework of reality that otherwise remains unrecognized. For instance, all drivers, Anthony Giddens argues, have at some point experienced passing a serious car accident at the roadside, and immediately felt engulfed by anxiety. Although there is no reason to slow down, everyone reduces their speed for the next few kilometers, displaying extra caution as they retract and reflect on the endless uncertainties threatening their own lives, as if some kind of unarticulated memorandum of mutual understanding and coexistence had been torn to shreds in front of their eyes. At some point, as they continue to drive on, the moment passes and normal speed is gradually resumed (Giddens 1992: 55). This is because, under normal circumstances, when the terror of unresponsiveness and the rupture it creates has lost its intensity, most people manage to revert back to another experiential reality; a taken-for-granted reality, in which one has a sense of one's presence in the world as real, alive, and continuous, and a sense of the outside world as consisting of a permanent, reliable, and substantial whole (Laing 1973: 39). D. W. Winnicott describes this basic trust in the foundations of personhood and outside reality as a product of the all-important— yet somehow also unconscious and effortless—intersubjective encounters between the human infant and its primary caretaker. Here, a well-groomed hope is patiently installed: a hope that what is needed, materially, socially, and existentially, will potentially be available—although perhaps not at the exact moment the desire is felt (Winnicott 1962: 138–40). However, this sensation of outside responsiveness, Michael Jackson argues, not only pertains to the social world, but also to the world at large; to every source of life that human beings may turn to for attention, regardless of ontological status (Jackson 2002: 341). To put it differently, and follow Giddens once again, human beings stand in a continuous relationship with "a shared—but unproven and improvable—framework of reality" that precedes engagement with the outside world. This is a framework that is "simultaneously sturdy and fragile," but which has an assumed nature, susceptible to exchange and moral of nature, that makes it possible to venture into the world with a sense of purpose and wholeness (Giddens 1992: 36), "knowing" that around every corner waits not an endless abyss of arbitrariness and negation, but rather a possibility, an opening, something that matters to one's continued well-being. And if not, as is often the case in life, one can accept the loss in the hope that there is always a next time, and a next time after that.

Fear and Trembling

The paradoxical creation and strained maintenance of this moral world is also the focus of Kierkegaard's *Fear and Trembling,* and as the title of the thesis implies, giving up everything in the face of powers beyond one's control is no small effort. Nevertheless, the alternative, Kierkegaard suggests, is even worse. Against nihilism and religious orthodoxy—the two popular positions he was writing against at the time, following Moe Rasmussen—Kierkegaard argues that, "If an unfathomable, insatiable emptiness lay hid beneath everything, what would life be but despair ... if one generation succeeded the other as the songs of birds in the woods, if the human race passed through the world as a ship through the sea or the wind through the desert, a thoughtless and fruitless whim ... how empty and devoid of comfort would life be!" (Kierkegaard 1985: 49). And yet the religiously orthodox person, Kierkegaard argues, seeks exactly this kind of fundamental rupture between himself and his surroundings, in that he sees little or nothing of value in the outside world. Quite the contrary: he has banked everything on the afterlife. The nihilist too—the ancestor of modern utilitarian man—has severed his ties to the world, and to the past and the future, and lives in a fragmented, solitary moment, perhaps taking pleasure in some sort of defeatist agency, as if knowing that everything is pointless and useless somehow makes one the co-creator of the inevitable outcome.

Following Kierkegaard, if one's understanding of the world is based on this quintessentially modern rupture between oneself and a cold and unresponsive world—a world that gives no hope or assurance that one's needs are accommodated, or one's efforts and appeals responded to—then how would one carry on with even the simplest tasks of everyday life, without falling prey to radical uncertainty or the "despair" of "insatiable emptiness"? Though the rupture may be upheld discursively, nourished by bouts of alienation, it provides little direction for human actions and relations and says little about the social and existential "truth" of human experience. In human lives, Jacques T. Godbout argues, giving and giving up to powers beyond our control appears to be the fundamental human response to this unequal balance of power between human wants and needs, and the unresponsiveness of outside reality whereby a living and reverberant moral horizon substitutes the hollow and whimsical external world. Though Kierkegaard's treatise and prescription to the challenge is fundamentally a religious one, resigning everything to God and taking it back by an act of faith, he does ask questions of anthropological importance, as Moe Rasmussen suggests. At the core of Kierkegaard's analysis of a moral and practical default reality, we also appear to find symbolic exchange encounters that keep emptiness and arbitrariness at bay and substitute infinite options with mutual obligations. To get on with normal day-to-day business, human beings give and give themselves up to the powers that overwhelm them, creating hope that not everything is possible but that one's surroundings are attentive and benign, or at least refrain from unconventional actions that will destroy hope in the "fragile" but "sturdy" contract.

The Gift of Death

But how does the sacrifice of Isaac by Abraham translate into everyday secular existence? This is a question that Kierkegaard devotes some attention to, as Moe Rasmussen notes, though it is not really systematically explored and remains perhaps a little unclear. Kierkegaard's enigmatic example of an everyday "knight of faith," who has given everything up and taken it back "on the strength of the absurd," is depicted in the prosaic image of the tax collector (this ancient symbol of oppression and materiality is surely not chosen by coincidence). His "sacrifice" consists in not having pot roast for dinner after having fantasized about pot roast, walking home through Copenhagen. Why would Kierkegaard choose to compare such a provocatively insignificant "loss" to Abraham's sacrifice of his son by his own hands—unless, of course, carrying loss well (which means not giving up hope that tomorrow will be another day, another opening), in whatever minuscule scale, is the paradigmatic clue to "infinite resignation"? The everyday demands of the existential give and take of life, at once sustaining and depriving a person, is a fundamental challenge that rings through existence and constantly threatens to lay bare the "insatiable emptiness" of life and to which human beings can only respond by giving up—though sometimes people are made to give up more than can be reasonably or ethically asked with no assurance that life will be brought back to acceptable terms. But the crucial demand is that the "sacrifice" has to be real and absolute and thoroughly "absurd." In the Isaac and Abraham story, it is only when God has seen that Abraham offers him *the gift of death*—the death of something even more precious than his own life—that he sends an angel to intervene. Abraham is stopped only when there is no longer any question of whether he had resolved to kill Isaac on God's command, and the sacrifice therefore was consummated. Only then is life, and the world of human ethics, suspended by the hideous sacrifice, restored (Derrida 1995: 72).

In everyday life too, Derrida argues, demands that take one outside the order of human ethics are the most "common thing" in the sense that to meet the demands of the outside world, and the powers one is sustained by, one must turn one's back on what one owes absolute commitment (Derrida 1995: 67). To confirm social worlds, one has to "give death" to what one loves—one's most precious and private matters—without calculation or certainty that life will be returned to a normal state. Yet, Derrida struggles to come up with strong examples of this sacrifice in its mundane expressions. From a Senya Beraku perspective, however, this existential dilemma in its most deadly and dreadful incarnation is played out in contemporary high-risk migration to Europe, which I will explore in the following section. Against the growing unresponsiveness of the outside world—whether it's the now-barren West African marine environment or the global shadow lands of late modernity (Ferguson 2006)—the deadly migrant voyages to Europe "gives death" to somehow re-establish a horizon of hope and once again rejuvenate life. That is to say, to confirm village life one has to risk one's own life in the desert or on the high seas; place it in the hands of God, as the migrants literally say, and not just one's own life, but something more precious, the entire family's future.

Everything Has Collapsed

To return to Senya Beraku, even a well-proven and trusted world is not immune to the shock of unresponsiveness. For years now, canoe fishing in Senya Beraku, and the whole West African region, has been radically declining, and the immediate effects are felt not only on a social and economical level but also on an existential level. So, while jobs in the fishing industry are disappearing, and families are struggling, the fishermen are concerned with certain changes in the marine environment; the composition of reality, as it were, is somehow disintegrating. Thus, many say the sea has not just become difficult to predict, even capricious, but it has also undergone a physical transformation, emphasizing how insufficient response to one's needs and desire changes one's perception of the environment. Now, some fishermen argue, the sea is "lighter," "too swift," and "thin" as if no longer rich with promise, and slow with familiarity but indeed characterized by "emptiness" in both the literal sense and in the symbolic sense that it offers no shelter for local aspirations in a changing world. Possibly fueled by the many millenarian churches in Senya Beraku, there is a belief that the decline in fishing signals the end of world, which may be true in an existential sense. Everything appears lost and the situation somehow unchangeable.

Talking to James Otoo, 37, a seasoned fisherman from Senya Beraku in February 2013, brought home the reality of the radical decline in West African canoe fishing.

"Everything has collapsed. People are dying. It's like a big disaster has come upon us," he said.

James Otoo explained how he was trained as a fisherman by his father and started his education by scooping out water from the hull

of the canoe, and then later handled the outboard motor. Gradually, he
was taught "to read" the waves and the seabirds and assess correctly
the movement of a school of fish, and to cast the net.

"I have really lost out. I never took a proper education because the
fishing provided for us. Now, the fish are gone, and I don't have anything and I can't read or write."

He blames the outside trawlers and the Chinese and the "Whites"
for ruining their catch by ploughing up their fishing grounds and for
using dragnets that "destroy the sea."

"We know that they are under pressure in their own countries, and
that is why they come here. They are fighting for survival, but so are
we. Soon, we will be forced to do anything to survive, armed robbery
or taking that crooked road to Europe."

James Otoo is the father of four children, and he is trying to put
them through school so that they will have an education. He works
mostly off Ivory Coast now, but the fishing is collapsing there too, and
his plan is to make an attempt for Libya "if God would only bless him"
with sufficient funds to make it across the desert. He knows it is dangerous but he feels he cannot just "sit down" and do nothing.

As another fisherman told me, "Come back in ten years, and you'll
find nothing here." This is perhaps Kierkegaard's nihilistic nightmare—a
place and its people fading into oblivion, and blown aimlessly like "the
wind through the desert" (Kierkegaard 1985: 49).

The Future Is Dark Here

As mentioned earlier, one of the more dangerous and spectacular strategies for avoiding the upheavals in village life (and perhaps, more generally, for pursuing the hopes and dreams of many younger people in
African countries "abandoned to their fate" in the political economy
of the globalized world [Cohen 2006: 1]) is high-risk immigration to
Europe.[1] Here, focusing on the question of hope and sacrifice, I will explore how bringing new life to local worlds that are under pressure often
comes at great cost. In the wake of the Arab Spring, rickety boats from
North Africa are once again landing in great numbers on the shores of
southern Europe, many others disappearing on the way. But although
risking one's life in the desert and on the Mediterranean is an extreme
measure, it is not unusual that reaffirming social worlds, as Derrida
argues, will bring one into the realm of sacrifice (Derrida 1995: 69).

During one such death-defying voyage in 2003—so an informant
told me during fieldwork among undocumented West African migrants

in Naples, Italy—one passenger declared upon departure that he would eat sleeping pills to avoid the horrors of drowning in the Mediterranean should the overcrowded boat capsize on the way. If, on the other hand, the boat arrived safely, he would wake up as a new man, having made it to the destination that is expected to radically alter one's circumstances, and bring one in tune with the hopes and dreams of social and material advancement that are so extraordinarily difficult to achieve in many parts of Africa (despite the fact that the realities of undocumented migrant life in Europe often turn out to be a huge disappointment, and even more so because of the social and existential expectations associated with the journey). For some reason, this short anecdote of somehow cheating death, waking up a new person in a new world, has stuck in my mind ever since. There is no doubt that the desire to advance in life without encountering the risk of death, or at least, by altering one's state of consciousness, without encountering the fresh and unique terror engendered by the nearness of death, is one reason why the story was remembered and retold, to the amusement of most of its listeners. Yet the story, and the smiles it evoked, revealed not only the desirability of painless and effortless transformation but also a deep-seated understanding of such transformations as not being achieved easily, and certainly not in a state of oblivion, but always in a state of "anguish." Gift giving with all its perils and ambiguities, including, apparently, a suspension of the ethical to the demands of the Other, inevitably involves "anguish" in the sense that "only one who draws the knife gets Isaac" (Kierkegaard 1985: 57).

To be sure, migrant experience is all about sacrifice and about giving up one's life. Leaving home and loved ones, gambling with safety on the road and on the high seas; living from hand to mouth in a strange land, where one is barely tolerated socially or politically, or, as in Greece, a target of violent attacks by the extreme right. To have a life and a future at home one has to sacrifice one's social position and human dignity and become a faceless nobody on the bottom of society in the big cities of Europe.

Yet, the dangerous path from Senya Beraku to southern Europe does not guarantee the desired transformation, to some its more like jumping from the frying pan into the fire.

Immanuel, whom I met in Treviso in Northern Italy in the summer of 2013, came from Senya Beraku in 2002 and found work in a Diesel jeans factory. His job consisted of making new denim trousers look worn (in itself a somewhat cruel irony that poor West Africans are hired to make our clothes look used—as if they are somehow experts, being beaten and battered by the road and the lack of opportunities at home—because Europeans have disassociated themselves with the kind of "dirty work" that would in reality wear out our clothes, reserving it for the migrants, while at the same time retaining a curious desire to associate ourselves with manual labor on a purely aesthetic level) but the chemicals involved gave him pains, and in 2008 the work was shut down and he has been "in the house" ever since. Fortunately, he was a tailor in Ghana, and he survives on making small repairs on his fellow migrant's clothes and shoes.

This fall, Immanuel's plan is to go from factory to factory and ring the buzzer and say "cerca lavoro" (looking for work), and hope something good comes out of it. Sometimes they will let him in, he explains, to fill out forms, and tell him to go home and wait, and they will call if they need an extra set of hands but most of the time they will just tell him to leave straight away.

The family at home—his wife, the children, and his parents—they do not understand, he explains. How can somebody be in Europe with no job? That puts tension on him from all sides, and makes him feel crazy at times.

"The future is dark here. I have to force myself to go somewhere else. If you don't have a job it's like you're sick person, a mad person, and you'll start talking to yourself."

It is not uncommon to hear Ghanaian migrants worry about insanity as a result of the trauma of unresponsiveness; that is, the insanity of having given up so much, having tried so hard, and having received so little, or nothing, in return creates a deep "frustration" that may cause one to lose one's bearings. Suddenly, the absurdity of it all, the pointlessness of suffering, comes back to haunt the migrants—how crazy indeed to "draw the knife" in this cold and indifferent world where the doors are shut to poor people from Africa no matter where they turn, and the dream of belonging to a larger whole is slipping further and further away with every step one takes. When the sacrifice is carried out continuously and with no response, what is left except the "insatiable emptiness" that undermines human lives to the extent that any kind of transcendence is lost, any kind of reliable and continuous whole gone, and the self is utterly alone in the world with no other voice than one's own disintegrating self, talking nonsense into thin air.

Engaging life by giving, and giving up—like the migrant workers who put their lives on the line in the desert, and on the Mediterranean, and on the factory floors of southern Europe—is destined to be a vulnerable attempt of creating obligations in the outside world because there is the very real risk of rejection and the immediate suffering it creates. When the communion with the wellspring of existence, whether it is the empty sea or the labor market of the crisis hit manufacturing industries of Italy, is impossible to obtain, a complete breakdown can appear. You can become a mad person, talking to yourself. This is perhaps the dark side of Abraham's sacrifice of Isaac; sometimes the loss is simply not replaced, and one has to find a way of "handling the situation well" or suffer the consequences.

To most Guan migrants, like Immanuel, the answer often lies elsewhere. There is another destination that one has to try to reach where the conditions are believed to be less hostile. Usually it is Germany, the United Kingdom, or Scandinavia. The point is that most destinations, even the point of departure, now appear intermediary, except perhaps the United States, which is viewed as the ultimate destination to many Ghanaians, and the marginality that the migrants fled in their own country appears to accompany them everywhere they go, as does the terror of giving up everything to powers beyond one's control without sufficient recompense. This migrant experience of being eternally on the move—and if not physically moving then feeling the earth drift away from under one's feet as in the slowly disintegrating fishing village of Senya Beraku—has become a globalized migrant predicament, argues Zygmunt Bauman. Yet, the dangerous migrant journeys are unlikely to bring respite and respect to those on the move as "the moats separating them from the sites of their desire and of dreamed-of redemption grows deeper, while all the bridges, at the first attempt to cross them, prove to be drawbridges" (Bauman 1998: 89).

Conclusion

In this chapter I have explored a framework of reality based on, and maintained by, symbolic exchange encounters—a fundamentally premodern practice that seems to contravene and create connections in the face of overwhelming and objectively unresponsive powers. In the case of the Senya Beraku fishermen, I have discussed how sacrifice and unmitigated physical engagement creates a sense of obligation in the environment. On a broader existential level, I have argued that this form of exchange, the moral worlds it affirms, and the hope it creates— by resigning everything infinitely and "taking it back on the strength of the absurd" (Kierkegaard 1985: 65)—is concerned with human beings clawing back a modicum of control in face of this underlying emptiness that may appear, at any time, as a sudden rupture of unresponsiveness and call into question the very meaning and fabric of existence. Apparently, however, giving oneself over to powers beyond one's control is always haunted by fear of deprivation and loss; fear that one's effort may not be reciprocated. Even so: "To embrace the experience of giving up objects and people, and to know the begetting and the renewal such an experience offers, is finally to serve the apprenticeship of death. And of the gift." (Godbout 2000: 222). Kierkegaard confesses that he himself is not ready to make this double movement, nor does he possess the necessary courage: "To be able to lose one's understanding and with it the whole of the finite world whose stockbroker it is, and then on the strength of the absurd get exactly the same finitude back again, that leaves me aghast" (Kierkegaard 1985: 65–66).

Finally, I discuss whether migrant "sacrifice" on the Mediterranean and on the factory floors of southern Europe could be viewed as frustrated attempts to create obligations in the otherwise indifferent political economy of the globalized world. One major difference stands out, namely that God called upon Abraham. Migrant deaths, understood as symbolic sacrifices, have not been called or wished for by the current political economy, and they are perhaps not desired precisely because they have the potential to challenge the foundations of power (Baudrillard 1993). Yet, giving death to power in the globalized world—substituting, for instance, the slow demise of African village life with a sudden and violent death on the sea—cannot be completely ignored, as the political responses to the terrible deaths off Lampedusa in the summer of 2013 has shown, though a feeling of routine has crept in long ago, justified by certain dehumanizing stratifications of a social, moral, and racial order. Migrant deaths are regrettable but also comfortably distant and somehow unavoidable and therefore not likely to produce any serious commitment. Kierkegaard's thesis naturally could not anticipate this situation where human "sacrifice" to the powerful Other has no consequence or rather where the migrant body has become "immortal" as John Berger forcefully argued long ago. Migrant workers cannot be killed or sacrificed because they are interchangeable; "they are not born: they are not brought up: they do not age: they do not get tired: they do not die. They have a single function—to work" (Berger 1971: 64).

Notes

1. There are, of course, other ways of dealing with the decline. Some leave fishing; some deploy new unsustainable equipment. Elsewhere I have described the details of these developments, and the dangerous journey via Libya across the Mediterranean to Italy, as well as the losses it entails (Lucht 2011).

REFERENCES

Baudrillard, Jean. 1993. *Symbolic Exchange and Death*. London: Sage.
Bauman, Zygmunt. 1998. *Globalization: The Human Consequences*. Oxford: Polity Press.
Berger, John. 1975. *A Seventh Man*. Harmondsworth, UK: Penguin Books.
Cohen, Daniel. 2006. *Globalisation and Its Enemies*. Cambridge, MA: The MIT Press.
Derrida, Jacques. 1995. *The Gift of Death*. Chicago: University of Chicago Press.
Ferguson, James. 2006. *Global Shadows: Africa in the Neo-Liberal World Order*. Durham, NC: Duke University Press.
Frankfurt, Harry. 1988. "Freedom of the Will and the Concept of a Person." In *The Importance of What We Care About*. Cambridge: Cambridge University Press.
Giddens, Anthony. 1992. *Modernity and Self-Identity: Self and Society in the Late Modern Age*. Cambridge: Polity Press.
Godbout, Jacques T. 2000. *The World of the Gift*. Montreal: McGill-Queen's University Press.
Heidegger, Martin. 2002. *Being and Time*. New York: Harper San Francisco.
Henrich, Dieter. 1982. *Selbstverhältnisse. Gedanken und Auslegungen zu den Grundlagen der klassischen deutschen Philosophie*. Stuttgart: Philipp Reclam jun.
———. 1999. *Bewusstes Leben. Untersuchungen zum Verhältnis von Subjektivität und Metaphysik*. Stuttgart: Philipp Reclam jun.
Ingold, Tim. 2006. "Rethinking the Animate, Re-Animating Thought." *Ethnos* 71: 9–20.
Jackson, Michael. 2002. "Familiar and Foreign Bodies: A Phenomenological Exploration of the Human-Technology Interface." *Journal of the Royal Anthropological Institute* 8: 333–46.
Kant, Immanuel. 1999. *The Critique of Pure Reason*. Cambridge: Cambridge University Press.
Kierkegaard, Søren. 1980. *The Sickness Unto Death*. Translated by Howard V. Hong and Edna H. Hong. Princeton, NJ: Princeton University Press.
———. 1983. *Fear and Trembling*. Translated by Howard V. Hong and Edna H. Hong. Princeton, NJ: Princeton University Press.

————. 1985. *Fear and Trembling.* Translated by Alastair Hannay. London: Penguin Books.

————. 1992. *Either/Or: A Fragment of Life.* Translated by Alastair Hannay. London: Penguin Books.

Laing, Ronald D. 1973. *The Divided Self: An Existential Study in Sanity and Madness.* Harmondsworth, UK: Penguin Books.

Lévi-Strauss, Claude. 1969. *The Elementary Structures of Kinship.* London: Eyre & Spottiswoode.

Lucht, Hans. 2011. *Darkness before Daybreak: African Migrants Living on the Fringes in Southern Italy Today.* Berkeley: University of California Press.

Luhmann, Niklas. 1999. *Tillid: En mekanisme til reduktion af social kompleksitet.* Copenhagen: Hans Reitzels Forlag.

Strawson, Peter. 1959. *Individuals: An Essay in Descriptive Metaphysics.* London: Routledge.

Winnicott, Donald Woods. 1962. *The Child and the Outside World.* London: Tavistock Publications.

EPILOGUE
Anthropology and Philosophy in Dialogue?

Anne Line Dalsgård and Søren Harnow Klausen

It has been a challenge for anthropologists and philosophers to talk productively together, not just in general but in this book as well. In the opening chapter for this volume Cheryl Mattingly and Uffe Juul Jensen offer a careful and extended treatment of some of the troubles implied as well as some possible avenues for improving the conversation. We intend to follow up on their questions and add our perspective on the exercise that this book represents. The discussions in the preceding chapters have led us to ask: What could be learned in philosophy by more "craftsmanlike" inquiry into the lives of everyday agents and inquirers? What could be gained in anthropology by a more speculative, challenging engagement with philosophical concepts and theories? And is there a more inspiring, more committed, and perhaps also more exigent collaboration yet to be tried out between anthropology and philosophy? This is what we will reflect upon in the following.

Taking our own questions seriously we do not always agree, coming not only from different disciplines but also from very different epistemological positions, but as we see it, this is a strength rather than the opposite. However, both seeing a valuable potential in a dialogue between our different approaches and disciplinary histories, we hope to outline at least some features that will invite further discussion and common exploration. We begin by identifying some of the expectable barriers for a dialogue, be they defined in terms of habit or as real epistemological differences. We then proceed to sketch out several borderline cases and new developments, including some of the endeavors presented in this volume. Finally, we raise a number of questions for future mutual inspiration. All this is done from quite a humble position, acknowledging the massive impossibility of gaining a full overview, while at the same time seeing a need to make attempts in such a direction. We ask readers to bear in mind that ours is an interest in a dynamic working relationship, not in taking a bird's-eye view for the sake of epistemological order and control.

Before progressing any further we should say that obviously it is hazardous to write in general on "philosophy" and "anthropology" as if they were distinct, internally coherent disciplinary approaches. It is even more so as we—a philosopher and an anthropologist—are writing together, searching for a kind of joint perspective on the differences and similarities between these two idealized entities. Nevertheless, this is what we do in the following. Our present attempt to explore the interface between our disciplines is instigated by experiences from two different disciplinary encounters: the collaboration (including intense discussions and disagreements) between Klausen and Dalsgård in the Danish Independent Research Council, and a research collaboration undertaken by Dalsgård and the philosopher Anne Marie Pahuus in 2007.

Dalsgård has, over the years, maintained a keen interest in phenomenology, affect, and materiality (for instance in Dalsgård 2004), and hence hers is a particular standing in anthropology. While also having a background in phenomenology, Klausen has been working within a broadly analytical tradition, defending classical notions of objectivity and knowledge from various sorts of relativist or "postmodern" criticism (see for instance Klausen 2004). These differences do not, however, pose any hindrance to mutual respect and joy in seeking to understand things together. About the shared report resulting from her collaboration with Pahuus, Dalsgård wrote: "We were two writers with very different professional 'tendencies': I wrote in an ethnographic concrete, specific, and at times personal style, while Pahuus leaned towards the philosophic-universal, more generalizing style…. The latter often challenged the anthropological tendency to present analysis as 'only tentatively asserted, full of reservation and qualifying detail' (Van Maanen 1988: 303), in recognition of the partiality of all ethnographic knowledge, while this ethnographic hesitation at times was too pedestrian for the philosopher" (Dalsgård 2008: 150). These tendencies—to emphasize the concrete and experience-based or, in a kind of impatience with the particular, to strive for the identification of universals and the objective moral good—are probably the most prominent characteristics of the two disciplines. However, to emphasize these almost stereotypical characteristics too will insistently (as stereotypes always do) blur a deeper understanding of the situation. As we shall see in the following, the relationship between anthropology and philosophy is more complex than that.

Why Now?

We find that the time is ripe for the two disciplines to approach and challenge each other. The exploratory collaboration in this book is encouraged both by the internal development of the two disciplines and by more general trends within the arts and sciences. There is currently a strong movement toward interdisciplinary collaboration (and in some cases toward "transdisciplinarity," meaning the transgression of disciplinary boarders and the merging of older disciplines into new and hybrid ones), as it is widely recognized that interdisciplinary approaches are called for in order to solve the often complex—or "wild"—problems posed by contemporary societies. The call for interdisciplinarity is sounded by stakeholders outside academia (politicians and other policymakers, managers, NGOs, and so on) and also at the core of research and academic discussions, where an experience of inadequacy in responses to concrete challenges prompts a search for more multifaceted approaches. At the same time, the pull toward interdisciplinarity also spurs reflection on the traditional methodologies and identities of specific disciplines, in addition to which, as always, close encounters serve to make the differences more vividly clear. But having said this, the question remains of how concrete interdisciplinarity can be brought to unfold in a fruitful way. As we see it, this will take not just an egoistic need, but also a common interest and a good deal of daring.

Most philosophers have come to agree that their discipline needs empirical input. They are in a collective rush to get out of the armchair, engage the real world, and base their theorizing on more robust evidence. The traditional methods of mainstream analytic philosophy, i.e. conceptual analysis driven by intuitions and thought-experiments and wide reflective equilibrium, are widely considered insufficient or even unreliable, and even those who still advocate a form of conceptual analysis are at pains to show that it is really also a kind of empirical study. It remains an open and hotly debated question, however, *where* exactly philosophers ought to go in order to obtain the empirical evidence they crave. The most popular choice right now seems to be experimental psychology and, more generally, cognitive science (one pioneering work was Goldman (1986); and Knobe and Nichols (2008) have recently set the agenda for a new wave of "experimental philosophy"). Yet this tendency may seem problematic, or at least it has significant shortcomings, since the evidence provided by cognitive science is obtained in artificial and decontextualized settings. Especially those philosophers who have always been keen to maintain a degree of historical and cultural sensibility, and who recognize the importance of context and situation, may prefer to turn to a discipline which, by contrast, studies human life in real-life settings. This makes anthropology an obvious choice, even though, as we shall see, it is not an easy match for philosophers, either.

Anthropologists, on the other hand, have always found inspiration in philosophy. It is fair to say that philosophy is the foundation without which anthropological curiosity would never have arisen. Rather than providing the answers, however, philosophy has inspired anthropological questions, which anthropologists have answered by way of ethnographies and theories developed on the basis of these queries. Most anthropologists have found philosophical striving toward universal answers to be too narrow and shortsighted, even though the search for a universal human condition is by no means absent in anthropology. Classical, modernist works like Edward Tylor's *Primitive Culture* ([1871] 1920) and James Frazer's *The Golden Bough* ([1890] 1971), and later works by Alfred Radcliffe-Brown, Claude Lévi-Strauss, Claude Meillassoux, and Maurice Godelier shared this aspiration. However, since the 1970s the notion of cultural relativism promoted by Clifford Geertz and later the critique raised by Edward Said's *Orientalism* (1978) and James Clifford and George Marcus's *Writing Culture* (1986) have, partially for political and/or ethical reasons, made this aspiration appear less legitimate. The tensions between universalists and cultural relativists in anthropology, which have thrived throughout the last century, have found new ground, for instance in recent discussions on the uses of phenomenology, which is accused of either being a recipe for purely descriptive studies, or being a Eurocentric reference to an existential pan-human "we."

Be that as it may, whatever theoretical viewpoint may be dominating in anthropology, a certain hesitation toward philosophical tidiness is always detectable. Variety and ambiguity are basic conditions in the production of anthropological knowledge and, just as in Liisberg and Bubandt's dialogue, the anthropologists must insist on the "if-ness" of the generality of their analysis, as when Bubandt (this volume) writes "*If* there are multiple modernities out there, there are also other political and cultural epistemologies of the new and of trust" (our emphasis). Bubandt calls his contribution a "counter-ethnography," challenging Liisberg's universal notion of trust, but while writing forth his Indonesian ethnography he progressively stabilizes Liisberg's concept as a concept that is worth challenging. In this process, the philosophical concept attains an ambiguous status as effectively useful but never fully true. Let us take a closer look at the possibilities for more profoundly engaging in, and mutually committing to, an exchange of viewpoints along and across these lines.

So Close . . .

The two disciplines obviously have a lot in common, yet this is not something either discipline would readily admit. Although in principle philosophy is concerned with the whole of reality, and thus has a vastly broader subject area than anthropology, in effect it has always centered on human nature, and particularly on human affairs such as morality, freedom, knowledge, thinking, and so forth. Some would say that this is so by necessity; that the very idea of transcending the human point of view is incoherent (and, if one takes into account the fact that anthropology is not only concerned with social relations, but also with the role of material objects and physical surroundings in human life, that the apparent difference vanishes altogether). Others will insist that although philosophy is always practiced by human beings, and in particular circumstances, this does not preclude it from trying to describe (and even succeeding in describing) the world as it is in itself (Klausen 2004)—but they, too, will have to concede that an overwhelmingly large part of the philosophical tradition has, as a matter of fact, been occupied with questions that are preeminently human concerns and arise within the human life-world.

Many works by the great philosophers of the past contain elaborate descriptions of the human condition and specific human ways—ranging from Aristotle's description of the life of the rational animal in the city-state, with its emphasis on the role of friendship, the exchange of gifts, participation in public affairs, and the like, over David Hume's portrait of humans as being driven more by habit, sympathy, and desire than by cold reason, and to Martin Heidegger's analysis of the human being as situated in a specific world and understanding itself through its dealings with everyday objects and tasks. Both anthropology and philosophy have been concerned with the tension between the local and "peculiar" and the more pervasive features of human existence, and with the question of how and to what extent human practices and human understanding differ across cultures.

The theoretical basis of the more relativist, some would even say romantic, discipline of anthropology is very similar to that of contemporary philosophy. Franz Boas's insistence that each culture should be assessed on its own terms, and not judged according to an allegedly objective (and de facto ethnocentric) standard, echoes Johann G. Herder's earlier plea for the autonomy and equal standing of cultures, which has informed later hermeneutics and much of continental philosophy in general. Bronislaw Malinowski's recommendation of participatory observation, of adopting the native's point of view, likewise resembles a line of thought that has informed large parts of twentieth-century philosophy, not only hermeneutics and the philosophy of Jürgen Habermas, but also recent Anglo-American philosophy (the primacy of an insider or participant perspective has been a central theme in the work of, for instance, Peter Winch and other Wittgensteinians, Peter F. Strawson, John McDowell, and Robert Brandom). Consequently, while the "human being" of philosophy has been marked by a Western notion of the self (in anthropology termed "peculiar" [Spiro 1993: 107]), even relativist anthropology has always insisted upon applying the human being as such as a foundation for its theories, emphasizing the varieties of human existence while resisting any attempt to view people and societies in a hierarchical manner. Both disciplines thus somehow start with the recognition of a shared human nature.

Moreover, at the same time as traditional philosophy may have been marked by a universalist and rationalist tendency, which did not sit well with anthropology, recent influential currents in philosophy—across the analytic-continental divide—emphasize situated and embodied cognition and the role of emotions and values in allegedly rational activities; a tendency that points strongly toward a further rapprochement with anthropology. Even if we consider those branches of anthropology that are leaning more toward sociology, we find plenty of parallels in modern philosophy. Marcel Mauss's interest in the structural aspects of human interaction was adopted by the structuralist movement in philosophy, whose influence is still felt. Indeed, the main inspiration to poststructuralism in French philosophy may be said to have come not from linguistics, as is commonly assumed, but rather from structural anthropology. (Consider the pivotal role played by Lévi-Strauss, who, not to forget, was first educated in philosophy, as was his intellectual heir, Pierre Bourdieu.)

Of all the influential currents in modern philosophy, phenomenology may come closest to the methodological ideals of anthropology, with its strong focus on lived experience and its notion of the life-world. Indeed, since the late 1980s anthropologists have made extensive use of the works of particularly Maurice Merleau-Ponty, William James, and John Dewey, and also Alfred Schutz's social phenomenology (see review by Desjarlais and Throop 2011). Even a more analytical thinker like Charles S. Peirce has informed important anthropological works (among others, E. Valentine Daniel 1996). Despite this, in a recent summary of the theoretical development in anthropology Kirsten Hastrup argues that phenomenology has often been taken by anthropologist to be a purely descriptive discipline. She asserts (especially pivoting on the anthropologist Michael Jackson) that it should rather be seen as a methodological resistance toward any form of theory fetishism that allows theory to dictate practical knowledge and as such, she states, phenomenology must be at the root of any anthropological endeavor (Hastrup 2004b: 17).

It should come as no surprise, though, that philosophical investigations tend to be more abstract (in the sense of generalizing) than anthropological studies are, and that anthropologists often engage in closer empirical studies and end up giving more emphasis to local irregularities and the challenges they pose to existing theoretical assumptions. Nor should it be any revelation that anthropologists mostly abstain from making normative judgments about the good life. According to the received view, anthropology studies that which *is*, not that which ought to be (Wolcott 1999: 181). Philosophy, on the other hand—especially the branches of ethics, political philosophy, and epistemology—is commonly defined as a normative enterprise. It looks beyond the actual practices of people, searching for better and more rationally justified alternatives. But these differences do not suffice to explain the mutual estrangement of these disciplines. At best, they point to a sensible division of labor. Moreover, it is now commonly accepted by most philosophers that philosophy should be somehow informed by empirical studies (and this is conceded even by relatively conservative philosophers in the analytic tradition like Frank Jackson [1998] or Timothy Williamson [2007]). Also, several recent, particularly American, anthropologists inspired by Nancy Scheper-Hughes, Paul Farmer, and others, have explicitly and unabashedly taken a normative stand, not only describing different practices, but sharply criticizing social injustice in and between societies as structural violence.

A less dramatic normativity can be discerned on at least two levels of the anthropological endeavor: at the ethical, epistemological level and at the level of societal morality. For instance, two anthropologists, both defending the primacy of experience, yet ending up with different conclusions, are Michael D. Jackson (among other works 1998, 2005, this volume) and Nigel Rapport (1997, 2003). Whereas Jackson argues that "we," the academics, the Europeans, and other superiors, should not lay claim to a privileged position in the definition of the world and what life should be, Rapport argues that for both empirical and moral reasons anthropology must recognize the individual, "as an actor with an identity over and above his or her membership in social groupings and cultural traditions" (2010: 84). Jackson insists on a relativist, non-judgmental perspective as an ethical prerequisite for cultural analysis, even though, primarily in his later works, he also purports a universal, ontological rather than ethical, "existential imperative" (2005, this volume). Rapport, on the other hand, argues for a non-relativist position, safeguarding the individual's universal ontological existence (2010: 85).

To say that one discipline is normative, the other not, is therefore not quite fitting. It could be said, however, that in terms of difference, normativity in anthropology most often takes the shape of a defense of concrete people, while philosophers are mainly concerned with laying down general norms that are independent of context. There are, however, exceptions even to this, as a significant movement in contemporary ethics has argued against the "principlistic" tradition in ethics, and, much in the spirit of the anthropological approach, insisted that ethical judgments are irredeemably particular, just like the human beings and situations with which they are concerned (cf. Nussbaum 1990; Dancy 2004).

. . . And Yet So Far

In spite of the many commonalities, researchers from the two disciplines are not immediately attracted to each other's methods and aims, but tend to view them with suspicion or reservation. And to the extent that they do use texts from the other discipline, these tend to be older works that have already been firmly scrutinized, criticized, or further developed (cf. for instance the work of Michele Moody-Adams on morality, culture, and philosophy (1997), which takes anthropology to be E. E. Evans-Pritchard, Ruth Benedict, and Margaret Mead, and also the recent widespread fascination with Gilles Deleuze in anthropology). However, this mutual estrangement is not really surprising, as it follows more or less logically from the traditional self-understanding of the two disciplines. Let us take a closer look at some often-claimed differences:

1. Anthropologists argue that philosophers base their all-including "we" on very limited experience with the world. To the degree that philosophical analysis includes empirical data, such data represents a particularly European (some would say male) perspective.

2. Philosophers suspect that anthropologists tend to exaggerate the peculiarity of the cultures they are studying. Their work is marked by a relativist bias that prevents them from seeing important similarities.
3. Anthropologists think that philosophers do not really allow themselves to be analytically challenged by the disorder of life. Exploring a secure body of written texts, philosophers attempt to control the amount of clutter and confusion they are confronted with.
4. Philosophers find that anthropologists do not respect the systematic unity of their thought. Picking here and there in the philosophical corpus, anthropologists tend to play fast and loose with concepts the precise meanings of which depend crucially on their theoretical context.
5. Philosophers tend to seek definitive evidence (for instance in the natural sciences), while most anthropologists accept that anthropological evidence is only partially true. The social context and the role of the researcher, among other factors, make anthropological evidence a kind of invention that is far from scientific proof.

These stereotyped yet widely perceived differences point in various directions. We shall consider just a few, namely methodology (wonder), conceptualization, and ontology, which in different ways touch upon these differences.

Wonder

If we look at the place that wonder holds in the two disciplines, then according to what may have been the most influential of all accounts of the nature of philosophy—that of Aristotle—philosophy begins with a state of wonder. ("It was their wonder, astonishment, that first led men to philosophize and still leads them" [Aristotle 1924: 982b12]. There is an even earlier, almost univocal, passage in Plato: "for wonder is the feeling of a philosopher, and philosophy begins in wonder" [1973: 155 d].) This may be more than an abstract ideal; as far as we can tell, the actual genesis of philosophical reflection fits this account. Philosophy in the Western style first emerged in the Greek colonies, on the borders of Greek civilization. It can thus be seen as a response to cultural encounters, and as a way of coping with the difficulties and incomprehensibilities that arose when the Greeks were confronted with conditions like Asian despotism and other "barbaric" forms of life. This called for a more inclusive and flexible kind of thinking than their traditional ethnocentric one.

Yet there is no doubt something to the allegation that philosophers are playing it too safe. By almost any standard, contemporary philosophy does not seem particularly daring. Part of this may be explained by that fact that it has become more professionalized (which applies to anthropology as well). In order to gain international acclaim, philosophers are now required to meet narrow standards and mimic the established research paradigms. There is less room for sweeping thoughts, and experiments may seem too risky. But the reasons for the philosophers' lack of daring may go deeper. Philosophy begins with wonder, but it is designed to cope with the sense of wonderment and, if possible, make it go away. It aims to reduce complexity, to find a few fundamental principles behind an apparently messy and unfathomably complex reality. It is a demystifying enterprise. Even those currents in modern philosophy that embrace the mysterious or paradoxical character of reality tend to treat it in a rather abstract and simplifying manner (for instance by conceiving of it in general terms like *la différence, das Ereignis,* and so on). Often philosophers are tempted to make things more simple than they actually have evidence for doing; to deny or ignore the obtrusive details, or to exorcise problems by fiat (cf. Wittgenstein's exclamation: "Das Rätsel gibt es nicht" [1963: 65], or the widespread habit in much of twentieth-century philosophy of "feigning anesthesia" [Dennett 1991: 40], such as ignoring the otherwise obvious facts that people are conscious beings and that there is such a thing as a subjective point of view).

It is a striking fact that even those contemporary philosophers who officially advocate bringing in empirical facts about the world seldom go far beyond traditional armchair philosophy when it comes to their actual practice. The program of social epistemology promises both to study and to improve real-life practices, yet most work in this tradition has been confined to abstract foundational issues. Michael Devitt has been an ardent proponent of "naturalized" epistemology, rejecting the privileged role of conceptual analysis—but when confronted with apparent empirical evidence for cross-cultural variation in semantic intuitions, he reacts by quickly explaining away its potential significance, and then ends up staunchly defending the particular brand of armchair expertise traditionally assigned to philosophers and linguists (Devitt 2006).

Ethnographic data, on the other hand, always represents an excess, an ambiguity, and a complexity that the anthropologist may wish to preserve (Engelke 2008: 17). Or as Jackson puts it: "To fully recognize the eventfulness of being is to discover that what emerges in the course of any human interaction overflows, confounds and goes beyond the forms that initially frame the interaction as well as the reflections and rationalizations that follow from it" (2009: 236). According to Jackson, the relationship between experience and episteme becomes particularly critical in moments of unfamiliarity or even estrangement in the field, but even in less dramatic circumstances, does *doing* ethnography involve seeing the familiar in unfamiliar ways (Forsythe 1999). This necessarily creates data that has no predestination. The anthropologist may turn her interest toward it, over and over again, and find new perspectives, and accumulated experience and ever-ramifying journeys of the imagination may change her interpretation of events heard of, observed, or lived through. Field data can be said to be timeless, as such data can always be analytically remobilized, even though the practices it describes may have changed (Strathern in Holbraad and Pedersen 2009: 383). As part of the anthropological experience the data cannot be put to rest, but may continue to be productive, although not necessarily within the same theoretical framework as originally intended.

The sense of wonder and questioning that carries thought forward is thus celebrated in anthropology and placed at the core of concept development to a much higher degree than in contemporary philosophy. While the philosopher may be engaged in systematization and maintaining coherence, the anthropologist will be drawn toward further exploration of those extra, unwieldy bits and pieces and their creative potential.

Concepts

Anthropologists and philosophers often seem to have a different understanding of *concepts,* though quite a few of the theories officially endorsed by philosophers ought to be compatible with the notions that anthropologists hold. Even those philosophers who strongly emphasize the importance of the context and deny that there is such a thing as *the* concept of, say, justice or knowledge (or that the concept has a single and immutable meaning), hardly pay attention to—not to mention let themselves be challenged by—the actual differences in usage and understanding. They often keep assuming that there is such a thing as "our" notion of justice or democracy, for instance, allowing the scope of "us" or "we" to remain indeterminate, but potentially universal. Rarely do they acknowledge that there may be a Western bias in the "standard" notions of democracy, justice, or a person, or self. Even the very

notions of philosophy or morality are not widely challenged, but more
or less taken for granted.

Anthropology, on the other hand, has made extensive use of philosophical concepts (drawn from thinkers like Heidegger, Foucault, Derrida, Deleuze, and recently Zizek), yet always—as with any use of theory
in anthropology—giving priority to ethnography. The kind of interest
anthropology has brought to philosophy is not the same as the philosophers' interests (Willerslev 2011: 506). From an anthropological point
of view it may be fully legitimate to write, as Rane Willerslev does: "I
am not concerned with the internal coherence of Deleuze's thinking
or with his position within the larger body of philosophy. My concern
is simply to use him as a source of inspiration for challenging basic
anthropological understandings of what constitutes the genuinely real
in human existence" (2011: 506). From a philosophical point of view,
this seems too facile. Some of the reservations it engenders may stem
from the fact that philosophers, even those of the more analytical sort,
tend to place a strong emphasis on exegetical correctness. This is characteristic for large parts of the humanities: Because researchers have an
intrinsic interest in—and often a veneration for—works and authors of
former times, it can be difficult for them to accept the fact that there can
be productive misinterpretations, especially in their own field. They are
less prone to adopt the lesson of philosophical hermeneutics, that all
interpretation involves a "fusion of horizons," and that to understand
at all means to understand differently (Gadamer 1960)—or at least they
will opt for a conservative reading of it, insisting that one should not
deliberately strive to produce alternative understandings, but merely
acknowledge that interpretation will, at any rate, transform the object
of interpretation, behind one's back so to speak.

But worries may run deeper. Some might argue that serious concern for internal coherence is a fundamental criterion of good research,
which should apply to all fields, and that nothing good can come from
simply disrespecting it. Though this is a thought that comes easily to
the philosophically schooled mind, it surely requires qualification. Adherence to a strict criterion of coherence (e.g. requiring perfect consistency, as well as the absence of anomalies; see BonJour 1985, 93ff.)
would have hampered progress in the sciences across the board. Just
consider the development of quantum mechanics, or of modern mathe-
matics under the spell of Russell's paradox and Gödel's theorem, which
were apparently doing fine on a shaky or even paradoxical foundation.
Yet there remains the apprehension that there are serious and less serious ways of doing "bold" research—and that anthropologists like Willerslev seem to do theirs too light-heartedly. One way to phrase this is to

say that although the concern for coherence might be trumped by other concerns, such a move should always be accompanied by serious scruples, such as recognizing that one is going up against some otherwise very compelling principles, or that a significant price is being paid. In order to be truly bold, the philosopher will argue, one must perceive a real danger, and acknowledge that something valuable might also be lost. In any case, it is telling that Willerslev himself speaks of using Deleuze as a source of *inspiration*. This confirms the philosopher's suspicion that he is not *using* philosophical theories in the standard sense, which means *applying them* to the field of anthropology. Rather, he is stimulated by them in the same way researchers can be inspired by quotations, works of literature, images, metaphors, and so on.

The anthropologist will probably reply that rather than neglecting the importance of coherent thought, he is preoccupied with a different project. He may be engaged in large-scale comparison, as Willerslev is here, "juxtaposing phenomena bearing a cross-cultural resemblance ... which may potentially re-open insights into the very issue of what constitutes the real" (Willerslev 2011: 505). In this case the anthropological project is a reconceptualization of ethnographic data through imaginative experiments with lateral comparison, and philosophy (Deleuze) is used as a starting point for speculation. The anthropologist could just as well insist on the bodily, sensorial, and practical nature of everyday life as material for thought—both the native and the anthropological thought—and a piece of furniture, a word, an envelope, or a hand gesture might therefore, when taken seriously, inspire just as much as any philosophical concept. The aim of this kind of imaginative experiments is not a systematic, conceptual ordering of the world, but an exploration of possible ways of overcoming the immediate realism of social life. A concept, then, creates conditions and is, concomitantly, created itself by the repercussions of its use. Few philosophers seem to subscribe to this notion of the concept where it figures as a thing among things in a shared (by anthropologists and their interlocutors alike), though not necessarily parallel, striving to understand existence. On the other hand, the anthropological imagination often shrivels and dies when confronted with the philosophical "purifying and polishing of concepts," as Friedrich Nietzsche (probably) teasingly puts it (Deleuze and Guattari 1994: 5).

Philosophers might retort, when charged with naively taking for granted a more or less universal and uniform meaning of concepts, by pointing out that this may indeed be true, but that it can hardly be avoided, and that anthropologists are not much better in this respect. One does not have to buy into an overambitious "transcendental" argument for the indispensability of a shared conceptual scheme (see, for instance, Davidson 1973) in order to make the point that almost any discussion of differences, transgressions, confounding, overflow, polysemy, and the like will, as a matter of fact, proceed from, and eventually return to, a common and often more conventional conceptual background. It is interesting to note that even an anthropologist like Jackson, who has strong relativist leanings and insists on the "innumerable differences in shaping a human life" (this volume), has no great difficulties discussing *the* human condition with a philosopher (Wentzer in this volume), and actually ventures to make claims about "natural justice" and a general "existential imperative." This should not be seen as inconsistent or self-undermining, as Jackson's notions are probably not intended to have a stable or uniform core meaning—or in any case their extreme generality means that they will be exemplified by very different real-life phenomena. But it does point to an irresolvable tension between the particular and universal aspects of conceptualizing, both of which are probably necessary, but which are emphasized differently by anthropologists and philosophers.

Culture, Ontology, and Evidence

Both naturalist and non-naturalist philosophy should be able to accommodate or cooperate with anthropology—naturalists because they have no fear of basing their theories on empirical findings; non-naturalists because they posit (and focus on) a peculiar realm of essentially human affairs and notions (as in the non-naturalist or "soft naturalist" theories of Brandom [1994] and McDowell [1994]. Surely the naturalist turn in philosophy has paved the way for an integration of anthropological findings. Yet since naturalism is often associated with a more or less scientistic or objectivist outlook, these "anthropological findings" do not, however, tend to be of the same sort as those typically produced by actual anthropological studies. Philosophers tend to be rather selective, often deliberately choosing those anthropological results that support their universalist assumptions (cf. Klausen 2004, which relies strongly on the—arguably tendentious—survey of Brown 1991).

Moody-Adams's *Fieldwork in Familiar Places* (1997) is a fine example of how philosophers have used findings from anthropology, even though this work might reasonably be said to take a rather conservative approach, using the empirical material to bolster conventional philosophical claims rather than to challenge them. The same goes for recent attempts in epistemology and the philosophy of language to take account of cultural differences (for example Machery et al. 2004). Although these studies may seem provocative, perhaps even revolutionary, when regarded from the perspective of traditional philosophy, they consist in rather simple examinations of the beliefs and attitudes of cultural groups—which are, in turn, conceived of as homogenous, that is, perceived in a more or less "essentialist" fashion—and rely on conventional framing of the views and problems treated. It can also be argued that they are confined to artificial experimental settings; they are not based on *fieldwork*, which is arguably what could lead to genuinely challenging results.

When philosophers make use of anthropological works, they mainly employ what Moody-Adams calls "descriptive anthropology" (1997: 4), characterized by quite an *altmodisch* concept of culture. Within anthropology, culture has been a contested concept since the 1980s. The "ontic-dumping" of the concept, that is, the everyday use of it to denote the particularity of a certain (often stigmatized) group of people, has created a cautiousness within the discipline. This was why Lila Abu-Lughod (1991) proposed a "writing against culture," arguing for an attention toward individual lives and complex social dynamics rather than typifications of cultural patterns and forms. Many anthropologists have later disagreed with this (in their perspective) paralyzing unease, and worked toward a restoration of culture as an analytical concept. One of them is Christoph Brumann, who, in his article "Writing for Culture: Why a Successful Concept Should Not Be Discarded" (1999), concludes that "any scientific concept is a simplifying construct and has its costs, but once the advantages have been found to outweigh these costs it should be employed with clear conscience" (1999: S13). However, this turbulence and re-installment of the concept in anthropology seem to have gone unnoticed amongst many philosophers, who tend to use the concept, at best, as was once proposed by Max Weber, and later made known by Geertz (1973: 5), as a web of significance that people have spun for themselves.

This notion of culture echoes Evans-Pritchard's assumption that all the beliefs of the Azande "hang together ... In this web of belief every strand depends on every other strand, and a Zande cannot get out of its meshes because this is the only world he knows ... It is the texture of his thought" ([1937] 1976: 194–95; cf. Moody-Adams 1997: 45). This is a kind of cultural solipsism. It squares with certain influential views in modern philosophy, notably the later Wittgenstein's doctrine of language games, which, at least on some fairly standard interpretations, treats language games as autonomous units of meaning, whose constituent parts can only be understood by adopting an insider perspective. Yet as argued by Moody-Adams, and by many anthropologists before her, this is both conceptually and empirically implausible. The empirical evidence suggest that the beliefs of the members of a culture, for instance the Azande, often differ considerably, and that there are always, at the very least, points of interaction between different belief systems.

The idea of *a* web of *significance,* that is, culture as singular, uncontested, and existing on the level of meaning ("culture as text"), certainly does not sit well with later discussions in anthropology on globalization, materiality, the virtual, and ontology (to mention but a few issues), which have marked anthropology in the 1990s and 2000s. A turn toward presence, affect, and non-representation in neighboring disciplines (geography, say, or literature) has resonated in anthropology recently, and new tendencies in philosophy, tentatively grouped under the label "the speculative turn" by Bryant, Srnicek, and Harman (2011), seem to coincide with this interest in a reality outside human interpretation. It should be said, though, that the tendency in philosophy to go beyond interpretation, language, and "culture" actually predates the parallel movement in anthropology by several decades. From the early 1960s onwards, the resistance toward ontology began to soften (see, for instance, Loux and Zimmerman 2003: 2–3), and some philosophers have since embarked on still more daring ontological enterprises and contributed to the so-called material, corporeal, and spatial turns in the humanities. Thus, it is evident that "philosophy" (and "anthropology" as well) is never a coherent, unified line of thought but covers a broad variety of approaches, some still occupied with webs of significance, while others discuss the reality of the real.

Even though the notion of a culture as a homogenous unity has been criticized in both disciplines, certain problems pertaining to the study of "cultures" persist. For example, it is still an important question to what extent cultures—or, to put it more neutrally—human life can and should be studied in a "detached," objectifying way, or whether a more involved, participatory standpoint should be taken. Advocates of the existence of "human universals," such as Donald Brown (1991), employ the more detached stance, which allows the anthropologist to posit the presence of invariants in human affairs, despite the fact that these may have found no expression, or perhaps even gone completely unnoticed, by the people under study. Expectedly, philosophers, who are likewise prone to seek hidden unities in the apparently manifold, have welcomed this approach. The defenders of universalism in anthropology do not deny (or at least do not present any evidence against the view) that the *self-understanding* and *experience* of different people may be extremely different. They explicitly choose an "etic" approach, that is, an approach informed by their own analytical concepts. This allows them to attribute familiar concepts to people, even though these people have no words for the relevant concepts in their own language, and even though they might not show any overt sign of recognizing the conceptual distinctions in question (Brown 1991: 48–49). Though it remains debatable to what extent experience is determined by language and what it takes to manifest that one grasps a concept, this could be a justifiable move also for empirically oriented philosophers and probably lead to illuminating results.

In anthropology, the "etic" approach has always been a tool for inquiry. Doing anthropology is by no means just an exercise in collecting native statements about the world. A theoretically informed analytical framework is also what helps the anthropologist transcend, or at least defamiliarize, her own native ("emic") point of view. But the answer to most anthropologists is seldom universalism. Not that everything is relative and nothing universal; in fact, a common anthropological stance builds on the recognition that nobody exists in a cultural vacuum, neither native nor observer, i.e. she recognizes a universal condition for human world-making. Rather, contemporary anthropology thrives on the stubborn suspicion that any universal category always implies a surplus, i.e. something that does not fit in and which necessarily will spin off more questions and trials. Where most philosophers may be satisfied with different data to nuance and consolidate their ideas, anthropologists, ideally, thus search for the data that shake these ideas and provoke new questions. Rightly combined, these apparently divergent interests may constitute a highly creative wrangling between consolidation and subversion.

Like the notion of culture, the analysis of empirical data presents challenges as well as opportunities for future collaboration. Philosophers, particularly those in the analytic tradition, will probably continue to borrow from the more or less "positivistic" notions of evidence-based research common to experimental psychology, cognitive science, and empirical sociology. But anthropologist could counterbalance this tendency by not only showing them that fieldwork can—and does—produce robust evidence (Engelke 2008: 2), but also by teaching them how to analyze such evidence in a manner which, at best, does justice both to its uniqueness and to its more general significance. The goal is not that philosophers should simply adopt the anthropologists' methods or point of view, but rather that anthropology should play its part in the shaping of philosophy's evidential canon. In a wording that might, once again, sound a bit lofty, it might assist philosophy in finding itself, in as much as philosophers are, in theory, acutely aware of the need for interpretation and contextualization but have difficulty when it comes to applying this stance to concrete empirical studies.

The challenge posed to anthropologists and philosophers in this volume has indeed related to the role of anthropological evidence and discussions, which has its origins in more general tendencies. Philosophers may draw on empirical research, but they confidently leave it to others to develop detailed description of social realities. The problem is that anthropologists, although confident within their own circles, have felt a certain uneasiness about their relationship with the positivist style of inquiry in the social sciences, at least since the so-called crisis of representation in the 1980s (Marcus and Fischer [1986] 1999: 22), and they have never really developed an adequate language for describing the kind of evidence produced. Anthropological knowledge cannot be empirical knowledge as understood in the conventional positivist fashion (Hastrup 2004a: 461). But how, then, can it be used by other disciplines, such as philosophy, which are prone to take the anthropological findings as "proofs" of existing realities? The more anthropology engages in cross-disciplinary collaborations, the more—or so it seems—the question of evidence in the generation of anthropological knowledge will need clarification. As Matthew Engelke recently remarked, "reflection on the concept of evidence might give us a language with which to engage colleagues in other human sciences, the humanities, and the natural sciences, as well as actors and interest groups in the wider world" (Engelke 2008: 3). This language, however, is still in the making.

The status of anthropological evidence as always partial, perhaps suggesting possible realities rather than proving them, works well with philosophy, especially as long as both disciplines are involved in the exploration of existential dilemmas and ethical reflection, where each individual case has its own particular significance (see Jackson and Wentzer, this volume). It creates more friction when the philosophical ambition is generalization, as is seen in Pedersen's and Meinert's dialogue in this volume. But as they ask: "Does Ugandan distrust challenge Løgstrup's theory of trust or does Løgstrup's perspective on trust challenge our perspective on Ugandan realities?" (this volume). In their collaboration, it became clear that their disagreements concerned the ontological status of the human life-world, and that neither of them could really submit to the viewpoint of the other. But as they conclude, if the aim is to enlarge theoretically sound understandings of real human life, then some kind of interaction has to take place. Their model is one of cautious rapprochement.

Room for Closer Interaction

One could say that "theoretically sound understandings of real human life" cannot but be the aim for philosopher and anthropologist alike. But as we have seen, theoretical soundness is not understood in a uniform manner, neither within each discipline nor between the two, and without a comparable foothold an attempt to enter into dialogue can lead to a multitude of misunderstandings. One response to this could be to accept that, as already noted, misunderstanding is not only a passable way forward, but may even lead to original results.

As we have seen above, anthropologists and philosophers subscribe to very different uses of theories and concepts. Philosophy could ask questions, which should then be answered by the social sciences, including anthropology (Bourdieu is said to have proposed this "rubbing" with social reality), but far too often it is not philosophers who pose the questions. Rather, it is anthropologists who both ask and answer the questions, with philosophers then attempting to improve on the anthropologist's answers. Ideally, philosophy could be prompted by the findings of anthropology to ask new questions, which would then be subjected to fieldwork by anthropologists. Philosophers could take on the anthropological challenge by accepting that the way concepts like democracy, trust, hope, or a person are understood differs between—and even within—societies, and then proceeding to work out the implications of these different notions and to systematically reconstruct them. One example of this kind of interaction can be found in Lucht's chapter, which applies Søren Kierkegaard's notion of hope (as elaborated by Moe Rasmussen) to Lucht's own fieldwork in a Ghanaian fishing village. This example shows both how philosophical notions can serve to highlight phenomena that might otherwise have gone unnoticed, and how they might be developed so as to acquire a more concrete meaning and become empirically operationalizable—as well as how the philosopher's notions are likely to be stretched. Some scholars of Kierkegaard would probably object to Lucht's use of the very subtle and complex notions of "resigning everything infinitely" and "taking it back on the strength of the absurd." This objection could, however, potentially provoke a philosophical rethinking of Kierkegaard into "Kierkegaard + Ghana," and hence renew the concept of hope. This would be in accordance with Deleuze and Guattari's notion of concepts as always encompassing their future development, as a dormant quality (Deleuze and Guattari 1994).

A different approach would be for the two disciplines to meet on the field of anthropology. Philosophy could help to develop hypotheses

and conceptualize fieldwork experiences. But it would have to submit to the norms of standard empirical research: concepts and theories
must be replaced if they do not serve to explain the empirical findings.
This ought to be acceptable to philosophers, considering their widespread advocacy of the method of "reflective equilibrium." And yet in
practice they are often averse to making substantial changes in their
conceptual framework; they tend to proceed in a top-down-manner.
Successful interaction with anthropology will probably require a more
bottom-up approach (Pedersen in this volume), and perhaps even the
philosopher's participation in the anthropological fieldwork. Anthropological fieldwork is a craft that has to be learned (Ingold 2008), and
like any other craft it takes "talent, training, and practice to become a
competent field researcher, and careful data-collection and analysis to
produce reliable results" (Forsythe 1999: 129). But good fieldwork also
requires sound operationalizable theory. Consequently, ethnographic
descriptions informed by philosophical concepts that are in part elaborated by philosophers in the process—and not merely borrowed by the
anthropologists—might be an example of genuine cooperation, and not
just mutual inspiration, between the two disciplines. The exchange between Raffnsøe and Miyazaki exemplifies such a feedback loop between
anthropology and philosophy, with Raffnsøe borrowing the notion of a
gift from anthropology (Mauss) and using it to shed new light on the
notion of trust, which Miyazaki then relates to his own studies of Fijian
gift-giving and uses to further develop the notion of hope, which could
again feed into a philosophical analysis. If this process were allowed to
go on, it might lead to the formation of a new transdisciplinary enterprise, more flexible and culturally sensitive than traditional philosophy,
but also more systematic than traditional anthropology. A possible field
for such collaboration is also suggested by contemporary philosophical theories of both propositional and practical knowledge (see, for instance, Hetherington 2006; Klausen 2009). Anthropologists are already
using to the notion of knowledge (for an early study, see Barth 1975)—
and will probably know more about different meanings and practices
of knowledge formation and knowledge use in real-life settings—but
by employing and testing the particular (and often neglected) understanding of knowledge that has been developed in analytic philosophy,
a new and promising approach might be found.

For the philosopher, a more ambitious empirical approach could be
applied to a wide range of philosophical topics in service of the discipline itself. Until now, empirical data has mostly been used, in more
interdisciplinary contexts, to study things like "negotiation of meaning" or "negotiation" or "construction" of identity. While such studies

are, without doubt, relevant to philosophy (meaning and identity being key issues in philosophy), there is no reason why the empirical
approach should not be extended to, say, processes of knowledge exchange or knowledge formation, or to the study of moral practices as
such (that is, practices considered as involving moral judgment and
the conferring of statuses—blame- or praiseworthiness, goodness or
badness—on individuals or groups). Figuring out what "philosophical
fieldwork" could consist in seems more and more vital to the discipline
since, as Moody-Adams (1997: 11) puts it, "there is often more to be
learned from what Walzer calls the 'workmanlike' moral inquiries of
everyday agents and inquirers than from the disengaged speculation so
common in contemporary moral philosophy." However, the role of the
anthropologists in this undertaking would be mainly that of inspirator;
a role that many anthropologists would probably find unsatisfying or
even dubious due to a strong (and, to the anthropologist, legitimate)
identification with the method of fieldwork.

A fourth approach could be more experimental and suggest new
prospects rather than analyzing the empirical present. Here we are
thinking of a kind of laboratory where philosophers, anthropologists,
and third parties could engage in a common exploration of possibilities.
Mattingly's and Jensen's contribution to this volume could be seen in
this light. They propose a cosmopolitan philosophical anthropology,
because as Mattingly argues elsewhere: "Perhaps the moral ordinary
is more subversive and creative than Aristotle (a member of an elite,
after all) realized or would have approved. Perhaps there is a way to
understand the moral ordinary as a resource for critique and transformation as connected to a 'we,' an 'I.' Perhaps, too, there are resources
that everyday persons sometimes draw upon to discover contingency
in what seemed necessary or to experiment with moral possibilities
that transgress or expand their moral universe" (Mattingly 2011: 12).
Another example of innovation springs from Dalsgård's and Pahuus's
fieldwork, where informants participated as equals with the researchers
in exploring the usefulness of Aristotle's concept of happiness. Here
neither Aristotle nor the informants could be said to be wrong, and
the interaction brought about a new understanding. Practiced in this
fashion, fieldwork is no longer just a study of what is, but also an intervention exploring what could just as well be. A more future-oriented,
engaged academic commitment might spring from such an exercise.

The current pull toward interdisciplinarity is clearly linked with institutional and political issues; an aspect that some find disheartening.
A possible reaction to the technocratic demand for "strategic" interdisciplinarity is to shun collaboration and stick to one's own discipline.

And even if one acknowledges the importance of interdisciplinary dialogue, it can be argued that at least a partial or temporal disciplinary insulation could be a good thing. It might help to develop and sharpen particular ideas and approaches, thus ensuring that the disciplines can provide input to the interdisciplinary dialogue that is both sufficiently qualified and original. But as the dialogue between anthropology and philosophy shows, there is often a basis, indeed even a need and an urge, for more collaboration within the disciplines themselves. We therefore propose to influence events by fostering interdisciplinarity with a human face, engaging in more curiosity-driven forms of collaboration. Indeed, it is not unlikely that even the more strategic settings, that is, work on the "grand societal challenges," can prompt new theoretical developments and fruitful interaction between the disciplines. The dialogues in this book have focused on trust and hope; what could be more relevant where the problems vying for our attention include climate change, heightened levels of stress and depression, religious conflicts, and disillusioned youth.

The dialogues also show that interdisciplinary collaboration, even when founded on the sincerest of intentions and an apparent abundance of common ground, will always be difficult. The first optimistic approaches may lead to frustration and disappointment, as it turns out that the other party is not really interested in the same issue after all, or does not contribute in the way that was expected. Breaking old habits and experiencing a loss of one's sure foothold is seldom a pleasant process. But there *is* reason to be hopeful. Experience shows that with sufficient perseverance, initial misconceptions and misplaced expectations will be replaced by a new understanding of what the disciplines really have to offer one another (Sjölander 1985). Even without coming together in an orderly and coherent way, the interaction may spur inspiration and theoretical innovation precisely by way of creative misunderstandings and the need for clarity. Necessity, as we know, is the mother of invention.

References

Abu-Lughod, Lila. 1991. "Writing against Culture." In *Recapturing Anthropology: Working in the Present,* edited by Richard G. Fox. Santa Fe, NM: School of Anthropological Research Press.

Aristotle. 1924. *Metaphysics.* Vol. 8 of *The Works of Aristotle.* Translated by W. D. Ross. Oxford: Clarendon Press.

Barth, Fredrik. 1975. *Ritual and Knowledge Among the Baktaman of New Guinea.* New Haven, CT: Yale University Press.

BonJour, Laurence. 1985. *The Structure of Empirical Knowledge.* Cambridge, MA: Harvard University Press.

Brandom, Robert. 1994. *Making it Explicit.* Cambridge, MA: Harvard University Press.

Brown, Donald E. 1991. *Human Universals.* New York: McGraw-Hill.

Brumann, Christoph. 1999. "Writing for Culture: Why a Successful Concept Should Not Be Discarded." Special issue, *Current Anthropology* 40, no. 1: 1–27.

Bryant, Levi, Nick Srnicek, and Graham Harman. 2011. *The Speculative Turn: Continental Materialism and Realism.* Melbourne: Re.Press.

Clifford, James. 1986. "Introduction: Partial Truths." In *Writing Culture,* edited by James Clifford and George E. Marcus. Berkeley: University of California Press.

Clifford, James, and George E. Marcus, eds. 1986. *Writing Culture.* Berkeley: University of California Press.

Dalsgård, Anne Line. 2004. *Matters of Life and Longing: Female Sterilisation in Northeast Brazil.* Copenhagen: Museum Tusculanum Press.

———. 2008. "Verfremdung and Business Development: The Ethnographic Essay as Eye-opener." *Being Seen: Paradoxes and Practices of (In)visibility,* conference proceedings, no. 1: 146–59. Available at http://onlinelibrary.wiley.com/doi/10.1111/j.1559-8918.2008.tb00102.x/abstract.

Dancy, Jonathan. 2004. *Ethics Without Principles.* Oxford: Clarendon Press.

Daniel, E. Valentine. 1996. *Charred Lullabies: Chapters in an Anthropography of Violence.* Princeton, NJ: Princeton University Press.

Davidson, Donald. 1974. "On the Very Idea of a Conceptual Scheme." *Proceedings and Addresses of the American Philosophical Association* 47: 5–20.

Deleuze, Gilles, and Félix Guattari. 1994. *What is Philosophy?* New York: Columbia University Press.

Dennett, Daniel. 1991. *Consciousness Explained.* London: Penguin Books.

Desjarlais, Robert, and Jason C. Throop. 2011. "Phenomenological Approaches in Anthropology." *Annual Review of Anthropology* 40: 87–102.

Devitt, Michael. 2006. "Intuitions in Linguistics." *British Journal of the Philosophy of Science* 57, no. 3: 481–513.

Engelke, Matthew. 2008. "The Objects of Evidence." *Journal of the Royal Anthropological Institute (N.S.):* 1–21.

Evans-Pritchard, E. E. (1937) 1976. *Witchcraft, Oracles and Magic among the Azande.* Oxford: Oxford University Press.

Forsythe, Diana E. 1999. "'It's Just a Matter of Common Sense:' Ethnography as Invisible Work." *Computer Supported Cooperative Work* 8: 127–45.

Frazer, James G. (1890) 1971. *The Golden Bough: A Study in Magic and Religion.* London: Macmillan.

Gadamer, Hans-Georg. 1960. *Wahrheit und Methode.* Tübingen: Siebeck Mohr.

Geertz, Clifford. 1973. *The Interpretation of Cultures.* New York: Basic Books.

Goldman, Alvin I. 1986. *Epistemology and Cognition.* Cambridge, MA: Harvard University Press.

Hastrup, Kirsten. 2004a. "Getting It Right: Knowledge and Evidence in Anthropology." *Anthropological Theory* 4, no. 4: 455–72.

———. 2004b. "Introduktion: Antropologiens Vendinger." In *Viden om Verden,* edited by Kirsten Hastrup. Copenhagen: Hans Reitzels Forlag.

Hetherington, Stephen, ed. 2006. *Epistemology Futures.* Oxford: Oxford University Press.

Holbraad, Martin, and Morten Axel Pedersen. 2009. "Planet M: The Intense Abstraction of Marilyn Strathern." *Anthropological Theory* 9, no. 4: 371–94.

Ingold, Tim. 2008. "Anthropology is Not Ethnography." *Proceedings of the British Academy* 154: 69–92.

Jackson, Frank. 1998. *From Metaphysics to Ethics.* Oxford: Clarendon Press.

Jackson, Michael D. 1998. *Minima Ethnographica: Intersubjectivity and the Anthropological Project.* Chicago: Chicago University Press.

———. 2005. *Existential Anthropology: Events, Exigencies and Effects.* New York: Berghahn Books.

———. 2009. "Where Thought Belongs: An Anthropological Critique of the Project of Philosophy." *Anthropological Theory* 9, no. 3: 235–51.

Klausen, Søren Harnow. 2004. *Reality Lost and Found: An Essay on the Realism-Antirealism Controversy.* Odense: University of Southern Denmark Press.

———. 2009. "Applied Epistemology: Prospects and Problems." *Res Cogitans* 6, no. 1: 220–58.

Knobe, Joshua, and Shaun Nichols, eds. 2008. *Experimental Philosophy.* Oxford: Oxford University Press.

Loux, Michael J., and Dean Zimmerman. 2003. "Introduction." In *The Oxford Handbook of Metaphysics,* edited by Michael J. Loux and Dean Zimmerman. Oxford: Oxford University Press.

Machery, Edouard, Ron Mallon, Shaun Nichols, and Stephen Stich. 2004. "Semantics, Cross-Cultural Style." *Cognition* 92: 1–12.

Marcus, George E., and Michael M. J. Fischer. (1986) 1999. *Anthropology as Cultural Critique: An Experimental Moment in the Human Sciences.* Chicago: Chicago University Press.

Mattingly, Cheryl. 2011. Working paper presented at Aarhus University.

McDowell, John. 1994. *Mind and World.* Cambridge, MA: Harvard University Press.

Moody-Adams, Michele M. 1997. *Fieldwork in Familiar Places: Morality, Culture, and Philosophy.* Cambridge, MA: Harvard University Press.

Nussbaum, Martha. 1990. *Love's Knowledge.* New York: Oxford University Press.

Plato. 1973. *Theaetetus*. Translated by J. McDowell. Oxford: Clarendon Press.

Rapport, Nigel. 1997. *Transcendent Individual: Towards a Literary and Liberal Anthropology*. London: Routledge.

———. 2003. *I am Dynamite: An Alternative Anthropology of Power*. London: Routledge.

———. 2010. "Apprehending *Anyone*: The Non-indexical, Post-cultural, and Cosmopolitan Human Actor." *Journal of the Royal Anthropological Institute (N.S.)* 16: 84–101.

Said, Edward W. 1978. *Orientalism*. London: Routledge and Kegan Paul.

Sjölander, Sverre. 1985. "Long-term and Short-term Interdisciplinary Work." In *Interdisciplinarity Revisited*, edited by L. Levin and I. Lind. Stockholm: OECD.

Spiro, Melford E. 1993. "Is the Western Conception of the Self 'Peculiar' within the Context of the World Cultures?" *Ethos* 21, no. 2: 107–53.

Strathern, Marilyn. 2004. *Partial Connections: Updated Edition*. London: AltaMira Press.

Tugendhat, Ernst. 2010. *Anthropologie statt Metaphysik*. München: Beck.

Tylor, Edward B. (1871) 1920. *Primitive Culture*. London: John Murray.

Van Maanen, John. 1988. *Tales of the Field: On Writing Ethnography*. Chicago: Chicago University Press.

Willerslev, Rane. 2011. "Frazer Strikes back from the Armchair: A New Search for the Animist Soul." *Journal of the Royal Anthropological Institute (N.S.)* 17: 504–26.

Williamson, Timothy. 2007. *The Philosophy of Philosophy*. Oxford: Blackwell.

Wittgenstein, Ludwig. 1963. *Tractatus logico-philosophicus*. Frankfurt: Suhrkamp.

Wolcott, Harry F. 1999. *Ethnography: A Way of Seeing*. London: AltaMira Press.

CONTRIBUTORS

Nils Bubandt is Professor of Anthropology at Aarhus University. He is author of *Democracy, Corruption and the Politics of Spirits in Contemporary Indonesia* (Routledge, 2014, published in Indonesian by Yayasan Obor Press in 2017) and *The Empty Seashell: Witchcraft and Doubt on an Indonesian Island* (Cornell University Press, 2014), as well as co-editor (with Anna Tsing, Heather Swanson, and Elaine Gan) of *Arts of Living on a Damaged Planet* (University of Minnesota Press, 2017). With Mark Graham, he is editor-in-chief of the academic journal *Ethnos*.

Anne Line Dalsgård is Associate Professor at Aarhus University. Based on extensive fieldwork done in Northeast Brazil since 1997, she has published extensively on motherhood, youth, violence, affect, and temporality. She is author of the book *Matters of Life and Longing: Female Sterilisation in Northeast Brazil* (Museum Tusculanum Press, 2004; Editora UNESP, 2006).

Michael D. Jackson is Distinguished Professor of World Religions at Harvard Divinity School. He is the author of numerous books on anthropology, including the prize-winning *Paths Toward a Clearing: Radical Empiricism and Ethnographic Inquiry* (Indiana University Press, 1989) and *At Home in the World* (Duke University Press, 1995), and has also published three novels, a memoir, and eight volumes of poetry. His latest books are *Walking to Pencarrow: Selected Poems* (ColdHub Press, 2016), *As Wide as the World is Wise: Reinventing Philosophical Anthropology* (Columbia University Press, 2016), *The Work of Art: Rethinking the Elementary Forms of Religious Life* (Columbia University, 2016), *and How Lifeworlds Work: Sociality, Emotionality and the Ambiguity of Being* (Chicago University Press, 2017).

Uffe Juul Jensen is Professor of Philosophy at Aarhus University. He is Director of the Centre for Health, Humanity, and Culture at Aarhus University, and a visiting professor in the Department of Social Science, Health, and Medicine at King's College London. He is the author or editor of several works on epistemology of science, the philosophy of biomedicine and medical ethics including *Videnskabsteori 1–2* (*Epistemology of Science 1–2*, Berlingske Forlag, Copenhagen, 1973), *The Philosophy of Evolution* (Harvester Press, 1981, co-edited with Rom Harre), *Practice and Progress: A Theory for the Modern Health Care System* (Blackwell Scientific Publications, 1987), *Changing Values in Medical and Heath Care Decision Making* (John Wiley, Chichester, 1990, co-edited with Gavin Mooney), *Sundhedsbegreber: Filosofi og praksis* (Philosophia Press, 1994, co-edited with Peter Fuur Andersen), *Activity Theory and Social Practice* (Aarhus University Press, Aarhus, 1999, co-edited with Seth Chaiklin & Mariane Hedegaard), and *Narrative, Self and Social Practice* (Philosophia Press, 2009, co-edited with Cheryl Mattingly).

Søren Harnow Klausen holds a doctoral degree in philosophy and is a Professor of Philosophy at the University of Southern Denmark. He is head of the research program "Knowledge and Values" and was a member of the Danish Council for Independent Research in the Humanities between 2008 and 2013. His works include *Metafysik* (Gyldendal, 1997), *Verfahren oder Gegebenheit?* (Attempto, 1997), *Filosofiens grundproblemer* (Gyldendal, 2000), *Reality Lost and Found* (University Press of Southern Denmark, 2004), *Hvad er videnskabsteori?* (Akademisk Forlag, 2005), and *På tværs af fag* (Akademisk Forlag, 2011).

Sune Liisberg is an external lecturer at the School of Communication and Culture, Aarhus University. He earned his PhD in philosophy and history of ideas in 2008, after presenting a thesis about Jean-Paul Sartre's phenomenological philosophy, and was the expert advisor, and author of the postscript, to the Danish translation of Sartre's *L'être et le néant* (*Being and Nothingness*) (Philosophia Press, Aarhus 2007; 2nd edition, Aarhus 2013; Oslo 2015). He has published on a variety of topics primarily within the fields of existential philosophy and phenomenology. From 2005 to 2009 he was also co-editor and editor-in-chief of *Slagmark,* a Danish academic journal in the history of ideas.

Hans Lucht is an anthropologist and senior researcher at the Danish Institute for International Studies in Copenhagen. He is the author of two published novels and the academic volume *Darkness before Day-*

break: African Migrants Living on the Margins in Southern Italy Today (University of California Press, 2011).

Cheryl Mattingly is Professor of Anthropology at the University of Southern California. She has been a Senior Fellow at the Institute for Advanced Studies, Aarhus University and is a 2017 Guggenheim Fellow. She has won numerous book prizes from the American Anthropoogy, including the Victor Turner Prize, the Stirling Prize and the New Millennium Prize. Major book publications include *Healing Dramas and Clinical Plots: The Narrative Structure of Experience* (Cambridge University Press, 1998); *Narrative and the Cultural Construction of Illness and Healing* (University of California Press, 2000, co-edited with Linda Garro); *Narrative, Self and Social Practice* (Philosophia Press, 2009, co-edited with Uffe Juul Jensen); *The Paradox of Hope: Travels Through a Clinical Borderland* (University of California Press, 2010), and *Moral Laboratories: Family Peril and the Struggle for a Good Life* (University of California Press, 2014).

Lotte Meinert is Professor of Anthropology at Aarhus University. She has been doing fieldwork in Uganda since 1994 and has published extensively on topics concerning social life, medical anthropology, education, time, and human security in East Africa. In 2009 her monograph *Hopes in Friction: Schooling, Health, and Everyday Life in Uganda* was published by IAP.

Hirokazu Miyazaki is Professor of Anthropology at Cornell University. His major publications include *The Method of Hope: Anthropology, Philosophy, and Fijian Knowledge* (Stanford University Press, 2004), *Arbitraging Japan: Dreams of Capitalism at the End of Finance* (University of California Press, 2013) and *The Economy of Hope* (co-edited with Richard Swedberg; University of Pennsylvania Press, 2017).

Esther Oluffa Pedersen is Associate Professor of Philosophy at the University of Roskilde. She has published the book *Die Mythosphilosophie Ernst Cassirers: Zur Bedeutung des Mythos in der Auseinandersetzung mit der Kantischen Erkenntnistheorie und in der Sphäre der modernen Politik* (Königshausen & Neumann, 2009), as well as several articles on trust, including "A Two-Level Theory of Trust" (*Balkan Journal of Philosophy*, 2010), and articles and anthologies on the philosophy of Ernst Cassirer, Immanuel Kant, and German philosophy more broadly.

Sverre Raffnsøe holds a doctoral degree (dr. habil.) in philosophy and a position as Professor of Philosophy in the Department of Management, Politics, and Philosophy at Copenhagen Business School. He is editor-in-chief of *Foucault Studies*. His most recent books are *Michel Foucault: A Research Companion* (with Gudmand-Høyer and Thaning; Palgrave, 2016) and *Philosophy of the Anthropocene: The Human Turn* (Palgrave, 2016). His recent work has appeared in *Journal of Political Power*, *Management and Organizational History*, *Organization*, *Outlines*, and *International Journal of Philosophy and Theology*.

Anders Moe Rasmussen is Associate Professor of Philosophy at Aarhus University. He is the editor of *Gestalten des Geistes: Kierkegaard im Kontext des Deutschen Idealismus* (De Gruyter, 2014, co-edited with Axel Hutter) and *German Idealism Today* (de Gruyter 2017, co-edited with Markus Gabriel), and the author of many articles on phenomenology and existential philosophy, dealing in particular with Søren Kierkegaard.

Thomas Schwarz Wentzer is Associate Professor of Philosophy at Aarhus University. He is the author of *Bewahrung der Geschichte: Die hermeneutische Philosophie Walter Benjamins* (Philo Verlag, 1998) and many articles within the field of philosophical anthropology, on phenomenology and hermeneutics, particularly dealing with Heidegger and Gadamer. He is the editor of *Finite but Unbounded: New Approaches in Philosophical Anthropology* (De Gruyter 2017, co-edited with Martin Gustafson and Kevin Cahill).

INDEX

www.ingramcontent.com/pod-product-compliance
Lightning Source LLC
Chambersburg PA
CBHW070911030426
42336CB00014BA/2375